# THE
# CONSUMER
# MOVEMENT

*Guardians of the Marketplace*

# SOCIAL MOVEMENTS PAST AND PRESENT

## Irwin T. Sanders, Editor

# THE
# CONSUMER
# MOVEMENT

## Guardians of the Marketplace

Robert N. Mayer

080700

Twayne Publishers • Boston
*A Division of G. K. Hall & Co.*

The Consumer Movement: Guardians of the Marketplace
Robert N. Mayer

Copyright 1989 by Robert N. Mayer.
All rights reserved.
Published by Twayne Publishers
A division of G. K. Hall & Co.
70 Lincoln Street, Boston, Massachusetts 02111

Copyediting supervised by Barbara Sutton.
Book Production by Janet Z. Reynolds.
Typeset by Compset, Inc., of Beverly, Massachusetts.

Printed on permanent/durable acid-free paper
and bound in the United States of America.

First Printing 1989

Library of Congress Cataloging-in-Publication Data

Mayer, Robert N.
The consumer movement : guardians of the marketplace
/ Robert N. Mayer.
p.    cm.—(Social movements past and present)
Bibliography: p.
Includes index.
ISBN 0-8057-9718-1 (alk. paper).
ISBN 0-8057-9719-X (pbk. :
alk. paper)
1. Consumer protection—United States—History.   2. Consumer
protection—History.   I. Title.   II. Series.
HC110.C63M38   1989
381′.32′0973—dc19        88-35226
CIP

# *Contents*

# *About the Author*

Robert N. Mayer is an associate professor of family and consumer studies at the University of Utah in Salt Lake City. His teaching and research activities focus on consumer behavior, consumer politics, and consumer policy evaluation. After receiving his B.A. in sociology from Columbia University, Mayer continued his studies in sociology at the University of California at Berkeley, where he also worked for a grass-roots consumer organization. His dissertation was an analysis of the social bases of public opinion and voting with respect to California referenda dealing with environmental issues.

In 1977 Mayer accepted a position at the University of Utah in a new interdisciplinary program emphasizing consumer studies. His research has covered a variety of subjects, from the acquisition of consumer values among children to the nationwide introduction of online computer services in France. His work has appeared in numerous journals, including *Journal of Consumer Affairs, Journal of Consumer Policy,* and *Journal of Consumer Research,* and he is an active member of the American Council on Consumer Interests and the Association for Consumer Research.

# *Preface*

If the ultimate standard for a social movement is the extent to which it changes the world for the better, then the consumer movement measures up well. For nearly a century, activists around the world have sought to improve consumer welfare by agitating for changes in business practices, government policy, and the behavior of consumers themselves. As a result, citizens enjoy a greater degree of safety, information, choice, and political representation than they would have otherwise.

All social movements face serious challenges in bringing about change, but consumerism may face more political obstacles than most. The task of mobilizing support is easiest for social movements that have a clearly defined goal, that attempt to deliver benefits to a narrow segment of society, or that address issues at the very core of a person's identity. Consumerism enjoys none of these advantages. It deals with a broad and shifting array of issues that affect just about everyone but in a diffuse fashion. Thus, most people favor the general goal of enhancing consumer welfare, but almost no one feels motivated or obligated to become a consumer activist. People assume that the consumer movement will persevere with or without their contribution.

If the prospects for consumer activism were completely bleak, however, there would be no subject for this book. Several factors have contributed to the success of the consumer movement. Contrary to popular belief, the relationship between buyers and sellers is not wholly adversarial. Consumers engage on a periodic basis in transactions with producers in which both parties presumably benefit, creating an incentive for sellers to keep their customers satisfied. The hand of consumerists is also strengthened by economic competition among sellers, which can lead to political divisions among them. Finally consumerism is able to tap both the economic self-interest and the social consciousness of consumers.

In writing from the vantage point of the late 1980s, it is tempting to describe the consumer movement in the past tense. Relative to past peaks of activity, consumer activism is currently experiencing a lull. Nevertheless, the quietude of the moment should not mask the continuing influence of the consumer movement. It has so transformed institutions and consciousness that many proconsumer actions now occur as a matter of course and without fanfare. For example, a variety of government and private organizations routinely act to ensure that advertisements are free of deceptive content and that consumer grievances are handled fairly. Thus, while the consumer movement does have a long and fascinating history, its current status and future prospects are equally important.

The analysis of the consumer movement begins in chapter 1 by considering different definitions of *consumerism* as well as the issue of whether it constitutes a genuine social movement. The chapter also elaborates on the dilemmas faced by social movements that purport to pursue the interests of the "public."

Chapter 2 provides a historical overview of consumerism in America, where the movement has been comprised of three waves, each one occurring during a period when rapid social change coincided with an upsurge in progressive social spirit. The key individuals and organizations in the contemporary consumer movement of the United States are introduced in chapter 3. The discussion sets boundaries on the movement and answers questions regarding its overall structure.

Chapter 4 turns to an examination of the ideas of consumerists. An ideological cleavage exists within the movement between "reformists" and "radicals." The two groups differ in what they perceive to be the most pressing consumer problems, how they explain the existence of these problems, and the measures they advocate to solve them.

The political dynamics of consumer issues are the subject of chapter 5. By examining the histories of several important pieces of U.S. consumer legislation, this chapter identifies the factors that influence success or failure when consumerists press for legislative or regulatory action. Chapter 6 uses the best available data to quantify the actual impacts of consumer policies on the economic well-being of consumers in the United States and presents some of the major criticisms of the consumer movement.

Chapter 7 highlights consumerism's international character. There is much to be learned from the approaches of consumerists in other nations. Taking a global perspective has the further advantage of directing attention to consumer issues that cross national boundaries, such as the exportation of products deemed unsafe for use in a country's domestic market. The book's final chapter addresses the future prospects of the consumer movement in the United States and elsewhere. Of particular interest are the conditions that may produce the next wave of consumer activism and the issues that are likely to constitute its rallying points.

The story of consumerism, like an evening soap opera, includes high-stake schemes, cover-ups, and double-crosses punctuated by car crashes, airline disasters, and poisonings. And like the soaps, the public follows the plot most attentively when the good guys are easily distinguishable from the bad. Unlike soap operas, however, the goal of consumerism is to empower people—both as individual buyers trying to get the most for their dollars and as a political force striving to rewrite the rules of the marketplace. If citizens don't like the plot of the consumerism drama, they possess the power to rewrite the script.

Writing a book on the consumer movement is a bit improbable given some aspects of my personal background. My father ran a small meat processing company, the very industry that was the target of the first consumer exposé, and he was always telling me how unreasonable and unnecessary government inspection of his processing plant was. The professor who served as my mentor, Franco Nicosia, taught in a school of business administration and continually emphasized the virtues of private enterprise and the evils of government regulation. Still, I couldn't escape the effects of coming of political age in the 1960s. Studying and participating in the consumer movement provided me—and I believe others—with a way to channel reformist political impulses without renouncing a middle class background.

Like the consumer movement itself, the research reflected in this book was conducted on a shoestring but benefited from a great deal of moral and intellectual support from editors, colleagues, students, and friends. Among the people whose help is easiest to call to mind are Stephen Brobeck, Jan Ellen Burton, John Burton, Greg Coon, Athenaide Dallett, Monty Friedman, Andrew Gitlin, Robert Herrmann, Stewart Lee, Erich Linke, Scott Maynes, Irwin Sanders, Daigh Tufts, and Cathleen Zick.

Throughout my life, there has been someone who has brought both insight and blind faith to my work: first my mother, Lily Mayer, and more recently, my partner, Carol Blackwell. I hope that Carol will quickly forget all the times that I "had to" work on the book rather than be with her.

I am grateful for permission to use the following: The cartoon "It was owned by a little old lady . . ." by Ed Stein, *Rocky Mountain News,* 1980. Reproduced by permission of Ed Stein. The cartoon "Deregulation Gives Consumers Greater Choices" by Dan Wasserman, © 1988 *Boston Globe.* Reprinted by permission.

*Chapter One*

# A Fragile but Enduring Movement

Modern consumers are Alices in a Wonderland of technological marvels where anything seems possible. In the cold month of January, Americans nonchalantly enjoy fresh strawberries flown in from New Zealand, while their homes are heated with natural gas extracted from the ground thousands of miles away. Nor does a consumer vacationing in some remote part of China find it remarkable when he can pay a street vendor with a credit card. Each year brings a cavalcade of new products and services that improve on last year's while costing less.

The technological complexity and vast geographical scope of the modern marketplace could give rise to feelings of suspicion and helplessness on the part of consumers. Yet, the modern consumer exhibits a tremendous level of confidence and trust. Few consumers stop to worry about whether their imported strawberries have been sprayed with a lethal pesticide or whether their credit card number will be misused by a merchant. Consumers go about their daily activities assuming that legal protections exist and are operative. They only take notice when their trust has been violated.

Consider the case of a fictitious American consumer, John Smith, waking up on a weekday morning. The lit cigarette that John was holding as he fell asleep did not set his mattress aflame because of strict federal flammability standards. In the bathroom, John opens a medicine cabinet holding medications in child-resistant containers. These containers were reassuring during a recent visit from his young nephew. After showering, John uses a hair dryer that is free from cancer-causing asbestos, owing to action by the Consumer Product Safety Commission. He also sprays

1

on deodorant with confidence because, thanks to the Food and Drug Administration, it does not contain any powerful skin irritants.

Entering the kitchen, John remembers a letter he has just received from the manufacturer of his coffeepot, asking him to return it as part of a government-mandated recall program. After prolonged use, the handle can become brittle and break, spilling boiling liquid on its owner. John will receive a replacement at no cost. Putting the coffeepot aside, he decides to have a bowl of bran flakes. He chose the brand he is eating on the basis of price, using the unit-pricing information required by his state in all grocery stores. The milk is still fresh, owing to John's consulting the open-dating information when he picked out the carton at the store.

John reads the side of the cereal box while he eats. Here is displayed a wealth of information regarding the cereal's ingredients and nutritional value. Again, the provision of this information is mandatory by virtue of the Fair Packaging Act as well as Food and Drug Administration rules regarding products sold with nutritional claims. After finishing his cereal, John places the milk container back into his new refrigerator, which still wears its bright yellow energy efficiency label. The label, required by the Energy Policy and Conservation Act, had allowed him to compare the annual energy costs of similar refrigerators made by different manufacturers. Returning to his bedroom, John selects a dress shirt and suit. Both come with mandatory care labels that are useful when it's time to launder them.

John leaves his apartment and gets into his car, where he is literally surrounded by the results of consumer protection laws and regulations. His seat belt, padded dash, collapsible steering wheel, sturdy bumpers, and safety windshield glass all come to him courtesy of the National Highway Traffic Safety Administration. He knows that some of the claims in commercials he hears on his car radio are exaggerated, but he vaguely recalls the Federal Trade Commission (FTC) is supposed to make sure that the ads do not contain outright falsehoods. Similarly, the fact that John will not hear a single cigarette commercial also reflects the government's consumer protection presence. Finally, the quality of the air he breathes is affected by a host of federal and state regulations, including the requirement that his car have a pollution control device and have its emissions monitored once a year.

John has been awake barely an hour, yet he has already reaped the benefits of dozens of consumer protection policies. If we followed him to a bank, a grocery store, a shopping mall, or an airport, we would encounter dozens, perhaps hundreds, more. These laws and regulations impose costs in addition to providing benefits, but without them, consumers would have to expend substantial amounts of money and time to avoid safety hazards and unwise purchases. Encounters with dangerous products and deceptive sales practices would eventually result in cynicism toward sellers. Instead, buyers in most modern societies carry out their business with a minimum of effort and a remarkable amount of trust, owing in no small part to the social movement known as consumerism.

## The Nature of Consumerism

The term *consumerism* has many meanings and connotations. In late 1976, a national survey conducted by Louis Harris and Associates and sponsored by Sentry Insurance (1977) asked members of the American public to define the term. For a large group of respondents (37 percent of the sample) consumerism was synonymous with consuming, buying, or using things. For many of them, the term suggested an excessive or obsessive interest in goods, akin to materialism. When Pope John Paul II, for example, decried consumerism as a form of personal enslavement, he was using the term in this pejorative sense. For the people in the Sentry Insurance survey, the phrase *consumer movement* came much closer to capturing the political and social movement aspects of consumerism. About two-thirds of the respondents associated the consumer movement with organizations or individuals fighting to protect the interests of consumers.

Ironically, the term *consumerism* was first used in the 1960s by opponents of the consumer movement who wanted to associate consumer activism with other dreaded "isms" such as communism and fascism (Lee and Zelenak, 1982; Magnuson, 1972; Morse, 1981). While few members of the business community still view consumerism as an un-American ideology, many would describe consumerists as self-appointed national nannies who wish to impose their values on others (Berger, 1988; Shephard, 1971; Winter, 1972). In contrast, management expert Peter Drucker (1969) calls consumerism "the shame of marketing," meaning that the movement's existence indicates that firms do not always do a good job of ascertaining and satisfying consumer desires. Even more affirmatively, consumerism has been described as a source of competitive advantage and profit (Fornell, 1978; Technical Assistance . . . , 1979, 1983).

Consumerism also means different things to the social scientists who study it. Although there is general agreement that consumerism consists of actions aimed at protecting and enhancing the rights of buyers, social scientists disagree concerning its scope. Some analysts limit consumerism to market transactions between buyers and private sellers; others argue that consumerism encompasses the consumer's transactions with governments, as in the case of garbage disposal services or education (Forbes, 1985; Mayer, 1981; Maynes, 1979). Furthermore, some students of the movement see it as a vehicle for increasing consumer responsibilities, not just rights (Stampfl, 1979). These responsibilities might include making well-informed choices, bringing product problems to the attention of manufacturers, and writing legislators to express support for a bill that is in the interest of consumers.

Regardless of its definition, there is some debate about whether consumerism is truly a social movement. Some sociologists think it is too politically tame, too reformist in its political goals, to bear such a label. For example, Foss and Larkin (1986) define a social movement as "involving at some point the use of physical force or violence against members of other social categories, their possessions, or their institutionalized instrumentalities, and interfering at least temporarily . . . with the political and cultural reproduction of society" (p. 2). Consumerism's claim to the status of a social movement is also challenged on the grounds that it is not marked by sufficient mass action. Someone using the civil rights and labor movements as a standard might find consumerism to be lacking in widespread, passionate, and spontaneous outpourings of grassroots consumer discontent. For example, former FTC chairman Michael Pertschuk (1982) prefers the term *consumer impulse* to *consumer movement* because "by and large the individual stake in the pursuit of consumer laws and regulations lacks the motivating energy of true political movements" (p. 11). Similarly, Stanley Cohen, who has sympathetically covered the consumer movement for the trade journal, *Advertising Age,* writes: "Consumerism's successes have rested on the persuasiveness of its cause rather than the political muscle it flexes. At best it has an elitist appeal" (1982, p. 61).

Some social movements admittedly have been more radical than the consumer movement and more characterized by mass action and total commitment. Yet it seems overly restrictive to require that an angry mob of consumers storm the corporate headquarters of General Motors demanding the head of its chief executive officer before consumerism can be termed a social movement. The movement's heavy reliance on the efforts of a small number of organizations located in Washington, D.C.

and New York City is no different from that of movements to protect the environment, promote nuclear disarmament, and advance the rights of children. Indeed, social movements run by full-time professionals who advocate for an unorganized constituency seem to be the norm in the contemporary United States (Berry, 1977; McCarthy and Zald, 1973; Walker, 1983).

Thus, consumerism does fall within most social scientific conceptions of contemporary social movements. It conforms to the requirements that it be "a purposive and collective attempt of a number of people to change individuals or societal institutions and structures" (Zald and Ash, 1966, p. 328) and that it operate "primarily through persuasive strategies and [be] countered by an established order" (Stewart, Smith, and Denton, 1984, p. 14). Accordingly, consumerism can be defined as a diverse and evolving social movement seeking to enhance the economic well-being and political power of consumers. This definition allows the terms *consumerism* and *consumer movement* to be used interchangeably. In addition, referring to a single movement suggests that a common thread runs through the consumer activism characteristic of different times and places.

## An Unlikely Social Movement

Because the consumer movement has enjoyed public support (Atlantic Richfield, 1982; Sentry Insurance, 1977) and maintained a continuous presence in the political arena for the past two decades, there is a tendency to take the movement's existence for granted. One might assume that it is well-financed, tightly organized, and free of both internal divisions and self-doubt, and thus ask why it hasn't accomplished more than it has.

In reality, the movement consists of a loosely knit band of individuals and organizations, deriving its sustenance more from moral outrage and a desire for justice than from extensive financial resources. Unlike organizations that represent a small number of businesses, each of which has an intense economic interest in the outcome of a public policy debate, consumer groups attempt to mobilize an inchoate mass of countless individuals, each of whom has only a limited economic stake in the outcome. Consequently, the mere existence of a consumer movement is noteworthy. That it has managed to survive for almost a century might be considered a political miracle.

## Conflict and Pluralist Perspectives

Not all social theorists would view the existence of a consumer movement as somehow remarkable. According to what can be called a conflict perspective, society is divided into groups with deep, enduring, and irreconcilable conflicts of interest, and social movements arise naturally to express these conflicts. Producers and consumers, for instance, are engaged in an unavoidable conflict in which one party's gain is the other party's loss (Ölander and Lindhoff, 1974). Producers may hold a considerable edge in terms of political power, including a governmental apparatus that serves their interests. But, the conflict perspective implies, just as workers will eventually win their struggle against owners, consumer protest will bubble up until true consumer sovereignty is achieved. Adherents of this perspective do not marvel at the existence, persistence, and achievements of the consumer movement. Indeed, they are more likely to question why the movement has been so timid and achieved so little. They criticize consumerists for focusing on the concerns of the middle class, for accepting existing market arrangements, and for giving what they consider the false appearance of addressing consumer grievances (Hornsby-Smith, 1986).

A pluralist perspective provides a different and, on balance, more convincing analysis of the dynamics of mobilizing consumer action. According to this view, political outcomes are determined by the interplay of numerous nongovernmental interest groups. The strength of each group depends on its ability to mobilize political resources—for example, to hire lobbyists, commission scientific studies, and strategically place campaign contributions. From the pluralist point of view, governmental actors have no prior political commitments or interests; they simply respond to whichever coalition of interest groups presses its case most effectively. Pluralist theory does not hold that all interest groups are equally endowed with political resources. Nor does it contend that the distribution of political power necessarily corresponds to the best interests of society. Indeed, pluralist theorists often point out that certain kinds of interest groups are at a serious disadvantage vis-à-vis others, especially those that, like consumerism, represent broad but weakly felt concerns. Yet pluralist theorists point to the fact that, under the right conditions, political institutions are responsive to these diffuse interest groups.

Convincing people to contribute to any political group is difficult, but certain kinds of social movements run into the "free-rider problem." The free-rider problem explains why providing public goods for members of a large group, each of whom has a relatively equal but modest stake in the good's provision, is so problematic. The problem of providing a public good is rooted in the fact that once it is provided, it is available to everyone regardless of whether they contributed to its provision. For instance, if a community installs a water treatment device to improve the quality of its water supply, all citizens will enjoy the cleaner water; receiving it will not depend on how much a person contributed in taxes. If a consumer group succeeds in passing a law that requires automobiles to be equipped with a padded dashboard and a collapsible steering wheel, all new car owners benefit from the new safety features, not just those people who worked for the law's passage.

Whereas the basis of the free-rider problem is the inability to exclude noncontributors from the benefits of a public good, the problem is compounded by the fact that the effect of a single individual's contribution toward the realization of a public good is usually imperceptible. When city officials urge citizens to reduce air pollution by taking the bus to work one day per week, individual commuters reason that the exhaust from their car on a single day isn't going to make much difference one way or the other. As long as everyone *else* does their part, the public good will be provided. Because noncontributors cannot be excluded from the benefits of the public good, an economically "rational" person will seek a free ride by feigning disinterest in the public good, hoping that others will bear the burden. The problem is that if enough people attempt to take a free ride, the public good will not be provided.

The free-rider problem is the reason governments must have the power to collect taxes. If it were left to citizens to voluntarily contribute to national defense or social insurance programs, the amount of money available for these programs would be paltry. Unfortunately for consumer activists, they lack the power to coerce contributions from the citizenry, but instead, must find other ways to overcome the free-rider problem. For some individuals, a sense of social injustice is sufficient to motivate participation. Others may be moved to make a financial contribution or volunteer time in the wake of a dramatic event or tragedy involving consumers. Still others may be induced to join consumer organizations by the offer of membership benefits such as a monthly magazine. And on occasion, consumer organizations receive support from foundations or government agencies (Walker, 1983). Nevertheless, the mobilization of financial and human resources is a constant battle for most consumer groups—as it is for environmental groups, honesty-in-government groups like Common Cause, feminist organizations, and charities—making their success in achieving even modest goals remarkable.

## Is Consumerism Necessary?

Our discussion of the difficulty of mobilizing a consumer movement presumes that such a movement contributes to consumer welfare. Some critics of consumerism, however, argue just the opposite, believing that the net impact of the movement has been negative. They say that it has produced some apparent gains for consumers, but at an unacceptably high cost in terms of higher prices, increased taxes, restricted consumer choice, reduced innovation, and countless rigidities in the free enterprise system (McKenzie, 1978; Weidenbaum, 1978).

Other critics of consumerism contend that its positive impact has been grossly exaggerated because the various outcomes attributed to it would have all come about, in time, as a result of self-interested behavior by sellers (Friedman and Friedman, 1979; Peltzman, 1974). A business wants satisfied customers who will purchase its products again, so it will not offer unsafe or shoddy goods. Similarly, a business's competitors will sue in court if it tries to gain an unfair advantage through deceptive advertising or predatory pricing practices, so government regulation is not needed. In short, the argument goes, the consumer movement has been unnecessary because the free enterprise system is already structured to protect the interest of consumers automatically.

Consumerists take strong exception to these criticisms. They vehemently assert that the benefits generated by their policies have far outweighed the costs (Green and Waitzman, 1979). And far from being unnecessary, consumerists argue, their presence has been vitally important in stimulating government action in defense of the health, safety, and pocketbooks of consumers (Bollier and Claybrook, 1986). What may appear as a firm's voluntary efforts to protect consumer rights is really the result of the consumer movement breathing down its neck.

## Beyond Rational Calculation

If we reject the view that consumerism is either undesirable or unnecessary, then the puzzle remains of why rational, self-interested individuals devote their energies to the movement. The usual answer is that consumer groups offer material incentives (such as salaries for the leaders, magazine subscriptions for the followers) or social incentives (such as organizational titles for the leaders, the chance to meet people for the followers) in exchange for participation (Berry, 1977; Clark and Wilson, 1961; Olson, 1965; Salisbury, 1969). The power of less tangible factors (what Salisbury calls "purposive incentives") such as altruism, moral outrage, guilt, and self-actualization is usually discounted.

Although material and social incentives are no doubt important in explaining participation in the consumer movement, such self-oriented incentives are probably insufficient explanations. Ethical or intellectual sources of motivation must be considered as well. But unless one intends to psychoanalyze the people who participate in consumer organizations, how can the role of ethical motivation in the consumer movement be investigated? The history of the movement provides a good starting point. One can examine the types of issues that have inspired the formation of consumer groups and the enactment of consumer protection legislation. One can also draw inferences from the social background of the people who have been attracted by the consumer cause. Later chapters focusing on conflicts within the consumer movement with respect to priorities and future directions also speak to the question of the moral basis of consumerism.

# Chapter Two

# Three Eras of Consumer Activism in the United States

For several reasons an analysis of the contemporary consumer movement must begin with an examination of the movement's historical roots. First, it is important to dispell the notion that the movement is only a recent phenomenon created by Ralph Nader. On the contrary, organized consumer action in the United States occurred in the nineteenth century, and consumer protection laws in some countries date back over two thousand years.

A second reason for considering the American movement's history is that features and outcomes of earlier eras of consumerism continue to affect consumers today. For example, the National Consumers League, founded in 1899, continues to promote and represent consumer interests. Similarly, the Federal Trade Commission and the Food and Drug Administration, arguably the most important consumer protection agencies in the United States today, were established before World War I.

Most important, many of the same dynamics that characterized earlier periods of consumer discontent have also marked more recent ones. Each of the three eras of consumerism in the United States can be understood as an expression of the dual Progressive ideas of humanitarianism and efficiency. In each era, the specific problems that catalyzed consumers grew out of fundamental changes in the nature of marketplace relationships, product technology, and consumer autonomy. Furthermore, the consumer movement has had to overcome the same problems—attracting public attention, generating organizational resources, stimulating government action—in each of its historical incarnations. Thus, attention to consumerism's past helps us appreciate its present challenges, deficiencies, and accomplishments.

## Caveat Emptor

Laws aimed at the protection of consumers are not confined to modern times (Forbes, 1987). Some prohibitions against adulterated food and false weights and measures are thousands of years old, such as those found in the Old Testament, the Code of Hammurabi, and the laws of India. European consumer protection statutes began to appear in the fifteenth and sixteenth centuries and were based on a very simple psychology of deterrence. For instance, sellers of adulterated milk in Austria were required to drink all of their own product. Similarly, French consumers were allowed to throw rotten eggs at those who had sold them. One can also point to several early examples of consumer protection legislation in the United States. The Constitution gave Congress the power to "fix the Standard of Weights and Measures," and various state laws were passed to allow inspection of foods, tobacco, liquor, leather, lumber, and gunpowder (Nadel, 1971).

Still, it would be a mistake to interpret early attempts to establish certain minimal standards of marketplace conduct as signs that an explicit concept of consumer protection existed. Government intervention in the economy was typically justified on the grounds of aiding the orderly flow of commerce. Consumer protection was only an incidental outcome (Nadel, 1971).

In some respects, the consumer's position was weakened as trade became more national and international in character. During most of the Middle Ages, consumers were to some degree protected by the moral strictures of the Catholic church, self-regulation by craft guilds, and consumers' own knowledge of products and local sellers. The law did not favor the consumer, but neither did it favor the seller; there was essentially no law covering consumer transactions (Preston, 1975). Then, the European kings, in their efforts to encourage the growth of trade, oversaw a shift in legal doctrine that favored sellers (for example, misrepresentations needed to be deliberate to be illegal and were therefore extremely difficult to prove). The dominant rule of the marketplace became "caveat emptor," or buyer beware.

# The First Era of Consumer Activism

The supply and demand conditions that underlay the doctrine of caveat emptor and limited government intervention on behalf of consumers changed rapidly in the latter decades of the nineteenth century. The ability to manufacture goods in large quantities and distribute them over long distances provided producers with the prerequisites for a truly national market. As indications of this transformation, the number of nonagricultural employees quadrupled between 1870 and 1910 and gross national product increased fivefold during the same period. As for consumers, not only was the U.S. population growing rapidly, but urbanization made consumers more concentrated and inexpensive to serve. In 1870, 25 percent of the nation's population resided in urban areas. By 1910, the figure was 46 percent (U.S. Bureau of the Census, 1975).

## Mass Production and Mass Consumption

In its initial stages, the industrial revolution in the United States was confined to basic industries such as petroleum, railroads, steel, and banking. By the end of the nineteenth century, however, mass production and mass distribution were applied to simple household goods, especially foods, cleaning products, and textiles. Indeed, the same people who worked in factories turning out industrial goods were among those who had the cash to purchase premade, prepackaged products. People bought clothing instead of making cloth and garments; they substituted kerosene lamps for homemade candles; they purchased coal instead of collecting and chopping wood; they ate meat that had been packed in Chicago rather than butchered in the backyard; they bought patent medicines rather than preparing their own home remedies (Cowan, 1983).

**Branding.** In addition to the transition from home-produced to mass-produced goods, there was a shift from the purchase of unbranded products, often sold in bulk, to branded and nationally advertised items. Consider the many products and companies that appeared in the late 1870s (Fichter, 1986). In 1876, Charles Hires introduced the nation's first popular soft drink. The history of Hires root beer itself illustrates the changes in modes of consumption that were taking place. Hires and his bride were on their honeymoon when he tasted a delicious tea and obtained the recipe for the blend of barks, berries, and herbs. After making some modifications, Hires introduced his herb tea as a "drug extract" of dry ingredients that the consumer had to boil in cheesecloth with

Table 2.1. Three Periods of Consumerism in the United States

| Period: | Turn-of-Century | 1920s and 1930s | 1960s and 1970s |
|---|---|---|---|
| Marketplace features: | National distribution<br>Branding of products | Mass production<br>Diffusion of electrical appliances<br>Image advertising | Product proliferation<br>Increased use of credit<br>Complex, new technology<br>Global production and consumption |
| New media of advertising: | Newspapers, magazines | radio | television |
| Main concerns: | Food and drug safety<br>Regulation of competition | Objective information<br>Representation | Product safety<br>Advertising's social impact<br>Avenues for redress |
| Key individuals: | Upton Sinclair<br>Harvey Wiley | Stuart Chase<br>Frederick Schlink<br>Arthur Kallet<br>Colston Warne | Ralph Nader<br>Esther Peterson<br>Michael Pertschuk<br>Sidney Wolfe |
| Important books: | *The Jungle* | *Your Money's Worth*<br>*100,000,000 Guinea Pigs* | *Unsafe at Any Speed*<br>*The Poor Pay More* |
| Consumer organizations: | National Consumers League | Consumers Union<br>Consumers' Research<br>Rural electrical coops | Consumer Federation of America<br>Public Citizen, Inc.<br>American Council on Consumer Interests |
| Major legislation: | Pure Food and Drug Act<br>Wholesome Meat Act<br>Federal Trade Commission Act | Food, Drug and Cosmetic Act<br>Wheeler-Lea Act | National Traffic Safety Act<br>Truth-in-Lending Act<br>Consumer Product Safety Act<br>Magnuson-Moss Warranty Act |
| Decline in activism: | World War I | World War II | Reagan administration |

water, sugar, and yeast. A few years later, he recast his tonic as a concentrate to which only water had to be added. In 1893, Hires herb tea
was first sold in a directly consumable form—in bottles. Finally, the product's name was changed to Hires root beer.

The 1870s also witnessed Henry Heinz's first bottle of ketchup and
Harley Procter's first bar of Ivory soap. By the year 1900, one could find
packages of William Wrigley's chewing gum, boxes of the Kellogg broth-
ers' corn flakes, and bars of Milton Hershey's wrapped chocolate. Add
to the list Campbell's soup, Kodak cameras, Coca-Cola, Van Camp pork
and beans, Postum, Cream of Wheat, and the National Biscuit Company's
first entrant into the prepackaged cookie market, Uneeda biscuit (Fox,
1984).

For the consumer, branding provided a certain degree of quality as-
surance and convenience, and combined with national advertising, it induced consumers to ask for particular versions of a good rather than the
generic good—Quaker Oats rather than just any raw oats. Thus, branding helped manufacturers expand demand for their products. It also
shifted power from retailers, who would buy in bulk from whomever
offered the best deal, to the manufacturers of desired brands (Pope,
1983).

## Problems of Industrialization

The rapid industrialization of American life entailed many benefits, but
it had its dark side as well. Two negative aspects in particular fed the
first wave of consumerism in the United States. The first problem was
achieving the "right" amount of competition in various markets. Neither
the extremes of monopolization by cartels nor chaotic competition in
which no firm was able to survive could be tolerated. Consumers shared
an interest with businesses and workers in having government policies
that regulated the degree and nature of competition in various industries.

The second problem that led to the initial wave of American consumerism was the safety and quality of the new, branded goods that were
being sold in national rather than local markets. Although most manufacturers of branded goods had an incentive to associate their names with
high quality, some disregarded consumer welfare. For example, to solve
the problem of transporting goods over long distances, chemicals might
be used to disguise stale or rancid meat. Other manufacturers simply
didn't care about repeat purchases—either because consumers had no
way to judge the efficacy of their product or because their product was
itself addictive. Patent medicines, which were typically useless and

sometimes contained narcotics, illustrate this case. To ensure the safety of foods and medicines would require the political mobilization of consumers fighting on their own behalf.

**Regulating Competition.** Finding the optimal level of competition was a problem that engaged many of the nation's brightest minds during the end of the nineteenth century and the beginning of the twentieth—men such as Supreme Court justice Louis Brandeis, Wisconsin senator and governor Robert La Follette, and President Theodore Roosevelt. Although the consumer stake in regulating competition was large, few of the people involved conceived of themselves as explicitly representing consumer interests. Some, like economist Henry Adams, viewed industrial overcapacity as the central problem of industrialization. For example, in the East, too many railroads were handling too little freight. Consumers might benefit in the short run from the intense price competition, but the long-run interest of consumers lay in the existence of stable industries. The solution to the problem of overcapacity, Adams argued, was the creation of state regulatory commissions staffed by impartial public servants (McCraw, 1984).

More directly sympathetic to consumer well-being were Brandeis, La Follette, and other members of the Progressive movement who reacted to the growing concentration of business power in both the the marketplace and the political arena. In general, the Progressives championed measures designed to increase the voice of large but poorly organized groups. These measures included direct primaries, the initiative and referendum system, tariff reform, laws protecting female and child laborers, programs to conserve natural resources, and, most important from the point of view of consumers, trust-busting.

The formation of trusts—combinations of large corporations within a particular industry with the intent of controlling production, prices, and profits—was, from the point of view of the firms, the most obvious and direct method of dealing with industrial overcapacity. This was the essence of the trust movement. In its extreme form, several firms might merge into one huge corporation capable of dominating an entire industry (for example, the Standard Oil trust). Providers of local utilities, such as transportation, heat, light, water, and sewage removal, exercised monopolistic control as well, often obtained through long-term franchises from local governments (Thelen, 1983). In 1907, moralist Edward Ross summed up the consumer's loss of self-sufficiency and the growth of trusts: "Nowadays the water main is my well, the trolley car my carriage, the banker's safe my old stocking, the policeman's fist my billy. . . . I let the meat trust butcher my pig, the oil trust mould my candles, the sugar trust boil my sorghum, the coal trust chop my wood, the barb wire trust split my rails" (p. 4).

Not all attempts to create trusts were successful. Nevertheless, the anticompetitive effects of the trusts were sufficient to stimulate government action. In 1887, the Interstate Commerce Commission was established to regulate the railroad industry, setting the precedent for independent regulatory agencies. Three years later, Congress passed the Sherman Antitrust Act, declaring trusts and other methods of monopolization illegal. The act was weakly enforced, however, and, ironically, the greatest wave of trust formation came in the two decades *after* its passage. By 1904, some 318 trusts were alleged to control two-fifths of the manufacturing assets in the United States (McCraw, 1984). It was only with the establishment of the Federal Trade Commission in 1914 that antitrust sentiment had the full weight of the government on its side.

**Regulating Products.**    The consumer movement as we know it today descends more directly from the late nineteenth- and early twentieth-century attempts to control food and drug adulteration than it does from the antitrust movement. Starting in the 1860s, scientists, physicians, and pharmacists agitated for regulation of foods and drugs by local boards of health (Okun, 1986). In some instances, businesses supported regulation, because it was difficult for the honest producer to compete with someone who sold adulterated products.

Federal action pertaining to food safety can be traced back to 1862 when Charles Wetherill set up a laboratory in the newly created Department of Agriculture to analyze samples of food, fertilizers, and other agricultural substances (Janssen, 1981). In 1865, a federal law was passed to outlaw the importation of diseased cattle and swine (Nadel, 1971). Concern with drugs can be dated back even farther. In 1848, the Import Drugs Act was passed to stem the tide of counterfeit, contaminated, diluted, and decomposed drugs being sold in the United States (Janssen, 1981). Despite these early precedents, the level of federal food and drug regulation was still inadequate, and state laws were often helpless to deal with goods shipped between states.

The rudimentary level of government control was matched by the primitive state of production techniques and products themselves. Ice was still the principal means of refrigeration. Milk was not pasteurized, nor were cows tested for tuberculosis. Patent medicines might contain opium, morphine, heroin, cocaine, or alcohol. Their labels did not indicate their contents but did claim they would cure every disease imaginable.

The efforts of the antiadulteration movement culminated in 1906 with the passage of the Pure Food and Drug Act and the Meat Inspection Act. These pieces of legislation owed their existence in no small measure to the efforts of one person, Dr. Harvey W. Wiley, who became head of the Department of Agriculture's Division of Chemistry in 1883. Drawing on the findings of his chemists, Wiley attempted to publicize dangers in the American food supply. In 1903 he established his "poison squad," a group of young male volunteers from the Bureau of Chemistry who ingested measured amounts of chemical preservatives with the purpose of observing their effects. The "experiments" generated substantial media coverage and helped awaken the public to food safety issues.

Wiley's efforts were supplemented by those of a number of citizens' groups, especially those composed of women. The National Consumers League, originally founded to improve the working conditions of women and children through selective boycotts, was one of these. The American Medical Association, perhaps worried about the competition from patent medicine manufacturers, also joined the fight (Nadel, 1971). Crusading journalists like Ida Tarbell and Lincoln Steffens (known as muckrakers) heightened public concern through cartoons, magazine articles, and editorials. Finally, President Theodore Roosevelt lent his support to the cause, knowing firsthand the difficulty of commanding soldiers during the Spanish-American War who were sick from adulterated meat rations.

Given the political resistance of food manufacturers and the lack of precedent for federal laws regulating the food supply, the struggle to pass consumer protection legislation might have dragged on longer had it not been for the publication in 1906 of Upton Sinclair's novel, *The Jungle*. His book is often referred to as the first consumer exposé, the forerunner of such books as Rachel Carson's *Silent Spring* and Ralph Nader's *Unsafe at Any Speed*. Yet, *The Jungle* became a consumerist classic largely by accident. Sinclair was far less concerned about the unsanitary conditions of the meat-packing industry than he was about the inhumane conditions under which the industry's employees worked and lived. True, exploitation of consumers and workers stemmed from a common source in Sinclair's mind, but the harm to middle-class consumers (those who had enough money to buy meat) was nothing to Sinclair in comparison to the daily horrors experienced by the novel's central characters, an immigrant family trying to work in Chicago's stockyards. To Sinclair's disappointment, the public outrage his book inspired was channeled into consumer protection reform. He is reported to have said, "I aimed for the nation's heart, but I hit its stomach instead."

The following passage from the novel describes the process by which ham that was spoiled beyond the point of concealment was made into sausage:

There would be meat stored in great piles in rooms; and the water from leaky roofs would drip over it, and thousands of rats would race about on it. It was too dark in these storage places to see well, but a man could run his hand over piles of meat and sweep off handfuls of the dried dung of rats. These rats were nuisances, and the packers would put poisoned bread out for them, they would die, and then rats, bread, and meat would go into the hoppers together. (p. 136)

Sometimes men, working in dark, steam-filled rooms, would fall into the cooking vats, and "when they were fished out, there was never enough of them left to be worth exhibiting—sometimes they would be overlooked for days, till all but the bones of them had gone out to the world as Durham's Pure Leaf Lard!" (p. 102).

Such descriptions ignited public outrage and provided the final push for the passage of landmark consumer legislation—the Meat Inspection and Pure Food and Drug acts of 1906. Eventually, however, World War I put an end to the first era of American consumerism, as the concerns of war supplanted those of peacetime consumption.

Thus, the first wave of consumer activism in the United States was a part of the broader Progressive movement. The regulation of large firms, whether to prevent them from suppressing competition or to force them to observe minimal standards of worker and consumer safety, was consistent with the Progressive theme of the "people" versus the "special interests." But for all its accomplishments—the formation of the first consumer organizations, the passage of the first consumer protection legislation, and the attacks on monopolies, trusts, and cartels—the first wave of consumer activism lacked the kind of consumer consciousness that was to characterize later periods of consumer protest. To the extent that people were beginning to recognize their distinct political interests as consumers, it was part of a more basic and in some ways reactionary critique of industrial capitalism. Consumer consciousness was rooted in agrarian values of family and community. It found expression in the establishment of consumer cooperatives and the attempts of the Populist movement to reunite production and consumption by eliminating middlemen, but consumer consciousness had not yet developed a modern, urban form (Thelen, 1983).

# The Second Era of Consumer Activism

Whereas the first wave of consumerism in the United States was an outgrowth of the massive changes wrought by the early stages of the Industrial Revolution, the second wave may be conceived as a response to that revolution's broadening impact—beyond the factories and transportation systems to the home, the domain of consumption itself.

## The Changing Character of Consumption

If the automobile assembly line epitomized the United States in the years before World War I, the electrification of the American home did so in the years following it. In 1907, only 8 percent of dwellings in the United States had electricity; by 1925, less than a decade after the war ended, 53.2 percent had electricity (U.S. Bureau of the Census, 1975). A household equipped with electricity was a household primed for the purchase of electrical appliances. Accordingly, the 1920s were marked by the introduction or accelerated diffusion of electric irons, washing machines, refrigerators, sewing machines, and vacuum cleaners. When a consumer purchased any of these appliances, it was likely to be for the first time, so the purchase decision was complicated by both inexperience and perceived technological complexity. An "automatic" electric refrigerator, for example, represented a quantum leap in complexity when compared to an icebox.

Electricity, however, was only one of several factors that combined to make consumer decisions more difficult in the 1920s. Many new "convenience" products were introduced during this period, especially foods, such as packaged desserts; cleansers, such as specialized laundry soaps; and personal hygiene products, such as toothpastes. Rising real wages provided consumers with the discretionary income needed to purchase both durable and convenience goods.

In addition to the new products themselves, consumer choices were further complicated by aggressive salesmanship, particularly in the form of advertising. Historian Stephen Fox (1984) describes the discovery of bodily functions as the most enduring effect of advertising in the 1920s. For example, the sellers of Listerine exhumed the word *halitosis* from an old medical dictionary in order to pump life into the sales of their antiseptic (Marchand, 1985). In addition to sweetening their breath, other advisers urged consumers to start worrying about their feet, underarms, and teeth.

More subtle but equally important in terms of making consumer choice more difficult were advertising-abetted notions that consumers had to select the "right" styles, colors, and ensembles. Most people were barely getting used to having bathrooms and centrally heated water when they were told by advertisements that plain white towels were a sign of unsophisticated taste. Advertising suggested the importance of coordinating the styles and hues found in even relatively private rooms such as the bathroom, kitchen, and bedroom (Marchand, 1985).

In short, a heightened need for consumer information resulted from rising real incomes, improvements in technologies, and widening choice. Yet, while the need for objective product information increased, the amount contained in national advertising decreased. The hallmark of advertising in the 1920s was an emphasis on "the results of a given purchase—health, happiness, comfort, love, social success—and the corollary disadvantages of not having the product" (Fox, 1984, p. 95). Advertising also sought to be artistic, comforting, entertaining—anything but informative (Marchand, 1985).

## Provision of Objective Consumer Information

It was in this climate of consumer noninformation that *Your Money's Worth,* by Stuart Chase and Frederick J. Schlink, appeared in 1927. The book depicted American consumers as operating in a world of "conflicting claims, bright promises, fancy packages, soaring words, and almost impenetrable ignorance" (p. 2). The authors attempted to expose the sales practices that wasted the consumer's purchasing power and robbed the nation of the true benefits of mass production. They railed against virtually any practice that made it difficult to weigh precisely price and quality—fraud, high-pressure salesmanship, nonfunctional styling, and planned obsolescence. The authors also decried product differentiation (the sale of brands differentiated only on superficial grounds) and a lack of standardization of sizes, forms, nomenclature, and practices. Chase and Schlink noted that a "housewife needing a sewing machine needle in an emergency might as well look for one in a haymow as on a neighbor's machine. Such needles are made in nine diameters . . . and in lengths varying by as little as one thirty-second of an inch" (p. 174).

The authors of *Your Money's Worth* offered a number of suggestions on how the consumer might drastically reduce the cost of living. Their recommendations included exercising healthy skepticism, making products at home, having the government set product standards, and establishing impartial testing laboratories. Chase and Schlink saw the federal government and universities as the most likely sponsors of such labs but ultimately hoped for private funding. In the interim, consumers were encouraged to follow Schlink's lead. He had set up "an experiment station," in conjunction with a community church in White Plains, New York, that prepared two confidential lists: "The first list carries products considered to be of good value in relation to their price; the second, products one might well avoid, whether on account of inferior quality, unreasonable price, or of false and misleading advertising" (p. 254).

The book generated hundreds of letters from people who wanted to know more about consumer products, and Schlink recognized that he now had the opportunity to expand his consumer club into a full-fledged consumer testing and information service. The new organization, Consumers' Research, Inc., received financial support from the patrons of several liberal magazines, and Schlink's friends added editorial and technical assistance. The confidential "Consumer's Club Commodity List" was thereby transformed into a magazine, *Consumers' Research Bulletin,* dedicated to product testing and information dissemination. Subscriptions went from 565 in 1927 to 42,000 five years later (Silber, 1983).

Again, in 1933, Frederick Schlink was co-author, this time with board member Arthur Kallet, of a book that would serve as a catalyst for consumer protest. The book, *100,000,000 Guinea Pigs: Dangers in Everyday Foods, Drugs and Cosmetics,* was a best-seller. As the title implies, it was an indictment of the way in which companies exposed unwitting consumers to untested new technologies. The metaphor of people as guinea pigs captured the feeling, fueled by the desperate conditions of the Great Depression, that consumers were at the mercy of larger forces (Silber, 1983).

Unfortunately, Schlink's skill as an administrator of Consumers' Research, Inc., did not match his prowess as an author. Schlink, with his wife and close friends making up a majority of the board of directors, held tight control of hiring, firing, editorial, and budgetary decisions. As the organization grew in size and diversity, debates emerged among staffers regarding its goals and future directions.

Following several meetings in which staff members discussed their grievances, the workers formed a chapter of the Technical, Editorial and Office Assistants Union in August 1935. When Schlink fired John Heasty for seeking union recognition, a strike broke out. Schlink rejected arbitration of the dispute; instead he used strikebreakers, legal injunctions, and armed detectives to control the magazine's offices and keep it operating. A number of the magazine's critics delighted in the fact that consumerists were at war with themselves (Silber, 1983).

With positions hardened, thirty employees, led by Arthur Kallet, decided to establish an organization to publish a new magazine, this time combining the interests of workers and consumers. The organization was called Consumers Union. Whereas Consumers' Research had ignored working conditions in evaluating products, the new publication would take them into account. Consumers' Research had shunned overtly political activity, but Consumers Union would engage in boycotts, educational campaigns, and political alliances. Finally, whereas Consumers' Research had created a gulf between workers and management, Consumers Union would govern itself collectively.

Consumers Union published the first issue of its magazine, *Consumers Union Reports,* in May of 1936. Only two years later, the circulation of *Consumer Reports,* as the magazine came to be called, surpassed that of *Consumers' Research Bulletin.* Under the steady hand of Colston E. Warne, who served as Consumers Union's president from 1936 to 1980, the organization grew steadily in circulation and reputation. As for Consumers' Research, its magazine is still being published, but it contains little product testing information and has less than one percent the 1987 circulation of *Consumer Reports.*

## Consumer Representation

The establishment of Consumers Union was one of the key events in the second era of consumerism in the United States. Another landmark, which occurred at about the same time, involved the attempt to provide consumer representation in the federal government. The Great Depression heightened the need to spend limited funds wisely and legitimized a critical attitude toward business practices. Perhaps more important for the future of the movement, the New Deal programs aimed at economic recovery established the principle of consumer representation. The most notable examples were the Consumer Advisory Board within the National Recovery Administration (NRA) and the Consumers' Counsel within the Department of Agriculture (Creighton, 1976). These advisory groups were created because New Deal programs involved an unprecedented degree of government planning and control over the economy. To prevent planning from being dominated by business and labor, representatives of the consuming public were needed. This was especially true because the thrust of many recovery programs was to raise prices and restore profits by restricting production.

But the New Deal efforts to establish consumer representation within government failed for several reasons. Since the consumer movement was still taking shape, it was difficult to define and identify consumer representatives. Once selected, consumer representatives had no clear program for achieving economic recovery. Specifically, the consumer's interest in low prices and high volume seemed out of step with other proposals for curing the Great Depression. Finally, administrators of New Deal programs like Gen. Hugh S. Johnson, head of the NRA, were not always convinced that a separate consumer point of view existed or needed to be articulated. Johnson believed, for example, that consumers (and workers) would be best served by making it profitable for industry to increase production (Creighton, 1976).

Despite these problems and the absence of any clear accomplishments by the consumer representatives, consumer representation during the New Deal did help clarify some important issues. Creighton (1976) attributes three such accomplishments to the consumer representatives:

They began to articulate the limits of the consumer's interest in a changing economy where the forces of the market could no longer be relied on to protect the consumer interest. Where there was to be government regulation of areas of the economy, they recognized the need for consumer advocacy to balance the influence of other special interests. And, finally, their inability to generate this support led them to the conclusion that the inherent weakness of consumers meant, inevitably, the need for government support to right the balance. (p. 27)

## Rural Electrical Cooperatives

While attempts to establish national-level consumer representation within New Deal programs had mixed results, grass-roots consumer action was successfully stimulated by another depression era project—the rural electrification program. The first step toward government-assisted rural electrification was the establishment in 1933 of the Tennessee Valley Authority (TVA), which was charged with developing the resources of the entire Tennessee River basin. In 1935, President Franklin Roosevelt created, via executive order, the Rural Electrification Administration (REA) with the goal of bringing reasonably priced electricity to the nation's farmers. Since the private power industry had already proved its unwillingness to tackle the problem, consumer-owned cooperatives emerged as the vehicle for achieving rural electrification, with the federal government lending money and providing technical assistance. The REA became a permanent entity in 1936 (Ellis, 1982).

The agency amassed an impressive record. In the seven years preceding the Japanese attack on Pearl Harbor in late 1941, the percentage of electrified farms increased from 11 to 38 percent, although part of the increase was attributable to efforts by private power companies. To many participants in the rural electrification cooperatives, their achievement was more than economic; it was social as well. The program drew together diverse people—from federal engineers to farmers—in a common cause (Ellis, 1982). When the spirit of consumer activism peaked again in the 1960s, rural electrification organizations provided the fledgling consumer movement with much needed financial and moral support.

## Stronger Legislation

Another major feature of consumerism between the two world wars was the strengthening of food and drug legislation. By the 1930s, the food and drug legislation passed in 1906 had been weakened by court decisions and rendered obsolete by technological changes in production and distribution. In particular, the government lacked the authority to control labeling and had to show that consumer deception was intentional in order to bar false claims. In 1933, President Roosevelt authorized Assistant Secretary of Agriculture Rexford Tugwell to submit a revision of the 1906 Food and Drug Act, but the proposed bill ran into heavy opposition from industry and advertising groups. It would take a five-year campaign of public education, as well as a tragedy, to achieve passage of the Federal Food, Drug, and Cosmetic Act in 1938.

To dramatize to the public the need for new legislation, the Food and Drug Administration (FDA) created an exhibit consisting of useless or dangerous patent medicines, cosmetics, and foods. The press gave the name "Chamber of Horrors" to the exhibit. In 1936, Ruth De Forest Lamb published her book *The American Chamber of Horrors,* carrying the FDA's message to a broader audience (Herrmann, 1970a). Although support for the legislation was gradually building, the final impetus for congressional action came from a tragedy. About a hundred people died when they took "elixir of sulfanilamide," the liquid form of a new sulfa-based drug. The drug apparently was safe in capsule form, but its liquid formulation contained a toxic solvent, diethylene glycol.

Even though the Food, Drug and Cosmetic Act of 1938 was subjected to numerous compromises, it was still a major improvement in several respects. The new law extended the FDA's jurisdiction to include cosmetics and therapeutic devices. Proof of fraud was no longer required to stop false claims for drugs. Most important, drug manufacturers were required to provide scientific proof that new products were safe (although not necessarily effective) *before* placing them on the market. No longer could consumers be used as unsuspecting guinea pigs.

One other significant piece of federal legislation was passed in 1938—the Wheeler-Lea Amendment to the Federal Trade Commission Act of 1914. The amendment empowered the FTC to regulate deceptive practices in addition to unfair ones. This had the effect of giving the FTC explicit jurisdiction over a wide range of harmful business practices, including deceptive advertising (Feldman, 1976).

As in the first era of consumer activism in the United States, consumer protection legislation in the second era resulted from a combination of long-term lobbying efforts, a political climate supportive of change, muckraking authors, and "fortuitous" scandals. And like the first wave of activism, the second was eclipsed by a world war. It was not until the 1960s that interest in consumerism was again rekindled.

## The Third Era of Consumer Activism

The decade following World War II was not hospitable to any forms of social protest, including consumerism. After the shortages of the war years, consumers were eager to start spending their wartime savings and make up for past deprivation. It wasn't necessary to have the best refrigerator for the money as long as you had a new one.

Nevertheless, one might have expected more consumer activism in the 1946–56 period than took place. Inflation increased consumer prices, especially during the first half of the period. Consumers were faced with difficult choices among new and technologically complex products. For example, two-thirds of American households had acquired their first television set by 1953 (Leuchtenburg, 1973). Similarly, consumers encountered complicated new service offerings in the postwar years, such as life insurance, installment credit, and the first credit cards (introduced in 1950 by Diner's Club). Inflation and the proliferation of consumer options had helped fuel the two earlier waves of consumer activism in the United States. Why not this time?

For one thing, McCarthyism—an ill-conceived and overzealous attempt to purge the United States of alleged communist influences—had a chilling effect on all social movements in the country, including consumerism. Anyone who criticized the practices of American businesses was likely to be labeled a communist and have his or her life ruined. Interestingly, the House Committee on Un-American Activities, the platform from which Sen. Joseph McCarthy launched his attacks, had been used in 1938 to investigate charges that Consumers Union was a communist front (Warne, 1982).

Still, consumer activism was absent from the American scene until the 1960s primarily because consumers were relatively satisfied. Despite inflation, real wages climbed after 1950. Not only were products readily available, but each year brought a new and improved version. Finally, the abundant economy provided American workers with more leisure time to enjoy their purchases.

### Rebirth of Consumer Protest

Given this level of contentment with the American standard of living, it is not surprising that the opening salvos in the third era of consumer activism were aimed not so much at the goods people consumed as at the methods by which products were promoted. In 1957, Vance Packard's *The Hidden Persuaders* indicted the advertising industry for using psychological techniques to manipulate consumers. Packard's charges of manipulation went beyond the marketplace to include political campaigns as well. The attack on advertising was intensified in 1958 with the publication of John Kenneth Galbraith's *The Affluent Society.* Galbraith was less concerned by the methods of advertising than by its social effects. He contended that advertising played a key role in making the United States an "unbalanced society" in which the pursuit of private goods overwhelmed the provision of public goods such as schools, museums, and hospitals.

The triumvirate of writers who helped spark the third wave of consumerism was rounded out by Rachel Carson. Her 1962 book, *Silent Spring,* focused on the damage caused by indiscriminate use of pesticides. Still other exposés were to follow in 1963. David Caplovitz documented the problems of low-income consumers in *The Poor Pay More,* and Jessica Mitford uncovered abusive funeral sales practices in *The American Way of Death.* Yet, by 1963, the spark for consumer protection had already jumped from the exposé writers to the halls of government.

### Federal Initiatives

**Kennedy's Consumer Message.** President John Kennedy's consumer message to Congress serves as a convenient starting point for the third era of consumer activism in the United States. The message, the first one by a president on the topic of consumer protection, was delivered on 15 March 1962. In it, President Kennedy enunciated a Consumer Bill of Rights, including the rights to (1) safety, (2) information, (3) choice among a variety of products and services at competitive prices, and (4) a fair hearing by government in the formulation of consumer policy.

Mark Nadel (1971) argues that Kennedy's consumer message is more important in retrospect than it seemed at the time. He claims that the message contained few genuinely new ideas and that consumer protection was not a high priority of the Kennedy administration. Robert Lampman (1988), one of the drafters of the message, disagrees. He notes that placing a high priority on consumer protection had been one of Kennedy's election promises. Prior to the 1962 message, he had already begun the process of making good on his promises by revitalizing several of the independent regulatory agencies and increasing consumer representation within government agencies.

**Amendments to Drug Safety Law.**  Even if the importance of Kennedy's consumer message was largely symbolic, 1962 did witness a concrete consumer protection achievement—the passage of the Kefauver-Harris Amendments to the Federal Food, Drug, and Cosmetic Act. In 1959, Sen. Estes Kefauver introduced a strong bill primarily directed at reducing drug prices rather than making drugs safer. Its chances of passage were remote; even Kennedy favored a much weaker bill. Then, a front-page story in the *Washington Post* revealed that only the efforts of a single FDA doctor, Frances Kelsey, had prevented the marketing in the United States of thalidomide, a drug that had produced birth defects when taken by pregnant women in West Germany and Great Britain.

The narrowness by which a thalidomide tragedy had been averted in the United States aroused public opinion and moved Congress to action. Senator Kefauver's legislation, although originally designed to address only economic abuses in the drug industry, ended up dealing with safety and effectiveness issues almost exclusively. The centerpiece of the 1962 amendments was the requirement that new drugs be tested for efficacy, as well as safety, before being released on the market (Nadel, 1971).

Despite Kennedy's consumer message and the passage of the Kefauver-Harris Amendment, the United States was not yet ready for another wave of consumer activism in 1962. There would be no further presidential initiative in the area of consumer protection until 1964 and no additional major pieces of legislation until 1966.

**A Presidential Adviser for Consumer Affairs.**   In 1964, President Lyndon Johnson appointed Esther Peterson, an assistant secretary of labor, to be the first special presidential assistant for consumer affairs. Having been schooled in the women's and labor movements, Peterson was not afraid to speak out in favor of proconsumer positions. As a result, she ruffled the feathers of business interests. The Advertising Federation of America, demonstrating a surprising lack of creativity, labeled her "the most dangerous thing since Ghengis Khan" (Negin, 1985). President Johnson was never completely comfortable with her aggressive style; he asked her to step down in the spring of 1967 and replaced her with Betty Furness, a one-time television personality. It was originally believed that Furness would be sympathetic to business positions, but she became an increasingly strong consumer advocate during her two years in the post (Creighton, 1976). Virginia Knauer became special assistant for consumer affairs in the Nixon and Ford administrations. Then Peterson was asked by Jimmy Carter to reassume her old post. Finally, Knauer was reappointed special assistant by President Ronald Reagan.

Regardless of who has held the position, the special assistant for consumer affairs has never wielded a great deal of influence. Nevertheless, continued existence of the position reveals the extent to which the consumer interest has been institutionalized in the federal government.

**Legislative Outpouring.**   The years 1966–68 witnessed the passage of several key consumer protection statutes. The string of legislative victories began with the 9 September 1966 signing of the National Traffic and Motor Vehicle Safety Act. The issue of auto safety had been languishing for more than a decade until Sen. Abraham Ribicoff called Ralph Nader to testify at a congressional hearing and the subsequent revelation that General Motors was spying on Nader (Whiteside, 1972).

Ralph Nader was to become the unchallenged leader of the American consumer movement, his name becoming almost synonymous with it. His 1965 book, *Unsafe at Any Speed,* is remembered as an exposé of safety defects in the design of Chevrolet's Corvair, but it was much more. It was an indictment of the entire automobile industry, and by extension other giant corporations, for ignoring the consumer's desire for a safe car and contributing so massively to air pollution.

Although Nader showed that a single concerned citizen could triumph against one of the world's largest corporations, he moved to institutionalize his guerrilla operation by establishing the Center for the Study of Responsive Law. The center served as the staging area for Nader's Raiders, typically idealistic students who spent their summers in Washington, D.C. The Raiders descended on federal agencies such as the Federal Trade Commission, Interstate Commerce Commission, and Food and Drug Administration. Their mission was to document the extent to which these regulatory watchdogs had fallen asleep on the job or, worse, become the tools of the very interests they were supposed to regulate.

Over time, an extensive mythology has grown up around Nader. His ascetic life-style is particularly intriguing. He shuns car ownership, lives in a rooming house in a low-rent district, reads only nonfiction, scrutinizes his food for dangerous additives, and has virtually no social life (Auletta, 1983). The nation's premier consumer advocate is the ultimate nonconsumer! He views consumption as a potential trap in which individuals trade their social commitment for a share of the good life. In many ways, Nader is far more devoted to the traditional values of hard work, thrift, individual responsibility, and civic involvement than many of the business leaders who have branded him un-American (Rowe, 1985). His single-mindedness has endeared him to journalists, but it has also caused friction with his coworkers and political allies, whom he expects to be as indifferent to material comfort and unwilling to compromise as he is.

With Nader and his associates shooting from the hip and distracting the opposition's attention, more moderate consumerists, particularly a number of consumer-minded members of Congress, succeeded in passing a series of major pieces of consumer legislation. In 1966, the Child Protection Act, banning dangerous toys from interstate commerce, and the Fair Packaging and Labeling ("Truth-in-Packaging") Act were signed into law. The Wholesome Meat Act and Flammable Fabrics Act Amendments were enacted the next year. In 1968, the Consumer Credit Protection ("Truth-in-Lending") Act, Interstate Land Sales Full Disclosure Act, Natural Gas Pipeline Safety Act, Poultry Inspection Act, and Radiation Health and Safety Act became law. And this was only the beginning.

The third era of consumer activism in the United States reached its peak in the early 1970s. The Consumer Product Safety Commission was created in 1972 to coordinate and strengthen federal efforts to protect consumers from unreasonable product risks. Consumer rights pertaining to credit were strengthened in 1974 with the passage of the Fair Credit Billing Act and the Equal Credit Opportunity Act. In 1976, premarket testing of all new chemical substances was mandated by the Toxic Substances Control Act.

Nader's popularity among the public provides an alternative indicator of the high-water mark of American consumerism's third wave. A Gallup poll conducted in January 1972 ranked Nader seventh among the nation's most admired people, immediately ahead of Pope Paul VI and Bob Hope (Gallup, 1972). A December 1974 Gallup poll asked a national sample of adults to name their preferred presidential candidate for the 1976 race. Nader was the ninth choice among Democrats, one place ahead of 1984 nominee Walter Mondale, and the fifth choice among independents, only one place behind 1972 nominee George McGovern (Gallup, 1978). The eventual candidate Jimmy Carter was far down on both lists.

Until about 1976, consumerists were highly successful in Congress, but during the Carter administration the movement lost its legislative momentum. Mark Green (1977), director of the Nader organization Congress Watch and one of Nader's most durable associates, attributed this shift to a public disenchantment with government (fueled by the Watergate scandal), a rejuvenated Republican party, and a more effective lobbying effort on the part of business interests. The consumer movement's declining fortunes in Congress, however, were partially offset by the appointment, for the first time, of consumer activists to high-level posts in federal agencies. But with Reagan's election four years later, the movement lost whatever grip it had attained on the government's regulatory apparatus, and 1980 thus serves as a convenient point for marking the end of the third era of consumer activism. This was also the year in which Nader turned over the reins of Public Citizen, an umbrella organization for a variety of consumer groups, to Dr. Sidney Wolfe.

## Causes of the Third Era of Consumerism

What brought about the third era of consumerism in the United States? Essentially two types of explanations have been offered. One emphasizes underlying conditions, citing the enduring and pervasive consumer problems that propel the growth of consumerism. The second focuses on the role of leaders ("political entrepreneurs") in resource mobilization, examining the process by which consumer organizations obtain financial support and media attention.

The tension between the two views is encapsulated in the question: Would there have been a third era of consumerism in the United States without Ralph Nader? Some would argue that Nader played an irreplaceable role in awakening public awareness of consumer problems. Advocates of the opposing view would assert that someone else would have emerged to lead the consumer crusade if Nader hadn't.

**Underlying Social Conditions.**   Analysts who believe that underlying societal conditions account for the emergence of consumerism's third era have highlighted the role of economic, technological, and social factors (Aaker and Day, 1982; Feldman, 1980; Herrmann, 1970b, 1980; Swagler, 1979). The economic factors included rising prices, an increasingly impersonal marketplace, a lack of seller accountability in markets that were already national and becoming international in scale, deceptive sales practices, intrusive and irritating advertising, and a low level of salesperson expertise. Among the technological factors, increasingly complex products and the growing presence of computers allegedly contributed to consumer apprehensiveness.

Economic and technological changes provided the sparks for consumer activism, but social factors supplied the fuel. The third era of consumerism ignited in a society of highly educated consumers whose expectations regarding quality of life were rising. Above all, a climate of social activism existed in which society's powerful institutions were no longer immune from criticism and in which citizens (at least, a politically active minority of them) sought ways to imbue their personal lives with a public purpose.

Consumer movements in the United States have always been part of much larger social reform movements. As we have seen, the first era corresponded with the Progressive Era, and the second with the New Deal; the third wave coincided with the Great Society. The connection between consumerism and the desire for social progress also exists at the individual level; support for consumerist goals is consistently associated with liberal political beliefs and high levels of community involvement (Barksdale and Darden, 1972; Herrmann and Warland, 1976; Mayer, 1976; Warland, Herrmann, and Moore, 1984).

Progressivism in general and consumerism in particular can be interpreted as attempts on the part of both society and individuals to reconcile the traditional American values of thrift, restraint, refinement, and concern for one's fellow citizens with the increasing affluence afforded by an industrialized society (Horowitz, 1985). Consumerism provides a particularly convenient means for resolving these tensions. It expresses traditional values of efficiency and humanitarianism while at the same time legitimizing the enjoyment of consumption. It allows individuals to eat their cake and feel good about it too.

**Political Entrepreneurship.** While not dismissing the importance of underlying social conditions, some commentators have attributed periods of consumer activism, and the third era in particular, to the actions of savvy individuals who have managed to sell the idea of consumer protection to the public. Political entrepreneurship has been displayed by government officials, particularly presidents and legislators.

Mark Nadel (1971) argues that President Lyndon Johnson supported consumer protection legislation because it was good politics in three respects. First, after spectacular success during 1964 and 1965 in enacting his legislative programs (Medicare, civil rights, aid to education), Johnson was facing an increasingly recalcitrant Congress and needed to reestablish his national leadership. Second, any new legislative programs could not be expensive because the federal budget was already stretched by escalating U.S. involvement in Vietnam and new social programs. Third, at a time when the nation was becoming polarized by the Vietnam War and racial conflict, there was a clear need for a consensus issue that would appeal to all segments of the population. Consumer protection legislation met these political needs, providing President Johnson with an inexpensive and popular means of regaining the momentum of his legislative program.

Michael Pertschuk, former chairman of the Federal Trade Commission, makes a similar argument regarding the reasons his mentor, Sen. Warren Magnuson, became a consumer champion. Nearly defeated in his bid for reelection in 1962, Magnuson enlisted Gerald Grinstein, a young Ivy League–educated lawyer, to revitalize his political image. The two men decided that a strong proconsumer record would serve this purpose well. In the fall of 1964, they asked Pertschuk to join the staff of the Senate Commerce Committee in the newly created position of consumer counsel. Pertschuk's assignment was simple: to build a positive consumer record for Magnuson and make certain that the senator received appropriate recognition for his achievements. Pertschuk apparently did his job well. By 1968, eight new consumer protection laws bore Magnuson's name as principal author.

The benefits of advocating consumer protection are not confined to members of the government. Activists in the private sector can derive personal satisfaction, fame, and employment as a result of their efforts on behalf of consumers. If the nation elects a president who is particularly proconsumer, consumer activists may even find themselves selected for high-level government posts (for example, Jimmy Carter appointed auto safety activist Joan Claybrook as head of the National Highway Traffic Safety Administration). Thus, both government officials and nongovernment activists can reap benefits by advocating consumer protection.

The fullest explanation of the causes of consumerism combines underlying social conditions with resource mobilization by effective political entrepreneurs. It would be a mistake, however, to dismiss the debate between the two views as purely academic, for it has important implications for whether and when a fourth era of consumerism will occur in the United States. One point of view encourages the analyst to keep a lookout for social conditions capable of creating the next wave of consumerism. The other perspective suggests that a new round of consumerist activity will require the emergence of new leaders who are capable of managing the transactions (such as arousing public interest, obtaining financial support, building alliances with other social movements) necessary for a successful social movement.

*Chapter Three*

# The Movement's Structure

The consumer movement in the United States has grown from a minor component of the turn-of-the-century Progressive movement into a fixture on the current American political scene. It has also expanded beyond the confines of a few highly developed nations and can now be found in virtually all market-oriented economies, developed and developing alike. Despite the movement's longevity and broadening influence, however, it remains loosely coordinated both within nations and on an international scale.

A social movement's structure is critically important. A movement's division of labor, degree of coordination, patterns of decision making, and sources of internal tension all affect how much it will achieve. For example, a movement in which all individuals and organizations devote their resources to performing the same activity will probably accomplish less than one in which there is a moderate amount of specialization based on the unique skills of each constituent part. In order to analyze the structure of the contemporary American consumer movement, a set of criteria must be developed for defining inclusion in the consumer movement. Then, working with these criteria, the individuals and organizations that make up the consumer movement can be identified and the quality of the movement's structure assessed.

## Defining the Consumer Movement

When a social movement first emerges, those people willing to be publicly associated with it often draw a great deal of criticism. By the time a social movement gains maturity and public acceptance, however, most everyone seems to consider themselves part of it. Phyllis Schlafly calls herself a "feminist," and members of the nuclear power industry describe themselves as "environmentalists." The same applies to the consumer movement, with cigarette companies defending their right to advertise as a means of safeguarding the consumer's right to be informed.

Given the expanding willingness of individuals and organizations to describe themselves as "consumerist" or "proconsumer," one needs a definition of the consumer movement that is discriminating yet sufficiently inclusive. One key issue is whether membership in the movement should be determined by self-designation or by general recognition from other movement participants. Another difficult question is whether a member of the movement must pursue consumer welfare as its primary goal rather than as one among several goals. A final problem is whether government agencies and officials should be included within the movement since so much movement activity involves applying pressure on government officials.

The most persuasive argument for a very broad definition of the movement is offered by marketing scholars Paul Bloom and Stephen Greyser (1981). Drawing on sociological theory (McCarthy and Zald, 1973, 1977), Bloom and Greyser compare consumerism to a product, like breakfast cereal or laundry detergent, that is in the mature stage of its life cycle and has experienced a high degree of market fragmentation. Following the analogy of a completely open market, Bloom and Greyser consider any organization (or individual) that conceives of itself as belonging to the consumer movement—regardless of its primary objectives and its governmental or nongovernmental character—as part of the consumerism "industry." Although their view may be overly inclusive, examining it provides a useful introduction to many consumerists.

Bloom and Greyser identify eight "firms" vying for public acceptance of their brand of consumerism: nationals, locals, feds, coops, reindustrialists, anti-industrialists, corporates, and deregulators. The nationals fall within any definition of the consumer movement one can imagine. They include large broad-based groups like the Consumer Federation of America, smaller multi-issue organizations like the National Consumers League and Ralph Nader's Public Citizen, and single-issue groups operating on a national level, like Action for Children's Television or GASP (Group Against Smokers' Pollution). The nationals are moderate to liberal in their political outlook, and their main products are lobbying and consumer representation in Washington, D.C.

The second category of sellers of consumerism, the locals, conduct their activities within states, counties, and cities. This category includes private consumer groups whose primary concern is the advancement of consumer rights. It also contains, however, people working in the mass media and government agencies for whom consumerism may be only one of several interests.

A third category, the feds, consists of federal agencies with programs designed to promote consumer welfare. In contrast to the nationals and the locals, the feds sell law enforcement and assistance in obtaining redress for consumer problems. As in the case of the locals, Bloom and Greyser do not confine membership in the consumer movement to nongovernmental entities.

The coops are private organizations that provide mechanisms through which consumers can pool their resources and obtain better information and/or better buys than they could have otherwise. Consumers Union, the publisher of *Consumer Reports,* and the Harvard Cooperative Society are representative of this category. The political philosophy of coops spans the spectrum from conservative to radical, including apolitical. The primary goal of the coops is the promotion of consumer welfare, but unlike the nationals and locals, they narrowly define consumer welfare in terms of direct economic benefits for their membership.

In the case of two additional sellers, consumerism is a relatively minor offering in a much broader product line. The reindustrialists, largely moderate to conservative in political philosophy, advocate strong government action to stimulate economic growth as well as greater cooperation between management and labor. Harvard economist Robert Reich (1987) is probably the best current representative of this version of consumerism, although his ideas were not yet prominent at the time Bloom and Greyser created their categories. The anti-industrialists, in contrast, are politically radical and sell citizen control of corporations and greater restraint in the use of technology. Represented by individuals like Nader associate Mark Green and California legislator Tom Hayden and by organizations such as Congress Watch and the Institute for Policy Studies, the anti-industrialists might describe themselves as belonging to a social movement designed to increase corporate accountability and economic democracy rather than improve consumer welfare per se.

The corporates, a seventh category, consist of consumer affairs offices in major corporations such as American Express, Coca-Cola, and Shell Oil. Their political orientation tends to be moderate, and their brand of consumerism consists of advising top management, educating consumers, and assisting in grievance resolution. In this category, Bloom and Greyser might have added Better Business Bureaus and organizations that specialize in improving consumer complaint handling by corporations (for example, the Technical Assistance Research Program Institute).

Counting business groups as a part of the consumer movement shows that Bloom and Greyser are willing to include entities from which traditional mainline consumer groups, such as the National Consumers League, the Consumer Federation of America, and Consumers Union, often try to distance themselves. For instance, these traditional consumer groups typically withhold voting privileges from business organizations and are very hesitant about accepting financial support from them.

The failure of the corporates to be generally regarded as part of the consumer movement by its central participants applies even more strongly to Bloom and Greyser's final category, the deregulators. Conservative in political orientation, they promote reduced government regulation as the best means of improving consumer welfare. Almost all deregulators advocate eliminating economic regulation of airlines, trucking, and licensed professions (exemplified by Alfred E. Kahn, Cornell University economist and former chairman of the Civil Aeronautics Board). Some deregulators seek in addition an end to social regulation concerning product safety and environmental protection (exemplified by Murray Weidenbaum, Washington University economist and former chief economic adviser to President Reagan). The American Enterprise Institute, a conservative think tank in Washington, D.C., provides the best illustration of an institution committed to deregulation in all its forms.

In sum, Bloom and Greyser take the view that membership in the consumer movement is by self-designation, and they include within the movement many groups and individuals for whom consumer issues are a secondary concern, including governmental entities. This inclusive definition has the virtue of recognizing that there is diversity and conflict within the consumer movement. Furthermore, who has the right to say that a particular organization does not belong to the movement just because other participants reject its conception of what is in the best interest of consumers? Still, if the terms *consumerist* and *consumer movement* are to have any political meaning, I believe that they should not refer to a "deregulator" who advocates abolishing the Consumer Product Safety Commission or to a "corporate" who cares about consumer welfare only to the extent that it enhances a corporation's profits. In contrast to Bloom and Greyser's approach, this chapter defines a movement core—

*primary activists* who are generally regarded as belonging to the movement, make the pursuit of consumer welfare their major goal, and are not part of the government. The term *secondary activists* is used to describe those participants, including members of other social movements and government officials, who contribute significantly to the movement but for whom the importance of consumer welfare is subordinate to other values.

## Secondary Consumerists

The movement's core of primary activists is surrounded by a variety of secondary consumerists, one group of which is composed of the social movements with which the consumer movement on occasion forms alliances. These movements include those advocating for organized labor, farmworkers, the elderly, the natural environmental, clean government, and corporate accountability. Of these, the most notable may be the American labor movement, which has frequently added its political clout to efforts to pass consumer information disclosure laws (Nadel, 1971; Pertschuk, 1982), and whose influence continues to be felt within consumer organizations (Mayer, 1984). Nevertheless, consumer protection cannot be considered one of organized labor's central goals.

In addition to consumerism's allied social movements, secondary consumerists also include members of a variety of occupational and industry groups. The rationale for excluding these groups from the movement core is that, although they may contribute significantly to the advancement of consumer welfare, their members are more tightly bound to professional codes or the interests of particular institutions than to the norms of the political activist. These groups of secondary consumerists may draw their members from the business community, academia, the newsrooms of print and broadcast media, public interest law firms, or legislative and regulatory bodies.

Some descriptions of the consumer movement include a few of these professional groups while excluding others. For example, a recent analysis of the consumer movement (Herrmann, Walsh, and Warland, 1988) places the academically oriented American Council on Consumer Interests (ACCI) squarely in the core of the movement. The members of ACCI typically engage in research and/or teaching with an eye to the welfare of consumers, but ACCI members see themselves as scholars and educators first and activists second. Indeed, ACCI's primary publication, the *Journal of Consumer Affairs,* frequently contains articles that challenge the prevailing wisdom among consumer activists or attempt to evaluate how well (or poorly) consumer policies are working.

Several analysts find it difficult to separate investigative and advocacy journalists from the core of the consumer movement (Nadel, 1971; Pertschuk, 1982). There is no denying the enormous influence of people like *Washington Post* columnist Morton Mintz and NBC television reporter Betty Furness. Still, the activism of journalists is constrained by their professional norms of objectivity and is often motivated by the desire for a good story as much as by belief in the consumerist cause. Journalists are distinguished from the other professional groups mentioned in terms of their ease of access to the public, not the depth of their commitment to consumerism.

The decision to place governmental consumer activists outside the movement core is also a controversial one. Many definitions of social movements implicitly exclude government actors, instead viewing elected officials and bureaucrats as the objects of social movement pressure (Foss and Larkin, 1986; Stewart, Smith, and Denton, 1984). A few legislators in the U.S. Congress, however, have pursued their own consumerist agenda, often initiating and shepherding legislation, with or without strong support from private consumer advocates (Nadel, 1971). Foremost among these legislative consumer advocates have been representatives Benjamin Rosenthal (Dem., N.Y.) and Henry Waxman (Dem., Calif.), and senators Philip Hart (Dem., Mich.), Warren Magnuson (Dem., Wash.), and Howard Metzenbaum (Dem., Ohio). (No Republican has yet attained equivalent stature as a legislative champion of consumers, but things may be changing. In 1987, Republican senator Robert Stafford of Vermont became the first member of his party to receive a perfect score from the Consumer Federation of America on his voting record.)

No matter how dedicated to consumers, legislators cannot devote themselves exclusively to consumer issues; there are just too many other pressing matters. Perhaps then the best case for including government actors within the core of the consumer movement can be made regarding members of agencies—such as the Food and Drug Administration, Consumer Product Safety Commission, National Highway Traffic Safety Administration—who are committed full time to consumer matters. For example, Dr. Harvey Wiley, chief chemist for the U.S. Department of Agriculture, devoted himself to exposing dangerous food additives. More recently, David Pittle, former chairman of the Consumer Product Safety Commission, was unstinting in his efforts to rid the marketplace of products like chain saws and power lawn mowers that exposed consumers to unreasonable risks.

Despite the substantial accomplishments of some regulatory officials, however, there are reasons they should not be classified as part of the movement's core participants. In an extreme case, a regulator may deliberately try to dismantle an agency or may hold views that are at odds with the mainstream of the consumer movement. Even when government officials are sympathetic to consumer protection, their primary responsibility is to enforce and implement laws. They cannot single-mindedly advocate the consumer's position but must search for the elusive "public interest." This is especially true in agencies, such as the Interstate Commerce Commission, where officials regulate the activities of a single industry and must somehow balance the welfare of both producers and consumers. But it applies as well to the so-called social regulatory agencies, such as the Consumer Product Safety Commission, where regulators are not always required to consider the effects of their rulings on the economic health of affected industries. These regulators must still follow certain administrative procedures and are not free to be uninhibited advocates for consumers.

The term *secondary consumer activists* in no way implies that their contribution to the consumer cause has been of minor importance. Any consumerist hall of fame would certainly include a number of legislators, regulatory agency chairmen, academics, public interest attorneys, and journalists. To understand the consumer movement and the reasons for its successes and failures, however, it is useful to designate a movement core and then examine its relations (supportive and conflictual) with secondary consumerists.

## The Core of the Consumer Movement

Having stripped away the outer layers of the consumer movement, one is left with those individuals and organizations who are generally regarded as part of the American consumer movement by the public and by other movement participants, have the advancement of consumer welfare as their primary goal, and are not part of the government. Because these core participants vary in the issues they confront, the geographic scope of their activities, and the extent of their accomplishments, they do not always seem to be part of the same social movement. Thinking of them as different parts of the same body provides a useful analogy—even if the right hand may not always know what the left hand is doing.

## Ralph Nader

If the anatomical analogy is apt, Ralph Nader would be the head of the American consumer movement. Not only is Nader's face the most readily recognized of any consumer activist, but his ideas have provided identity and direction for more than two decades (although his importance has waned in recent years).

Just as the human brain receives, processes, and retransmits neural messages, Nader has served as a clearinghouse for the consumer movement (Nadel, 1971). He receives information from angry consumers, his own researchers, industry whistle-blowers, and government informants. He then organizes and transmits this information through press releases, appearances on the mass media, testimony to Congress, and publications.

Nader has always been portrayed as a leader, but a solitary one. His humbling of General Motors when the giant corporation spied on him cast him in the image of David fighting Goliath. Magazine covers have portrayed Nader as an itinerant medieval knight. One of his more sympathetic biographers, journalist Hays Gorey (1975), describes him as "an American Pied Piper, a male Jeanne d'Arc. A Lenin, some would say, or—others—a Luther" (p. 147). Common to all these allusions is the theme of an intensely driven individual who obtains power not by election or delegation but by seizure and force of example. Nader has founded or originally sponsored at least twenty organizations (Gorey, 1975), but he prefers to follow his personal agenda rather than oversee the daily operations of a far-flung empire.

Many people have wondered about what motivates Ralph Nader. His critics are sure that he is either an anticapitalist fanatic, a publicity seeker, or a puritan prig. When Sen. Robert F. Kennedy asked Nader directly about his motivations, Nader said that when he saw the human carnage that results from automobile accidents, he couldn't help but think that the United States and its auto industry are capable of doing better. This gap between the actual and the possible incenses Nader and gives rise to his belief that corporate decision makers lack accountability and responsibility (Buckhorn, 1972).

Nader is baffled and angered by the repeated questions about what makes him tick. If he were trying to prevent cruelty to animals, no one would ask why, but because he objects to defective cars, diseased meats, and other forms of cruelty to humans, his motives are questioned. According to Nader, the more relevant question is why so *few* people care enough to be consumer advocates.

Nader was born in Winsted, Connecticut, on 27 February 1934, the youngest child of Lebanese immigrants, Nadra and Rose Nader. He excelled in school and went on to attend Princeton, where he graduated magna cum laude in 1955, and Harvard Law School. Nader did not acquire his moral principles and willingness to challenge accepted views from these Ivy League institutions, however. He rebelled against the conformity of his fellow Princetonians by refusing to wear white bucks; once he went to class in a bathrobe. Nader viewed Harvard Law School as nothing but a "high-priced tool factory" which turned out lawyers for banks and other large corporations (Auletta, 1983).

If any single aspect of Nader's personal background explains his motivation, it is his parents. His father, Nadra, was passionately committed to social issues and spoke out frequently at town meetings. The restaurant that provided the family's main livelihood was known as a place where one fed the mind as well as the body. At home, Nadra sat at the head of a dinner table that resembled a college seminar. Ralph's sister, Laura, herself a well-known anthropology professor, recalls that her father would pose some hypothetical social problem for the family to discuss. She is certain that the family "think sessions" helped launch her younger brother toward a career that involved fighting for social justice (Buckhorn, 1972).

Nader's interest in automobiles, his first target, was apparently piqued during law school. He devoted much of his third year there to studying auto safety. After law school, Nader worked briefly for a law firm in Hartford, Connecticut, where, among other things, he handled automobile accident cases. Between 1961 and 1964, he worked as a journalist and traveled extensively. While in Scandinavia, Nader was particularly impressed by the ombudsman form of consumer representation. Upon his return, he helped introduce a bill in the Connecticut legislature to establish an ombudsman, but the legislative campaign was a failure.

Despite the 1965 publication of *Unsafe at Any Speed,* Nader might have continued to labor in obscurity if it not been for a blunder by General Motors. Irked by his book and fearing that he would serve as a witness in civil suits brought by automobile accident victims, GM hired private detectives to find something that might discredit him. The affair blew up in GM's face when Senator Ribicoff, before whose subcommittee Nader was scheduled to testify on the subject of auto safety, found out about the detectives. After adverse publicity, and fearing more of the same, GM agreed to give Nader $425,000 to drop his invasion of privacy suit. Nader used the money to bankroll literally dozens of consumer organizations. David Sanford, a Nader associate turned critic, concludes that "General Motors quite unintentionally saw to it that Nader would become the most powerful and probably the most admired private individual in the country" (1976, p. 7).

## Consumer Federation of America

The Consumer Federation of America (CFA), a federation of more than two hundred organizations, best fits the description of the consumer movement's backbone. In addition to its relentless lobbying efforts before Congress and regulatory agencies, the CFA has served as a nerve center for the consumer movement, coordinating the actions of diverse organizations throughout the nation. They include private consumer organizations (whether national, state, or local in scope), local consumer protection agencies, public power groups and rural electric cooperatives, credit unions, and trade unions. The CFA operates a State and Local Resource Center that strengthens state and local organizations by supplying them with information, technical assistance, and financial support. For example, the center prepares a monthly mailing to state and local consumer groups and offers small grants for travel and other activities.

## Consumers Union

Consumers Union (CU), publisher of the product testing magazine *Consumer Reports,* might well be considered the heart of the consumer movement in the United States, for it has pumped critical resources into the body of the consumer movement—legitimacy, information, and financial support. By virtue of its scientific product testing, CU has balanced the advocacy of more strident consumer activists and lent legitimacy to the entire consumer cause (Silber, 1983). The information CU provides to its nearly four million subscribers not only helps individual consumers get their money's worth in the marketplace but also provides consumer groups with ammunition in their attempts to pressure government entities and businesses. For example, CU's product testing plays an important role in publicizing automobile safety problems, most recently those involving the Suzuki Samurai ("Warning: The Suzuki . . .," 1988). Finally, CU's financial resources have enabled it to launch several consumer organizations, including the American Council on Consumer Interests, the International Organization of Consumers Unions, and regional advocacy offices in Washington, D.C., San Francisco, and Austin, Texas.

## Antismoking Groups

If CU is the heart of the consumer movement, its lungs are represented by two organizations with appropriate acronyms: Action on Smoking and Health (ASH) and Group Against Smokers' Pollution (GASP).

The first is headed by long-time antismoking advocate John Banzhaf III, described by the *Washington Post* as one of the fastest legal guns in the East—"a litigation-firing, George Washington University law professor with a zest for galloping into other people's court fights in the name of the public interest" (Ringle, 1984). Using a variety of methods to reduce smoking and protect the rights of nonsmokers, ASH has testified before Congress and regulatory agencies, brought shareholder resolutions before corporations, educated the public, and engaged in litigation. In its early years, ASH focused on reducing smoking per se. More recently, it has enjoyed some success in asserting the rights of nonsmokers by establishing separate smoking areas on commercial airplanes and in restaurants.

In contrast to ASH, GASP is exclusively devoted to promoting the rights of nonsmokers. Whereas ASH concentrates on legal challenges to cigarettes before federal regulatory agencies, GASP is an association of local chapters that engage in state and local action to protect nonsmokers. For example, the New Jersey chapter of GASP has urged corporations to create smoke-free office space and picketed tobacco-sponsored events such as the Metropolitan Museum of Art's Vatican exhibit, backed by Philip Morris (Langway, 1983).

## Food Issues

The stomach of the consumer movement would have to be assigned to the Center for Science in the Public Interest (CSPI). Michael F. Jacobson, the holder of a Ph.D. in microbiology from MIT, and Bruce Silverglade, a former FTC attorney, lead this pesky, fearless, and effective organization. It has two complementary goals with regard to food, nutrition, and health matters: to educate the public and to influence government and corporate policy.

Although CSPI claims to receive 60 percent of its operating budget from its fifty-eight thousand members (Bergner, 1986), its priorities largely reflect the interests and expertise of its staff. Freed from the need to receive direct member approval for its actions, CSPI's staff takes more forceful positions on health matters than professional associations such as the American Medical Association or voluntary health organizations such as the American Cancer Society (Segal, 1986). The Food and Drug Administration, by virtue of its wide-ranging responsibilities for the health of the American public, is the most frequent target of CSPI's wrath. CSPI petitions, lobbies, and generates media pressure to prod FDA action regarding salt, caffeine, pesticides, preservatives, food dyes, and antibiotics in food.

The Federal Trade Commission, which has jurisdiction over food advertising, also feels the heat of CSPI attacks on a frequent basis. The consumer group has charged the FTC with being too lax with respect to nutritional claims in advertisements. It questions, for example, whether advertisers of high-fiber cereals should be allowed to state that their products reduce the risk of cancer, and it views the claim that eating more cheese will prevent osteoporosis as downright deceptive. A McDonald's advertisement that shows whole potatoes and bottles of milk and says that McDonald's uses just a pinch of salt in its french fries is, according to CSPI's executive director, Michael Jacobson, extremely deceptive, since McDonald's milkshakes contain even more sodium than its french fries do (Miller, 1987).

In addition to safety issues relating to food, CSPI focuses on alcohol and environmental pollutants. It advocates ingredient, caloric, and warning labels on alcoholic beverages, as well as raising alcohol excise taxes. It has also compiled a long record of fighting to reduce exposure to toxic substances, such as asbestos, in the home, workplace, and ambient environment.

## Other National Consumer Organizations

The anatomical analogy may have reached the limits of its usefulness, but to complete it, the arms of the consumer movement might be assigned to those national organizations not already mentioned. Typically headquartered in Washington, D.C., many of them were either founded or inspired by Ralph Nader. One arm consists of multi-issue groups; the other arm represents organizations dedicated to a single type of consumer issue.

**Multi-Issue Groups.** We have already encountered the most important of the consumer movement's multi-issue organizations—the Consumer Federation of America. Of the remainder, the most notable are: (1) the National Consumers League; (2) Public Citizen, including Congress Watch and the Litigation Group; and (3) the Center for the Study of Responsive Law.

The oldest of these groups is the National Consumers League (NCL). Since its formation in 1899, NCL has represented both consumer and worker interests before government and business decision makers. With nine decades of experience, NCL has achieved a level of legitimacy and respect unmatched by most other consumer organizations. Early in its history, NCL joined in the fight for minimum wage standards, child labor restrictions, and workplace safety requirements. In more recent decades, NCL has exercised its lobbying and educational skills in the pursuit of food and drug safety and consumer information requirements. Most recently, NCL has devoted its greatest attention to health care issues, especially access to affordable, quality care for all Americans.

Originally founded in 1971 by Ralph Nader, Public Citizen, Inc. is the most complicated of the multi-issue organizations because it conducts its own activities as well as serving as an umbrella for six additional organizations. Playing on the theme of David fighting Goliath, Public Citizen serves as an effective mechanism for obtaining contributions from members of the public. By the end of 1972, four of Public Citizen's most important subgroups had been established: Health Research Group, Aviation Consumer Action Project, Litigation Group, and Tax Reform Research Group. Congress Watch, the legislative lobbying arm of Public Citizen, was formed in 1973.

Besides serving as a means of generating funds and publicizing the activities of its constituent parts, Public Citizen has served as a platform for its presidents. Ralph Nader served in that role until 1980, when he was succeeded by Dr. Sidney Wolfe, the head of the Health Research Group. In 1982, Joan Claybrook, head of the National Highway Traffic Safety Administration under Jimmy Carter, became Public Citizen's third president. All three of Public Citizen's presidents have used their positions to speak out forcefully on a variety of consumer and citizen issues.

Within Public Citizen, the Litigation Group is in charge of waging court battles for health, safety, and accountability of government and businesses ("PC's Greatest Hits," 1986). In 1972, when Ralph Nader got bumped from an Allegheny Airlines flight to Hartford despite having made an advance reservation, the Litigation Group filed a lawsuit that eventually (in 1978) resulted in stricter rules against bumping passengers. In 1973, it won a court decision that President Nixon's firing of Special Watergate Prosecutor Archibald Cox had been illegal, and in 1983, it won a major Supreme Court case that invalidated the provisions of more than one hundred federal laws that would have allowed Congress to overrule regulatory decisions. In 1986, a Litigation Group lawsuit successfully challenged the Gramm-Rudman-Hollings deficit reduction law as unconstitutional. In the same year, the group set a potentially important precedent by obtaining a Florida Supreme Court ruling that insurance agents may share their commissions with customers.

The other general purpose department of Public Citizen is Congress Watch. Congress Watch is devoted to representing consumer interests in legislative forums as well as serving as a congressional watchdog, two goals that often go hand-in-hand. For example, by annually publishing the votes cast and campaign contributions received by every member of the U.S. Senate and House, Congress Watch hopes to both influence future votes and increase accountability for past ones. Congress Watch engages in traditional forms of legislative lobbying as well; it claims at least partial credit for a number of consumer and environmental protection laws, including fuel economy requirements for cars (1975), the Toxic Substances Control Act (1976), legislation giving state attorneys general the right to sue price fixers (1977), and establishment of the Superfund to clean up toxic waste dumps (1980).

During the Reagan administration, Congress Watch's successes were largely defensive in nature. In 1981, the group helped thwart the Reagan administration's attempt to bury the Consumer Product Safety Commission in the Commerce Department. In 1982, it stopped passage of President Reagan's Regulatory Reform bill which would have given the director of the Office of Management and Budget unprecedented control over the decisions of regulatory agencies. Then, in 1983, Congress Watch played an important role in ending congressional funding for the Clinch River Breeder Nuclear Reactor, a project that consumer groups considered a $8.8 billion boondoggle ("PC's Greatest Hits," 1986).

A final example of a national, multi-issue consumer organization is the Center for the Study of Responsive Law (CSRL). The center was the first Nader organization, having been formed in 1968 with Nader as its sole founding trustee (Burt, 1982). It has been described as "Nader's Brookings Institute," reflecting its primary function of conducting and disseminating research studies relating to the general question of the responsiveness of law and legal institutions to the needs of the public (Burt, 1982). In its early years, CSRL was the base for Nader's Raiders and their investigations of government agencies such as the Interstate Commerce Commission, Federal Trade Commission, and Department of Agriculture. Several of these studies, although initially dismissed as gross exaggerations of minor problems, were later verified by other investigators and resulted in substantial improvements in government programs. More recent targets of CSRL's investigations include industry-sponsored school materials ("hucksters in the classroom"), the postal service, meat and poultry inspection, and nursing homes.

**Single-Issue Groups.** Complementing the multi-issue consumer organizations are single-issue groups focusing on such areas as (1) automobiles, (2) airlines, (3) health, (4) energy, and (5) insurance. Although more than one consumer organization may exist to address problems in a particular domain, this overview of the consumer movement's structure will confine itself to only one organization in each of these issue domains.

1. One of the oldest single-issue groups is the Center for Auto Safety. Founded in 1970, the center has the simple but ambitious goal of reducing the forty-six thousand motor vehicle–related deaths and the 1.7 million disabling injuries that occur annually (National Safety Council, 1986). After obtaining information from consumer complaints and accident reports, it prods the Department of Transportation, especially the National Highway Traffic Safety Administration (NHTSA), into action.

The Center for Auto Safety has played a leading role in a number of auto safety controversies. One example was the alleged tendency of Ford Motor Company vehicles to slip spontaneously out of park, pop into reverse, and take off. By the National Highway Traffic Safety Administration's (NHTSA) estimates, 165 deaths and 3,000 injuries were linked to the alleged transmission problems as of 1980 (Emshwiller and Camp, 1988). The Center for Auto Safety sought a recall of the millions of Ford vehicles with this potential problem, but NHTSA allowed Ford to send out advisory letters and warning labels instead. The center's executive director Clarence Ditlow III called the decision "illegal and a farce" ("Consumer Group. . . ," 1981) and tried in vain to get NHTSA to reconsider its decision. In 1985, congressional auditors reported that 138 people had been killed in connection with the alleged defects *after* NHTSA's decision not to require a recall ("Ford Lists . . .," 1986).

In an unfortunate replay of the Ford episode, the Center for Auto Safety was the first to charge that Audi 5000s had a runaway acceleration problem. This time Audi recalled about 250,000 vehicles to install a shift-lock device that would supposedly remedy the problem. Center director Ditlow again found this response inadequate, describing it as just a "relabeling" of company-instituted service campaigns. Ditlow was particularly galled by Audi's offer to make a free audiocassette available to drivers to reacquaint them with proper seating position and operation of controls ("Audi's 'Runaway' Recall . . .," 1986). Ditlow urged the government to order Audi to repurchase its 5000-series cars, instead of blaming the victims of its design defects ("Audi, Told . . .," 1987).

2. What the Center for Auto Safety tries to do on the ground, the Aviation Consumer Action Project (ACAP) attempts to do in the air. Its purpose is to promote consumer interests in aviation, especially safety. Ironically, ACAP's most important achievement temporarily reduced its significance. It worked for the passage of airline deregulation legislation

and elimination of the Civil Aeronautics Board, the government body before which it frequently appeared in the name of consumers. Recent disenchantment regarding airline deregulation, however, has revitalized the role of ACAP (McGinley, 1987b; McGinley and Dahl, 1987).

3. The Health Research Group (HRG), a subgroup of Public Citizen, has taken on the sizable task of monitoring the medical establishment, drug industry, and health-related regulatory agencies in the federal government. Its efforts are directed at all three branches of government: it presents testimony to Congress, petitions regulatory agencies, and initiates lawsuits. In addition, HRG is actively involved in educating the public through its publications and media appearances.

Dr. Sidney Wolfe is the Health Research Group's point man. Like Clarence Ditlow, Wolfe began his work under Ralph Nader's shadow but has since emerged as one of the consumer movement's most effective and well-known spokesmen. He has appeared before Congress more than forty times to address issues ranging from generic drugs and medical record confidentiality to product liability laws and emergency planning in the event of nuclear accidents. Wolfe has been described as adversarial, unfair, self-serving, and someone who enjoys confrontation (Schorr and Conte, 1984).

The Health Research Group is particularly fearless when it comes to taking on the pharmaceutical industry, whether through publications such as *Pills That Don't Work* or by hounding companies such as the makers of Oraflex, an arthritis drug, and Bendectin, a morning sickness drug, to withdraw drugs from the market. HRG also promotes worker safety in addition to consumer safety. HRG and Public Citizen's Litigation Group won a court battle with the Occupational Safety and Health Administration limiting worker exposure to ethylene oxide, a deadly gas ("PC's Greatest Hits," 1986).

4. There are several single-issue organizations concerned with energy policy, including two within Public Citizen—Critical Mass Energy Project (CMEP) and Buyers Up. The first group is devoted to replacing nuclear power, which it regards as both dangerous and expensive, with alternative energy sources. Its bête noire has been the Clinch River Breeder Nuclear Reactor, which was finally abandoned in 1983. More generally, CMEP challenges the pronouncements of the nuclear power industry, fights for greater public participation in nuclear plant licensing, draws attention to the high concentration of ownership in the nuclear industry, and seeks improved emergency planning for nuclear accidents.

The primary purpose of Buyers Up, a recent addition to Public Citizen, is to provide consumers, primarily in the Washington–Baltimore area, with volume discounts on home heating oil. It is also intended to serve as a model for other communities to negotiate group discounts not only for home heating but for weatherization, home repairs, and even legal services and insurance.

5. In the field of insurance, consumers are primarily represented by the National Insurance Consumer Organization (NICO). Like many of the organizations discussed above, NICO is strongly associated with its president, J. Robert Hunter. In serving as an advocate for insurance consumers, Hunter draws on his experience both as administrator of the Federal Insurance Administration and as a member of the insurance industry.

Originally established to help consumers buy insurance wisely and to eliminate abusive insurance industry practices, NICO's attention has been redirected in recent years to the so-called crisis in commercial liability insurance. While the insurance industry has called for restricting legal doctrines such as joint and several liability (under which an injured person may recover the full amount of an award from one of several negligent defendants) and limiting recovery (including attorneys' fees, punitive damages, and awards for pain and suffering), NICO has been providing an alternative perspective. Hunter (1986) claims that the current crisis has been caused by the insurance industry itself. In particular, the industry sells policies too cheaply during periods of high inflation, expecting far to outweigh underwriting losses with investment gains. When inflation abates, the claims mount and may exceed receipts. Thus, Hunter's preferred solution to the insurance problem is better state regulation, not radically altering the tort system.

## State and Local Consumer Organizations

If the arms of the consumer movement are its national organizations, its legs, the state and local groups, give it a solid foundation in the everyday concerns of ordinary consumers. One leg might be assigned to the myriad groups—some quite durable, others rising and falling with a single, short-term issue—staffed by private citizens, typically adult volunteers. The other leg would then represent the student-run public interest research groups (PIRGs) that function on many university and college campuses.

**Grass-roots Consumer Groups.** According to the Consumer Federation of America (1987), there are currently more than four hundred state and local consumer groups, not including government agencies, engaged in consumer advocacy in the United States. Taken together, these organizations are said to represent over two million members. (It is not clear whether this total counts individuals only once who belong to more than one organization.) Not surprisingly, the states with the most consumer groups are also the most populous, California and New York. The majority were founded during the 1970s and therefore have managed to sustain themselves for more than a decade.

Some consumer groups are the extension of a single activist individual and carry out few regular programs. Others, however, have successfully passed the mantle of leadership several times and can even afford paid staffs. An example of the more durable local consumer groups is Consumer Action of San Francisco. Founded in the early 1970s to help consumers achieve redress for their individual problems, Consumer Action's volunteers advised consumers regarding their rights in door-to-door transactions and picketed unscrupulous car dealers. Gradually, the group developed the ability to conduct research and to lobby at the state level. Today, some of Consumer Action's activities are national in scope, such as its studies regarding banking charges. Moreover, its executive director, Ken McEldowney, serves as president of the Consumer Federation of America and testifies before Congress.

**CUBs.** A particularly noteworthy form of state-level consumer organization is the citizens' utility board, or "CUB." A CUB is designed to advocate on behalf of residential utility consumers before the state legislature, state courts, and, most important, the state public utility commission. The rationale for a CUB is that, just as a utility's costs of doing business are formally considered by a public utility commission, so should the ratepayers' ability to pay.

Many states have established consumer counsels to represent consumers in the rate-setting process, but they tend to be weak, underfunded, and worried about offending the state officials who hold their purse strings. What makes CUBs unique is their private financing mechanism. They are granted access to utility company billings for the purpose of soliciting membership. Dues are typically low (less than ten dollars a year), but when they are multiplied by tens of thousands of members, a CUB's budget can be substantial. The goal is to raise enough money to hire the services of accountants, lawyers, economists, and engineers—whatever professional expertise it takes to scrutinize and combat arguments made by public utility companies. The first and most active citizens' utility board is in Wisconsin, but additional CUBs have been established in Illinois, Oregon, and New York (Bergner, 1986).

Consumer advocates tend to place great stock in the potential of the CUB concept. They view CUBs as a decisive step toward the empowerment of citizens, just as labor unions empowered workers. In theory, there is nothing to prevent the CUB concept from being applied in other industries that are regulated at the state level, such as banking and insurance (Kohn, 1984).

**PIRGs.**   In 1970, Nader used his own funds to create an organization called the Public Interest Research Group. Its purpose was to engage in lobbying rather than research (Gross, 1975). Nader and his colleagues began working to establish similar organizations on college campuses to tap youthful idealism and promote activism at the state and local levels. The groups attract students who are interested in dealing with fundamental issues of equity, justice, consumer safety, and environmental protection. As of 1987, there were twenty-four PIRGs operating in the United States and two in Canada (Griffin, 1987).

They are typically funded by the students on a particular campus. Initially, students were automatically assessed for the PIRG on their campus unless they specifically declined to contribute. Although this system was highly effective, it was also coercive and unpopular; it has largely been abandoned.

PIRGs have tackled a wide range of issues, many of which are relatively distant from traditional consumer issues. For example, PIRGs have successfully lobbied to establish state-level superfund programs to clean up toxic wastes. They have also helped establish limits on campaign contributions to candidates running for state office.

## Assessing the Movement as a Whole

Having looked at the constituent parts of the consumer movement, it is now possible to pose questions about its overall structure—its size, degree of specialization, sources of cohesion and tension, and patterns of authority and decision making.

### Size and Membership

One can paint a very impressive but somewhat misleading picture of the size of the consumer movement. The Consumer Federation of America (1987) estimates that there are more than two million members of state and local consumer groups, to which one could add members of national consumer organizations like the National Consumers League.

There are also almost four million subscribers to *Consumer Reports*. In addition, surveys of the general public indicate that there are many "latent" consumerists, that is, people who support the goals of the consumer movement but do not actively take part in it. For example, in a 1982 national public opinion study (Atlantic Richfield Co., 1982), 87 percent of respondents felt that "people active in the consumer movement" had done either "a great deal of good" or "some good." Of course, talk is cheap, and answers to telephone interviews are even cheaper, but the number of consumer movement sympathizers could be substantial.

Despite this evidence of mass support, it is hard to escape the conclusion that the consumer movement's accomplishments derive largely from the intense activity of a few Washington-based individuals and organizations. Michael Pertschuk (1982), former chairman of the Federal Trade Commission and now director of the Advocacy Institute, avoids using the term *consumer movement,* believing that consumer advocacy has stemmed from political entrepreneurs rather than grass-roots efforts. In a survey of lobbyists for a variety of national public interest groups in Washington, political scientist Jeffrey Berry (1977) found that, more than any of the other public interest movements in his study, consumer groups were established because of entrepreneurial leadership rather than political or economic events.

Some consumer organizations do not even claim to have many members or to receive significant amounts of funding from individual contributions; these include the Center for the Study of Responsive Law, the Community Nutrition Institute, and the National Insurance Consumer Organization. Even when membership dues constitute a significant source of revenue for national groups, priorities are often set by a small number of leaders who themselves are rarely elected or subject to review. For example, the Center for Auto Safety reports receiving 40 percent of its revenue from its nine thousand members (Bergner, 1986), but in no way is the center member-controlled. Some organizations, such as the National Consumers League, periodically send out questionnaires to their members asking them to indicate the importance of various consumer issues, but this type of member feedback is strictly advisory.

Critics of the consumer movement tend to reinforce the impression that consumerism consists of a handful of self-appointed vigilantes of the free enterprise system. These critics tend to equate the consumer movement with Ralph Nader (Burt, 1982; Sanford, 1976) or a few highly visible individuals such as Joan Claybrook and Sidney Wolfe. Critics also claim the consumer movement enjoys little public support and could not

survive without tax breaks and government subsidies, such as payments
to the groups for their participation in regulatory proceedings (Bennett
and DiLorenzo, 1985).

Although the critics underestimate the extent of public support for the
consumer movement, they are correct in asserting that consumer organizations owe their existence more to the activity of a few highly committed individuals than to an outpouring of mass sentiment. In this
respect, the consumer movement conforms to a general tendency among
social movements, particularly in the United States. Sociologists John
McCarthy and Mayer Zald (1973) have observed the "professionalization
of social movements" whereby committed individuals earn a modest
but full-time living as leaders, speaking for largely unorganized
constituencies.

Jack Walker (1983), in an analysis of 564 political interest groups, am-
plified on the funding sources of "citizen groups," a category that includes
environmental, peace, clean government, and consumer groups. Citizen
groups obtained much of their revenue from what Walker termed "patrons"—individuals, private organizations (like foundations), and
occasionally government agencies. Whereas critics of the consumer
movement would point to this patronage system as evidence of the ar-
tificiality of consumerism's mass support, Walker views political patrons
as performing a positive function. They sponsor "newly emerging elements of society" and thereby make the American political system more
democratic.

Building on a base of widespread but unchanneled consumer discontent, the consumer movement at any given time is run by perhaps fifty
full-time professionals. Their continuing employment depends on their
ability to solicit dues-paying members, sell publications, and find patrons.

## Financial Resources

Although consumer activists, social scientists, and critics generally
agree that the movement's strength derives from an entrepreneurial elite
rather than mass action, they disagree regarding the depth of the movement's financial resources. Consumerists like to portray themselves as
living hand-to-mouth, if for no other reason than to elicit sympathy from
potential contributors. Critics of the movement describe it as "a huge
lobbying and opinion-making conglomerate" which uses the public interest label as a money-making tool (Burt, 1982).

Clearly, the wealthiest consumer organization is Consumer Union. In
1985, CU had 257 full-time staff members and an annual budget of $46.2

million (Bergner, 1986). Next is Public Citizen, including its six subgroups. The only other consumer organization with a budget of more than $1 million is the Center for Science in the Public Interest. Its 1985 budget of $1.3 million covered a total staff of 21 people. Most national consumer organizations have a budget of less than $500,000 and a paid staff of less than a dozen people.

Consumer advocates like to point out the disparity between their financial resources and those of "big business." For example, a 1978 article in *Consumer Reports* ("Business Lobbying . . .," 1978) compared the $352,000 spent on all forms of lobbying by the three major consumer lobbying organizations (Consumer Federation of America, National Consumers League, and Congress Watch) with the $1 billion spent by businesses on grass-roots lobbying *alone*. Even if one includes expenditures by Common Cause ($1.3 million), environmental groups ($1.4 million), and the advocacy offices of Consumers Union ($290,000), the ratio between consumer and business lobbying resources was still about 1 : 300.

Critics of the consumer movement, on the other hand, prefer to emphasize the fact that consumer groups don't spend all the money they receive. David Sanford (1976), a former Nader associate turned critic, reported that Public Citizen had accumulated more than $1 million in retained funds by the end of 1974, most of it invested in certificates of deposit. Sanford writes: "If Ralph Nader would speak to me, which he won't, I'd ask him why with so much urgent public business in need of doing, Public Citizen is amassing these riches and why Nader does not confide in contributors that he's keeping so much of their money in the bank" (p. 31). Sanford also intimates, without being able to prove it, that Nader was "dealing in Ford stock at about the time his book on General Motors was being published" (p. 14). Another Nader critic, Dan Burt (1982), accuses Nader-affiliated organizations of engaging in the speculative practice of "short selling," wherein one bets that the price of a particular stock will go down. It is bad enough, says Burt, that it's contributor money that is being gambled with; there is the disturbing possibility that short selling might be timed to take advantage of negative publicity generated by the very same consumer groups.

Despite these charges, it is difficult to conclude that the movement is extremely wealthy. Given the fragility of most social movements, can an organization be faulted for running a surplus and investing some funds for the future? Does it really matter that Ralph Nader owns some stock, even auto industry stock, or that consumer organizations perhaps engage in risky financial practices? The important point is that, relative to its political adversaries, the consumer movement is financially weak. It cannot hope to match the business coalition—or even a single powerful corporation—in terms of campaign contributions, paid consultants, lobbyists, advertisements, or public relations staffs. The movement employs its limited resources well, and it receives a lot of free publicity from the media. Nevertheless, it operates under tight resource constraints.

## *Efficiency and Division of Labor*

The purpose of any social movement is to bring about change, usually institutional change. Typically, social movements make their greatest demands on governments, sometimes seeking change in governmental policies per se, and sometimes pressuring governments to force change in the private sector. In order to press vigorously for governmental action, a social movement must accomplish the essential tasks of generating public support and mobilizing the resources (human, financial, and informational) necessary to compete effectively in the legislative, regulatory, and judicial arenas. What type of movement structure is most effective in accomplishing these basic tasks? Sociologists are divided on the question. Some argue that a centralized formal structure, with a clear division of labor among movement organizations, is most effective, especially when a movement wants to change social institutions rather than merely raise the consciousness of individuals (Gamson, 1975; Zald and Ash, 1966). Other analysts believe that decentralized social movements with minimal division of labor are more successful (Gerlach and Hine, 1970). A segmented, decentralized structure allegedly makes a movement highly adaptive by encouraging experimentation in tactics and competition among subgroups. Moreover, when division of labor is minimal, the movement is less vulnerable to the loss or cooptation of any single organization (Jenkins, 1983).

The consumer movement has avoided both centralized and decentralized extremes, but it clearly leans toward the former. The division of labor that has evolved within the American consumer movement is relatively specialized. The single-issue groups such as the Center for Auto Safety perform the front-line lobbying, research, and publicity functions of the movement. The fate of these organizations tends to ebb and flow, however, with the single issue to which they are dedicated. The long-term tasks of coordination, legitimation, representation, and fund-raising devolve to the multiple-issue groups, including the Consumer Federation of America, Public Citizen, and Consumers Union.

In some instances, the movement must draw on the skills and resources of its secondary activists and allied social movements. A consumer-oriented journalist might be willing to time an article to heighten the impact of a consumer organization's actions; a public-spirited attorney might donate his or her services to a consumer group; a labor union might lend its substantial political resources to convince a congressman to take a proconsumer position on a bill that affects the purchasing power of its members.

Although the consumer movement seems to have established a reasonably efficient division of labor, critics of the movement ascribe to it a greater degree of coordination and central control than really exists. Dan Burt (1982), for instance, turns the rhetorical tables on the consumer movement, criticizing it in terms usually reserved for corporations: "The Nader network . . . is characterized by interlocking directorates, transfers of funds among fellow organizations, a shared ideology, often shared personnel and facilities, and an abiding passion for secrecy" (p. 137). Burt's view is far too conspiratorial, however, and ignores important sources of tension and conflict among elements of the movement.

## Internal Strains

There are many sources of strain within the consumer movement, some of them personal ones. For example, some antismoking activists resent the fact that John F. Banzhaf III, executive director of ASH, has gained journalistic recognition as the leader of the crusade against cigarette smoking (Sapolsky, 1986). And, of course, Nader's fame has generated its share of jealousy as well (Sanford, 1976). In addition to the recognition and admiration he enjoys, Nader compounds the problem by being demanding and intolerant. In particular, his unwillingness to compromise—and his tendency to attack personally anyone who does compromise—has alienated many legislators otherwise sympathetic to the consumer cause (Pertschuk, 1982; Schwartz, 1979; Stein, 1979).

Other conflicts within the movement arise from the genuine ideological differences among consumer advocates. For instance, some consumerists believe their first duty is to promote the interests of low-income consumers, whereas other activists see their role as championing the interests of all consumers. (These ideological cleavages within the movement will be discussed in depth in the following chapter.)

In addition to strains within the core of the movement, there are important conflicts between the consumer movement and its allied social movements. For example, friendly relations normally exist between consumerists and representatives of organized labor. Labor unions aided in the passage of key consumer legislation during the late 1960s (Nadel, 1971) and came to the defense of the embattled Federal Trade Commission in 1980 (Pertschuk, 1982). For their part, consumer groups have always supported attempts to improve working conditions; the National Consumers League was even founded for this purpose. Yet, when it comes to the issue of trade protection from foreign competition, the two movements part company because trade restrictions protect jobs at the expense of higher consumer prices. The powerful Consumer Federation of America acknowledges its debt to organized labor by remaining silent in the protectionism debate, but other consumer organizations, such as Consumers Union, are willing to take a public position against trade restrictions.

A similar source of conflict exists between consumerists and environmentalists. Most of the time, the two movements work together to restrict pesticide use, encourage energy conservation, and institute recycling programs. Nevertheless, environmentalists seem to believe that consumerists are willing to sell out the environment for lower prices or greater consumer convenience. For example, *Consumer Reports* rates the quality of various brands of disposable diapers; environmentalists would prefer that CU reject all disposable diapers in favor of reusable cloth ones. For their part, consumerists sometimes accuse environmentalists of being insensitive to the problems of low-income consumers (Holsworth, 1980; Mitchell, 1985). Reducing air and water pollution is all very well, consumerists might say, but only after people's basic needs for food, shelter, and medical care are ensured.

The strains within the core of the consumer movement and the conflicts between consumerism and other social movements sap consumerism's strength, embolden its adversaries, and threaten its strategic alliances. Moreover, as the next chapter will demonstrate, these strains often reflect a fundamental ideological cleavage that runs through the consumer movement. Most of the time, however, the movement manages to contain internal conflict and maintain a good working relationship with other social movements.

*Chapter Four*

# The World according to Consumerists

The ideas that guide social movements run the gamut from radical to reactionary. Radicals are dissatisfied with the social order as it is and want to break decisively with existing institutions. Reactionaries also want massive social change but usually with the restoration of some idyllic golden age as their goal. Most social movements in the United States have tended toward the liberal, reformist portion of the political spectrum. There have been important exceptions, such as the labor movement at the turn of the twentieth century or the right-wing survivalists of today, but the dominant social movements of the post–World War II period—civil rights, feminist, antiwar, environmental, and consumerist—have been reformist in the sense of believing that social improvement can be achieved by working through rather than destroying society's basic institutions (Rossiter, 1962).

Reformist social movements often contain a blend of political philosophies. Their center is composed of individuals and organizations who are willing to work for gradual change through existing political channels, but there is usually a more radical wing (Broom and Selznick, 1975). This is true of the environmentalist movement, for example. The movement is best characterized by the reformist organizations, such as the Sierra Club and the Natural Resources Defense Council, that seek to pass environmental legislation and ensure its vigorous enforcement. The reformist center also encompasses groups that try to find common ground with big business—for example, enlisting the aid of affluent individuals and corporations in buying tracts of ecologically unique land. But the environmental movement also has a left wing consisting of organizations like Greenpeace, which throws its tiny boats in the path of huge whaling ships, and Earth First!, which advocates violent resistance to certain forms of land development (Rauber, 1986; Sale, 1986).

The consumer movement is characterized by the same pattern of ideological diversity. (The term *ideology* is used here to denote a relatively coherent perspective on the world that serves to justify political action [Blumer, 1951].)

Ideologies that promote social change have a number of common ingredients. First, they identify the extent and severity of certain social problems; the amelioration of these problems constitute general goals. Second, ideologies explain why the identified problems exist; these explanations typically contain assertions about the motives and behavior of various elements in society, such as consumers, businesses, government, the mass media, and technology. Third, in line with the reasons social problems exist, change-oriented ideologies propose specific solutions and preferred political tactics. Using these three components, this chapter illustrates and contrasts the two leading forms of current consumerist ideology—reformist and radical (although even radical consumerism is reformist when compared to some other social movements). The distinction drawn here between the two ideologies will be sharper than it often is in actuality. Nevertheless, participants in the consumer movement's core as well as secondary consumerists tend to fall into one or the other camp.

Within the core of the consumer movement, reformist ideology is often espoused by its leading organizations—Consumers Union, the Consumer Federation of America, and the National Consumers League. Among secondary consumerists, reformist views tend to characterize consumer educators, academics, government officials, and members of the business community. Individuals who exemplify reformist ideology are David Pittle, currently technical director of Consumers Union and formerly chairman of the Consumer Product Safety Commission; Esther Peterson, twice the presidential consumer adviser; Michael Pertschuk, currently head of the Advocacy Institute and formerly chairman of the Federal Trade Commission; and E. Scott Maynes, a Cornell University economist who has also served on the board of Consumers Union. The reformist core of the consumer movement also has a segment that not only accepts but warmly embraces the principles of the free market. These "corporate consumerists" include such people as Virginia Knauer, twice the presidential consumer adviser; the Society of Consumer Affairs

Professionals, whose members are consumer advisers within businesses; and *Consumers' Research* magazine, the precursor of *Consumer Reports*.

Whereas most consumer movement organizations find it safer to espouse reformist ideology, individuals are freer to articulate radical ideas. In a film entitled *America at Risk* (1984) and produced by Consumers Union, Ralph Nader is described as having brought "ideology" to the consumer movement. In reality, the movement always had an ideology; it was just never recognized until Nader infused it with a radical component. Nader's associate Mark Green, New York's 1986 Democratic candidate for the U.S. Senate, also belongs to the radical wing of the movement, as does journalist Morton Mintz of the *Washington Post*.

Although individuals tend to be more ideologically extreme than organizations, some consumer groups hold radical views. The Center for the Study of Responsive Law and Public Citizen are two organizations that often display a radical analysis of the consumer's predicament. Among secondary consumer organizations, none other than the National Council of Churches and the Interfaith Center on Corporate Responsibility have been described as radical "corporation haters" (Nickel, 1980) because of their opposition to the sale of infant milk formula to third world families who are unable to use the product safely. The radical wing of the consumer movement is smaller than the reformist wing, but it consists of highly influential individuals and organizations whose ideas have been widely disseminated.

## Problem Perception and Identification

### Reformists

To the reformist wing of the consumer movement, the most important consumer problems are those that inhibit the efficient operation of markets. When markets are performing at their best, consumers are free to choose among an array of products, rewarding with their purchases those firms that offer the highest level of quality for the lowest price. But in practice, according to reformists, consumers are prevented from playing their part in creating market efficiency. Instead of having accurate, impartial, and inexpensive information at their disposal, consumers are bombarded with advertisements, more than $110 billion worth annually in the United States alone (Lafayette, 1987). Compounding the problem is deception by unscrupulous sellers; abuses include short-weighting, bait-and-switch advertising (in which consumers are enticed with a great deal only to be switched to a much more expensive product), medical quackery, fraudulent get-rich-quick schemes, and high-pressure door-to-door sales pitches. Reformists within the consumer movement believe that these abuses are perpetrated primarily by small, marginal operators, not large mainstream American businesses, and that they cost consumers billions of dollars annually as well as injure honest competitors who play by the rules (Knauer, 1970).

It is not just inadequate and inaccurate information that constitutes consumer problems and prevents consumers from promoting market efficiency. The absence of speedy inexpensive avenues of redress discourages consumers from sharing their negative experiences with sellers (Maynes, 1979). During the early years of the contemporary consumer movement, reformists focused attention on legal doctrines that were clearly stacked in the favor of sellers. The holder-in-due-course doctrine, whereby consumers lost their rights once a credit contract was sold to a third party, was a prime example of such a law. Later, when consumer protection statutes were enacted, practical barriers to their use and enforcement became objects of criticism. For example, no one is going to spend a thousand dollars bringing suit against the manufacturer of a defective toaster. Similarly, today's "lemon laws" appear to give consumers tremendous benefits by stipulating that a refund or replacement may be appropriate when a new car requires constant repairs, but how many consumers are going to take on General Motors or Toyota in a legal battle?

Reformists within the movement largely subsume the problem of consumer safety under the problems of obtaining consumer information and pressing grievances. Without precise information regarding the safety features of products, consumers cannot buy the degree of safety they wish. In addition, when a lack of information results in consumers paying more than necessary for a product, they have less money to spend on optional safety features (for example, air bags in cars or more sensitive bindings on downhill skis). When effective means of consumer redress are not available, consumers will fail to alert firms to safety problems, thereby increasing the likelihood that other consumers will be injured before a firm realizes that corrective action is needed.

The problems of information and redress are less an indictment of free enterprise principles than a sign of their incomplete application, according to reformists. By the same logic, they are concerned about consumers who lack the knowledge, sophistication, or experience to function effectively in the modern marketplace—such as young children, the elderly, and recently arrived immigrants. For example, reformists denounce advertising aimed at children who are too young to understand its commercial purpose. In sum, reformists define as a problem any condition that prohibits consumers from being the true sovereigns of the marketplace.

## Radicals

Consumerists adhering to a more radical ideology also believe that the competitive free market would be nice in theory, but they believe that corporations control the market, not vice versa. Big businesses are viewed as equal to governments in terms of their power over the everyday lives of individuals. Unlike governments, however, giant corporations are unrestrained by mechanisms of accountability. As a result, consumers are overcharged, injured, and manipulated.

To a consumerist radical, the near-monopoly power of firms generates two major consumer problems: supracompetitive prices and subcompetitive quality, including hazardous products. According to radical ideology, America's basic industries are highly concentrated; each is controlled by a few giant corporations. Drawing on estimates by the Federal Trade Commission, Ralph Nader once argued that if industry concentration were reduced to the point where the four largest firms in any industry were limited to 40 percent of total industry sales, prices would fall by at least 25 percent. Sen. Philip Hart of Michigan estimated that this 25 percent figure was itself only about a quarter of the overall consumer loss that is due to unfavorable business and government practices (Nader, 1971).

Some of the methods by which firms charge inflated prices are straightforward, such as price fixing and mergers, but most of the methods are more subtle. For example, the cereal industry (in which Kellogg, General Foods, and General Mills account for about 85 percent of sales) was accused of being a "shared monopoly" which excluded new competitors, overcharged consumers, and reaped huge profits (Scanlon, 1970; "Monopoly . . . ," 1981). Some consumer activists, and later the Federal Trade Commission, claimed that the cereal companies' enormous advertising budgets made it impossible for new firms to enter the industry. Thus protected, the cereal companies used a number of practices to avoid price competition—for instance, announcing projected price increases far enough in advance so that all firms could raise their prices simultaneously, and encouraging grocers to arrange shelves by manufacturer rather than type of cereal (Bloom, 1978). The FTC's case against the cereal industry was eventually dismissed in 1981, however, on the ground that there was insufficient evidence of anticompetitive practices.

Radicals offer the pharmaceutical industry and its attack on generic, or "no-name," drugs as another illustration of the way in which powerful corporations freeze out competition. Generic drugs often sell for half the price of their brand-name equivalents. To protect their revenues, the major pharmaceutical companies have engaged in a campaign of disparaging generics and frightening doctors, pharmacists, and patients. For example, they warn pharmacists that lawsuits could arise if they don't dispense brand-name drugs ("The Big Lie . . . ," 1987).

Perhaps more galling to radical consumerists than instances of industries attempting to charge supracompetitive prices is when the government accomplishes the task for them. Examples abound. Trade restrictions raise the prices of domestically produced goods. Traditional regulation of airlines, trucking, and banking also has the effect of limiting competition and raising consumer prices. Occupational licensing by states may ensure consumers that service providers meet minimal levels of competence, but it also allows licensed professionals to charge higher prices.

Corporate domination of the marketplace, according to the radical, results in more than high prices. Without the threat of competition, firms have little incentive to produce products that are high in quality or to seek product improvements. Favorite consumerist targets include drugs and cosmetics that have little proven value (Kaufman et al., 1983) and automobiles that are inefficient in their use of energy and expensive to repair (Haddon, 1970). In the extreme case, firms market products that are unnecessarily hazardous to the health and safety of consumers, apparently believing that they will not have to answer for the practice. Recent entrants into the consumerist hall of shame include the Ford Pinto, which frequently exploded when hit from the rear (Dowie, 1977; Hills, 1987); the Dalkon Shield intrauterine device, which caused a variety of serious medical problems among its users (Engelmayer and Wagman, 1985; Mintz, 1985; Perry and Dawson, 1985); and infant milk formula's being sold in third world countries by several companies including Nestlé (Garson, 1977; Post and Baer, 1978).

Within radical ideology, corporate misconduct is deliberate, criminal, and systemic. It is epidemic, not episodic; characteristic of large corporations, not just fly-by-night firms. The tip of the iceberg is frequently visible, as when executives of the Beech-Nut baby food company knowingly sold millions of jars of fake apple juice for infants ("Two Guilty in Sale . . . ," 1988) or when Hertz Corporation systematically overcharged its customers for auto repairs by using phony damage claims ("Hertz's Reparations . . . ," 1988). Taken as a whole, "crime in the suites" (Mintz and Cohen, 1971) is considered by radicals to be far more abusive of citizens than crime in the streets (Claybrook, 1986).

In contrast to the reformists' forcus on a relatively narrow set of problems, such as lack of information and hazardous products, is the radicals' view of consumer problems as indistinguishable from a broader class of "citizen" problems like environmental pollution or exposure of workers to dangerous substances and conditions. The breadth of citizen problems, and their integral connection to consumers' problems, is seen in Ralph Nader's insistence that corporations "stop stealing, stop deceiving, stop corrupting politicians with money, stop monopolizing, stop poisoning the earth, air and water, stop selling dangerous products, stop exposing workers to cruel hazards, stop tyrannizing people of conscience within the company and start respecting long-range survival needs and rights of present and future generations" (1980, p. 367).

In sum, the consumerist radical believes that there is a basic asymmetry in the relative power of producers and consumers. The essential mission of the consumer movement is to correct that imbalance. Rather than justifying action on behalf of consumers in terms of economic efficiency, radicals appeal to the concepts of fairness, equity, and self-evident consumer "rights."

## Problem Explanation

Although reformists and radicals differ in the consumer problems on which they place the greatest emphasis, nearly all agree that there are serious consumer problems regarding safety, information, competition, and redress. Where holders of reformist and radical ideologies diverge more substantially is in their explanations of consumer problems. In trying to account for the problems' existence and magnitude the two wings take very different views concerning the role of consumers, businesses, government, mass media, and technology.

### *Reformists*
In the reformist view, consumer problems can best be explained in economic terms. Greed on the part of sellers takes its toll on consumers, but the more basic deficiencies in information and redress are attributable

to the imperfect functioning of markets. Classical economic theory claims that markets use economic resources to their fullest. This optimal allocation of resources is achieved when consumers are rational and fully informed; markets are competitively structured; a good's price accurately reflects all the costs of its production (there are no "externalities"); and transactions such as comparison shopping, returning merchandise, and bringing legal action are costless (Lane, 1983). Consumer problems exist and corrective government action is justified, according to reformists, to the extent that reality deviates from these conditions (Swagler, 1979).

**Information Deficits.**   Why aren't consumers fully informed? Sellers have an incentive to keep consumers selectively and partially informed. A car manufacturer may advertise its low prices, but it is not going to mention that its vehicles are neither durable nor energy-efficient. But the absence of accurate, timely, and precise consumer information has even deeper roots. In theory, consumers could provide themselves with information, but here we run into two of the assumptions of the classical economic model—the absence of transaction costs and of externalities.

Ignorance is expensive, but so is information (Stigler, 1961; Swagler, 1979). As a person begins to shop for a new product, a refrigerator, say, the first bits of information come relatively cheaply and are often highly useful. As the process of becoming informed continues, however, the cost of acquiring an additional piece of information tends to increase while its value tends to decline. As a result, the consumer is going to stop short of becoming fully informed, for that would be prohibitively expensive. Instead, the *rational* consumer is going to search for information only up to the point where the cost of acquiring an additional bit of information (which is one type of transaction cost) is equal to the anticipated benefits of that information. A consumer who is extremely pressed for time may not search for any information at all, but would be no less rational for that fact.

Even if one accepts the idea that consumers will never be fully informed, is it unrealistic to hope that consumers will be at least relatively well informed? That depends, in part, on how costly consumer information is to acquire. Some is prohibitively expensive. For instance, how many consumers can afford to test the treadwear of competing brands of tires before purchasing four for their car? Similarly, how likely are they to inspect personally the sanitary conditions of several local restaurants before deciding where to dine? Both types of information are important and useful, but individual consumers are unlikely to bear the heavy costs of acquiring them.

Why then doesn't some organization go into the business of selling this information? An organization could take advantage of economies of scale by conducting one set of tests or inspections and selling the information at a reasonable price to a large number of interested consumers. By this logic, one would expect product testing and the provision of impartial consumer information to be a booming business. In reality, product testing organizations, even Consumers Union with its four million subscribers, find it difficult to make ends meet, and there are only a handful of such organizations that survive without government subsidy. Although some consumers are willing to pay for consumer information in the form of a book or magazine, other consumers will try to obtain the information without paying for it. They may borrow the information from a friend, or they may rely on those consumers who do purchase information to keep sellers on their toes. After a while, the people who are paying for the production of consumer information may get fed up at subsidizing other consumers and decrease their purchases of consumer information. As a result of this free-rider phenomenon, impartial consumer information gets produced in very small quantities.

**Limited Redress.**   The problem of limited consumer redress can also be related to high transaction costs and externalities. Like being informed, pursuing a consumer complaint involves time, money, and psychic costs. These costs can be substantial, particularly when consumers must rely on the judicial system. A consumer may simply conclude that the likely costs of seeking redress are higher than the likely benefits. The rational consumer has no incentive to consider the fact that his or her complaint has the potential to benefit other consumers, for example, by leading a firm to correct a problem. Thus, like using consumer information, seeking redress for consumer problems involves external benefits and consequently occurs at suboptimal levels from a societal point of view.

**Limited Competition.**   Bound as it is to classical economic theory (Creighton, 1976), reformist ideology views the behavior of producers in essentially the same terms as consumers. Both buyers and sellers attempt to maximize their satisfaction ("utility") in relative isolation from other consumers or producers. Accordingly, when markets deviate from the ideal of perfect competition (that is, a market with many sellers as well as easy entry and exit), it is the result of firms engaging in honest, rational behavior rather than colluding or extracting special favors from the government.

One way in which firms reduce price competition is through "product differentiation," the attempt to create the impression that a product is drastically different from its competitors when in fact it is similar. Oil companies try to create strong consumer preferences for their products by implying that putting a tiger in your tank is somehow desirable, that you can trust your car to a man who wears a star, or that some new additive will make your engine run smoother or cleaner. These efforts at differentiation cover up the fact that most gasoline is, or was until recently (Owen, 1987), pretty much the same.

Price competition can also be limited when an industry is characterized by a few large firms. This oligopoly may arise for fairly innocent reasons. For example, large capital requirements or economies of scale may limit the number of competitors, as in the automobile, steel, aluminum, cigarette, and light bulb industries (McKenzie and Tullock, 1978). Oligopolists, however, tend to shy away from price competition, since a price decrease by one firm will force all other firms to lower their prices as well. In the end, no one's competitive position will have been improved, and all firms will be worse off. Conversely, there is a positive incentive for oligopolists to raise their prices—as long as everyone goes along.

Thus, a common thread runs through the reformist explanations of information deficiencies, limited redress, and limited competition. These problems are not due to business conspiracies but, rather, are attributable to imperfections in the market mechanism. Correct the imperfections, and consumer problems will disappear.

**The Role of Government.**   To a reformist, government is not part of the problem; it is a potential part of the solution. The government's role is to serve as an impartial arbiter of the competing claims of various groups. Reformists realize that substantial disparities exist among groups in their ability to make their case to the government. Business interests are well funded and well represented since they have a lot riding on the outcome of an issue. Consumers, in contrast, have hundreds of concerns in their lives, so their interest in an issue such as automobile bumpers will never be as intense as the industry for which bumpers are its daily bread (Rowe, 1985).

Like consumer problems themselves, the weakness of consumer representation is due to a marketplace imperfection, this time in the political market. Although all consumers might agree on the desirability of being represented, any one individual is likely to leave lobbying to others, knowing he will reap the benefits of their efforts. But, of course, if everyone tries to be a free rider, no representation of consumer interests will take place.

In short, the government arena is not a level playing field when it comes to a match between producers and consumers, but upsets sometimes occur. A scandal or accident may put business interests on the defensive; consumer representatives may cleverly outmaneuver business lobbyists; a civil servant or legislator may buck industry pressure and act courageously. Hence, despite the odds being stacked in favor of businesses, it is possible for consumer interests to prevail when a case comes before the government.

**Mass Media.** The American mass media are often accused of having a liberal bias and especially being seduced by Ralph Nader (De Toledano, 1975; Sanford, 1976). Nevertheless, the mass media have not always been friendly to the consumer movement. Consumer economist Richard Morse (1981) points out that the press was reluctant to cover early consumer movement events. Not only was the creation of Consumers Union not considered newsworthy, but the *Herald Tribune* and *New York Times* refused even to carry Consumers Union's paid advertisements. This indifference continued until well into the 1960s. As late as 1966, CBS was unable to find a national sponsor for a documentary on the need for legislation requiring the explicit disclosure of interest rates in a form that could be compared across different types of loans. Some stations aired the program without financial support from advertisers, but others declined. And when truth-in-lending legislation passed, the *Wall Street Journal* failed to consider it worthy of coverage (Morse, 1981).

The relationship between the mass media and the consumer movement has been far more congenial over the last two decades. Television has proved to be a particularly friendly medium, with consumer reporters becoming a standard feature of many news programs. Although the mass media cannot be counted on for sustained effort or follow-through, consumer activists have found media coverage to be an effective and, above all, free method of creating public awareness and arousing public sentiment. Hence, reformists view the mass media as an important if not wholly dependable ally.

**Technology.**    According to reformist ideology, technology is inherently neither villainous nor benevolent. It is a neutral tool that can be used or abused. Accordingly, reformists have criticized artificial sweeteners, expressed skepticism regarding the preservation of food through irradiation, and generally opposed the development of nuclear power. At the same time, they have embraced technological improvements such as air bags, smoke detectors, and solar power equipment. They see no reason to doubt that technology can be used to improve the quality of the consumer's life.

Reformists, then, are aware of a variety of obstacles to the advancement of consumer welfare. Markets fail to allocate some resources efficiently, corporations are insensitive to the social effects of their activities, consumers are poorly informed, the government is disproportionately responsive to the desires of businesses, the mass media are fickle in their coverage of consumer issues, and technology needs constant monitoring if its negative effects are to be avoided. Nevertheless, skillful political maneuvering, combined with a little luck, can result in significant consumer victories.

## Radicals

**The Irresponsible Nature of Giant Corporations.**    If reformists blame consumer problems on serious flaws in the market mechanism, consumerist radicals attribute the problems to the nature of giant bureaucratic corporations. The evils of corporate gigantism stem from two sources. First, corporations wield tremendous power, yet this power is essentially unchecked. A favorite contention of consumerist radicals is that big businesses *are* governments. Not only do corporate revenues rival those of many nations, but corporations also impose taxes (through their ability to control prices), take life (through their ability to ignore product safety), and drastically affect the quality of life and of the environment (Mintz and Cohen, 1971). Corporations exercise the same degree of power as governments, but they are exempt from public control and accountability. They become arrogant, secretive, heady, and corrupt. "Power has to be insecure to be responsive" (Nader, quoted in Klein, 1975), and corporate power is all too secure.

The second source of corporate villainy, as the consumerist radical sees it, is the shielding of individuals from personal responsibility for their actions; by their legal nature, corporations protect their members from personal liability. The problem runs much deeper, however. The vast size, geographic scope, and bureaucratic structure of the modern corporation creates an enormous gap between those who make corporate decisions and those who bear their brunt. From behind a veil of secrecy and unaccountability, all sense of individual responsibility evaporates and the worst in human nature is unleashed (Mintz, 1985). Corporate leaders and managers perpetrate violence, deceive consumers, charge outrageous prices, and destroy the environment—even though in their private lives they may be pillars of the community. The same person who wouldn't think of dropping a piece of litter on a neighbor's lawn might be willing to contaminate the entire Gulf of Mexico once he assumes his corporate identity (Rowe, 1985).

A perfect example of the separation of individual and corporate morality concerns Claiborne Robins, head of the A. H. Robins company, makers of Robitussin cough medicine, Chap Stick lip balm, and the infamous Dalkon Shield. As a private citizen, Robins was the picture of civic responsibility in Richmond, Virginia, where company headquarters were located. In June 1969, he gave $50 million, most of it in his company's stock, to the University of Richmond, one of the largest, if not the largest, gifts ever given by an individual to a private university. Although the university was the greatest beneficiary, Robins family largesse touched virtually every educational, cultural, and philanthropic institution in Richmond.

About the same time that Robins was donating $50 million to the University of Richmond, his company was acquiring the rights to market an intrauterine device which resulted in injuries to an estimated 200,000 women in the United States alone, including punctured uteri, severe pelvic infections, and sterility (Barrett, 1988). Under Robins's leadership, the company marketed the Dalkon Shield intrauterine device with virtually no testing, deceived physicians and the general public, silenced employees with misgivings about the product, destroyed documents that might prove damaging in court, and used every trick in the book to slow the course of regulatory and judicial action against it (Mintz, 1985; Perry and Dawson, 1985). Throughout the sordid episode, Robins and other company officials denied memory of and responsibility for crucial events in the marketing of the Dalkon Shield. During one trial, Judge Miles W. Lord, unable to contain his outrage and incredulity, said: "It is not enough to say, 'I did not know,' 'It was not me,' 'Look elsewhere.' Time and time again, each of you has used this kind of argument in refusing to acknowledge your responsibility and in pretending to the world that the chief officers and the directors of your gigantic multinational corporation have no responsibility for the company's acts and omissions" (Lord, quoted in Mintz, 1985, pp. 264–65).

Mark Green and John Berry's use of the term *corpocracy* (1985a) captures the radical's view of the two main sources of corporate corruption. First, the term means rule by corporations, thereby suggesting the enormity of corporate power and its similarity to the power of governments. Second, the term highlights the extent to which modern corporations function as remote and unresponsive bureaucracies. (It is also difficult to ignore the similarity between *corpocracy* and *hypocrisy*.)

**Apathetic Consumers.**     Reformists view consumers as rational beings. Consumer decisions are not always well-informed only because consumers are pressed for time and because useful consumer information is expensive to obtain. Radicals, in contrast, tend to view consumers as apathetic at best and brainwashed at worst. Nader has frequently expressed frustration regarding the difficulty of "motivating victims to end their victimization" (quoted in Ignatius, 1976). People should want to decide public matters for themselves, he says, but most don't want to be bothered with the responsibility. They prefer believing to thinking because the latter takes more effort. Nader admits that his notion of an active citizenry may be at odds with human nature (quoted in Klein, 1975).

At the same time that consumerist radicals like Nader want people to become more involved in public decision making, they display disdain for many of the consumption decisions that people actually make, such as smoking cigarettes, riding in a car without a seatbelt, eating bacon, or buying an automobile that gets only eight miles to the gallon. Radicals fault citizens who measure well-being in terms of the quantity of goods they own rather than the quality of their lives.

Ralph Nader's personal consumption style expresses an ideal that is far from that of the average American citizen. He owns neither a car nor a house. To save money on clothing, he bought twelve pairs of shoes and four dozen socks at the PX before leaving the army in 1959. As of 1983, he was still wearing one of the original twelve pairs and hadn't bought any additional pairs (Auletta, 1983). If his own behavior is any indication of his ideals, Nader wants consumers to become "secular monks," working for social change with indifference to material rewards (Rowe, 1985).

The belief that consumers are apathetic and passive is best seen in debates regarding advertising. Radicals claim that advertising is incredibly potent, capable of making consumers buy practically anything (Nader,

1984). Adult consumers are seduced by bogus promises of sex appeal, popularity, and social status (Packard, 1957; Gold, 1987). Therefore, banning advertising is often seen as an effective means of decreasing consumption of "bad" products like cigarettes and alcoholic beverages. Radical consumerists consider advertising directed at young children especially insidious and unfair. Research indicates that the majority of children under five years old don't fully understand the commercial nature of ads (Robertson and Rossiter, 1974; Ward, Wackman, and Wartella, 1977). Children are further confused by the use of characters from television programs to sell products. All told, radicals blame advertising for making the United States a nation of sugar-loving children and materialistic adults.

**Government Complicity.** According to radicals, not only are giant corporations as powerful as governments, but government, far from being a countervailing force to the enormous influence of business, doles out huge subsidies to corporations and ignores their misdeeds. Radicals describe the American economy as "corporate socialism" (Nader, 1971) in which government favors business by constraining competition. For example, the growers of agricultural products like oranges, almonds, and hops are allowed to restrict how much is grown and how much reaches the market, thereby propping up prices (Lenard and Mazur, 1985). Although the impetus for deregulation of agriculture as well as the airline, banking, and trucking industries is often attributed to conservative economists, elimination of industry-specific regulation has long been a goal of radical consumerists (Green and Nader, 1973).

Corporations also benefit from a tax system in which federal and local governments make enormous "tax expenditures" on businesses by forgoing the collection of certain taxes. Exempting businesses from taxation through depletion allowances is a case of a direct tax expenditure. Tax provisions that provide income tax reductions in exchange for investing in a particular industry work more indirectly. These provisions not only benefit taxpayers wealthy enough to take advantage of them but, more important, subsidize industry by reducing the cost of obtaining capital. All told, total tax expenditures in 1975, not all of which went to businesses, were estimated to be almost $100 billion (U.S. Congress, 1974).

An additional aspect of "socialism for the rich and free enterprise for the poor" is the way in which government bails out corporations when they flounder. The government's decision to rescue the Chrysler Corporation from the brink of financial disaster seems, in retrospect, to have paid off, but it is more than balanced by the money that has been lost in various attempts to bolster the nation's privately-owned railroads, for example.

Even government agencies explicitly established to protect consumer interests, like the Food and Drug Administration, the Consumer Product Safety Commission, or the National Highway Traffic Safety Administration, are seen by radical consumerists as serving the interests of big business. These agencies are subject to co-optation by the industries they are supposed to police. A "revolving door" between business and government contributes to agency timidity. Agency leaders are often recruited from the very industry they will regulate and therefore share its perspectives and priorities; when their term of government service comes to an end, administrators frequently move on to positions in the industry they once regulated.

President Ronald Reagan's top appointments in the U.S. Department of Agriculture (USDA) provide clear and recent examples of the revolving door in motion. Agriculture Secretary John Block was himself a hog farmer from Illinois. Assistant Secretary C. W. McMillan, in charge of meat inspection policy, had been executive vice president of the National Cattlemen's Association for twenty-two years before assuming his position in the USDA. Also closely involved in the meat inspection process was Deputy Agriculture Secretary Richard Lyng, a former president of the American Meat Institute. With these men in charge, it should not be surprising that the USDA implemented a new policy of industry self-regulation under which federal meat and poultry inspections were reduced from a daily to a "less-than-continuous" basis (Hughes, 1983). In short, radicals put little faith in government as a protector of consumers.

**Mass Media.** To the radical, the mass media are part of the problem, not part of the solution. Although it is true that the media tolerate a few proconsumer columnists and reporters, radicals find the overall quality of consumer coverage to be poor. The media live off advertisements urging people to buy; they are not going to bite the hand of their corporate sponsors.

Usually the influence of commercial sponsorship on news coverage and editorial content is subtle, but not always. In 1982, Paul Maccabee, music editor and reporter for a Minneapolis-based weekly, was fired for his coverage of a jazz festival sponsored by Kool cigarettes, in which he described Kool officials as "nicotine pushers" and noted that Duke Ellington died of lung cancer (Perry, 1982). In a 1987 incident, the managers of two radio stations in New York City and Philadelphia complained that Delta Air Lines had canceled their advertising contracts to punish the stations for poking fun at the airline's rash of potentially dangerous incidents, including one in which a pilot mistakenly shut down both engines (Bolt, 1987).

Radical consumerists are also distrustful of the mass media because the media are giant and highly profitable corporations themselves. The radicals resist the notion that the public airwaves can be given away freely to private interests to use as they see fit. Rather, broadcasters should be regarded as stewards of a public resource. They should be held to high standards of responsibility since the media have the power to define what constitutes "news" (Mintz and Cohen, 1976). If the citizenry cannot own and operate the mass media, which would be the ideal, the government should tightly regulate the media in the public's name.

**Technology.** To a radical, new technologies are considered guilty until proven innocent. Radicals are particularly suspicious of new pharmaceutical, chemical, computer, and genetic technologies. A case in point is the controversy over whether radiation should be used to preserve food. Proponents of food irradiation point out a number of possible benefits: less use of pesticides and fungicides, less risk of food poisoning from chicken and of trichinosis from pork, and lower prices because of longer shelf life. Most consumerists, however, have opposed the introduction of food irradiation. They fear that it will remove the stink that warns consumers of tainted products and will degrade vitamins and nutrients; most of all, they fear the unknown effects of irradiated food ("Fruit . . . , 1986).

In general, radicals are dubious about new technologies, believing that they tend to be controlled by large corporations and serve to increase corporate power. According to Nader (1984), if consumers controlled energy development, they would press for efficient, renewable, safe, and competitively priced energy sources, whereas corporate control results in just the opposite. Radicals' suspicions of technology arise also from their feeling that the human ability to develop technology has outstripped the ability to control its effects. For many years, radical consumerists warned of the dangers of nuclear power; then Chernobyl confirmed their fears. Similarly, radicals have used the December 1984 disaster at a chemical plant in Bhopal, India, as further evidence of humans' inability to control the technological genie (Karpatkin, 1986).

Radicals admit that some technologies have the *potential* to empower consumers rather than promote their dependence on giant corporations. Solar power is a darling of radical consumerists because it promotes consumer self-reliance. Similarly, new information technologies, such as two-way, interactive cable TV, could make consumers more informed before they make purchases and better organized when they share a grievance (Nader, 1984). Unfortunately, according to radicals, corporations recognize the liberating possibilities of technologies like solar power and quickly move to suppress them (Denman and Bossong, 1979).

The great fear of the radical consumerist is that technology's ill effects will incubate for twenty or thirty years, at which point the world will find itself drowning in toxic and carcinogenic substances. But radicals are hopeful. Working with environmentalists, they were able to pressure Congress into scuttling development of a supersonic transport plane. In addition, the tragic explosion of the space shuttle *Challenger* inadvertently strengthened their hand by further eroding faith in technology.

The array of forces that radicals believe confronts them is formidable. Corporations wield enormous power in both the marketplace and in government arenas, consumers are apathetic, the mass media are biased in favor of business, and technology is constantly coming up with new threats to humanity's future. Given this worldview, it is remarkable that radicals are able to maintain their sense of commitment; any victories against such powerful foes must severely test their humility. No wonder, then, that radical consumerists like Nader are frequently accused of self-importance.

## Solutions and Tactics

### *Reformists*

To state the difference in approach in starkest form, reformists believe that solutions to consumer problems can be achieved by working with businesses and through existing government institutions, whereas radicals feel that consumer protection requires changing government institutions or bypassing them entirely. Reformists accept the necessity of compromise; radicals view their role as adversarial in nature.

**Working Within the System.** The primary activities of the reformist take place in legislative, regulatory, and judicial settings. When the political climate is favorable, reformists press for new laws to broaden consumer rights, such as those requiring the disclosure of consumer information (for example, interest rates on loans, credit cards, and savings accounts). When the political climate is less hospitable, legislative lobbying by consumerists is often directed at fending off business-inspired attempts to weaken consumer legislation or to reduce the effectiveness of consumer protection agencies. Throughout the 1980s, for example, consumerists have had to block attempts to eliminate the "Delaney Clause," with its blanket prohibition against carcinogenic substances in the nation's food supply, and efforts to limit consumer rights of compensation in the event of a product-related injury.

Once a consumer-oriented law is on the books, reformist activity shifts to the regulatory and judicial realms in order to secure proper implementation and enforcement. In consumer protection matters, Congress commonly passes a broadly stated objective and then leaves the job of deciding on specifics to a regulatory agency. For example, in 1972, Congress passed the Consumer Product Safety Act, which established the Consumer Product Safety Commission with the mandate of protecting consumers from "unreasonable risks of injury associated with consumer products." This mandate gives the commission broad discretion in interpretation. First, what constitutes an unreasonable risk? Second, should a product be blamed when it is associated with an injury but doesn't cause it? Should football helmets be regulated because players get concussions in spite of wearing them?

When regulatory agencies have such broad discretion, a primary role of consumer organizations is to file petitions urging action on a particular issue and present testimony during rule-making proceedings. For instance, the Center for Science in the Public Interest has petitioned the Food and Drug Administration to require nutrition labeling on the wrappers of fast-food items, and the Center for Auto Safety frequently petitions the National Highway Traffic Safety Administration to recall a particular vehicle because of an alleged safety defect.

According to the Administrative Procedures Act, the bible of regulatory activity, all interested parties must be given an opportunity to provide input once a regulation is proposed. Consumer groups, as well as others, use this occasion to lobby for their particular positions. For a brief period in the late 1970s, some regulatory agencies even paid consumer groups to prepare testimony for their rule-making process (Mayer and Scammon, 1983).

When an agency is unresponsive to the position taken by consumer organizations, the groups may challenge regulatory decisions in the courts. For example, shortly after taking office, the Reagan administration rescinded a regulation that would have required passive restraints (air bags or automatic seatbelts) in all new cars. The rescission was challenged by the automobile insurance industry with strong encouragement from consumer and public health groups. The decision to scrap the passive restraint standard was overturned by a judicial ruling that the government's decision was "arbitrary and illogical" (Karr, 1982).

Consumer groups often engage in court battles at the state level, too. In 1986, for instance, the Public Citizen Litigation Group won a Florida Supreme Court ruling that allows insurance agents to share their commissions with customers. In 1976, the Litigation Group successfully challenged a Virginia law that banned advertising of prescription drug prices. Both court challenges were intended to save consumers considerable amounts of money.

The courts can be used to challenge presidential and congressional actions in addition to those of federal and state regulatory agencies. In contrast to radicals, though, reformists have no special preference for court action compared to legislative and regulatory lobbying. The courts are only one of several mechanisms of traditional interest group politics that can be used to promote consumer interests.

**Consumerists in Pin Stripes.**   The willingness to work with rather than against businesses is a relatively recent development within the American consumer movement. Some observers take this as a sign that consumerism has lost steam or, at least, has been derailed by the pro-business Reagan administration (Bradley, 1987). Another explanation is that having eliminated the most outrageous consumer abuses, consumerists must now be more resourceful in tackling the more esoteric and complex problems that remain (Belkin, 1985).

Reformists have been increasingly willing to accept funds from business sources. For example, the Consumer Federation of America published its *1987 Directory of State and Local Consumer Organizations* with the financial assistance of the Food Marketing Institute. Similarly, the National Consumers League used funds from Corning Glass Works, Nationwide Insurance, and Prudential Insurance Company to prepare a guide to hospice and home health care.

Consumer groups have also begun to broker deals with businesses. In 1986, for instance, several consumer groups negotiated a compromise with the chemical industry. In exchange for industry support for a review of certain pesticides, the groups agreed not to oppose lengthening the patent period for new chemical products (Bradley, 1987). Radicals like Ralph Nader oppose this form of consumer-business cooperation, believing it leads to co-optation (Belkin, 1985).

A final area in which consumer and business interests seem to be converging is consumer complaint handling by firms. Once, consumerists had to fight the notion that people who complained about products were antibusiness cranks whose grievances should be ignored. Today, many firms have become convinced that consumers' complaints are a valuable source of feedback and new ideas, and some firms now are even seeking them out (Brown, 1987; Malech, 1987).

## Radicals

Given their distrust of government's willingness and ability to control corporate behavior, radicals shy away from involvement in legislative and regulatory activities. (Witness Ralph Nader's continual refusal to run for political office despite his substantial popularity and name recognition.) If radicals must press their case through governmental avenues, they prefer the courts because the judiciary is supposed to be the "citadel of the minority," counting rights rather than votes (Nader, quoted in Klein, 1975). Thus, radical strategy focuses on three goals: (1) making regulatory proceedings more like judicial ones, (2) using direct economic pressure rather than governmental means to influence businesses, and (3) changing the very nature of corporate governance.

**Institutionalizing the Consumer Representative.**   According to radical consumerists, many decisions affecting consumers are made in pseudojudicial environments in which the consumer has no representation. For example, if the Interstate Commerce Commission is holding hearings on whether to raise shipping rates, the trucking industry will show up in force, but consumer advocates will be absent. Similarly, when state public utility commissions are considering a request for a rate increase, the telephone or power company is there with its economists and lawyers, but who represents the consumer? In the absence of effective consumer advocacy, regulators have little choice but to accede to the demands of business claimants.

Radical consumerists favor two means of promoting consumer representation and making the regulatory system adversarial in the true sense. During the 1970s, Ralph Nader's top priority (as well as that of many other consumerists) was the establishment of an agency to represent consumer interests before other government agencies ("Mr. Nader's New Year's Wish," 1974). The proposed agency was most commonly called the Consumer Protection Agency, but it was also referred to as the Agency for Consumer Advocacy and the Office of Consumer Representation. The agency would have no laws to enforce nor could it make new regulations. Its function was solely to improve consumer representation by serving as a sort of free-floating consumer attorney. Needless to say, business organizations regarded the proposed agency as a serious threat to their political influence and vehemently opposed it. They charged that such an agency would create legal and administrative chaos, delaying both governmental and corporate decision making (Vogel and Nadel, 1976).

During several sessions of Congress, the agency was nearly established, particularly in 1975 when a bill was passed in both the House and the Senate, but it died in the conference committee when President Gerald Ford vowed to veto it. When Jimmy Carter assumed the presidency, it seemed likely that the bill would finally pass. But the political mood of the nation had become increasingly antigovernment, and Ralph Nader had apparently alienated fence-sitting legislators with his unwillingness to compromise. The most important factor, however, in the agency's defeat was effective business lobbying, including promises of campaign contributions (Green, 1978; Schwartz, 1979; Stein, 1979).

Having failed to institutionalize a consumer voice in all federal regulatory proceedings, radical consumerists narrowed their ambitions. They turned their efforts to the state level and attempted to establish citizen utility boards, or CUBs (discussed in chapter 3), to represent consumer interests before public utility commissions. The establishment of CUBs suffered a serious setback in February 1986, however, when the U.S. Supreme Court ruled that state regulatory commissions may not require utility companies to enclose consumer group inserts in bills ("Utility Bills . . . ," 1986). It remains unclear whether state legislatures may impose such a requirement. Despite this setback for what Nader has called the "silicon chip of the consumer movement" (quoted in Bergner, 1986), consumer advocates are seeking new ways to establish consumer membership organizations to oversee state-regulated industries, like insurance and banking ("Senate Passes . . . ," 1988).

**Politicizing Consumer Purchasing Power.**     Holding that political power stems from economic power, radicals believe that consumers must effectively wield their collective purchasing power. Producer monopolies and oligopolies must be confronted by consumers organized as monopsonies (a sole buyer) and oligopsonies (a few large buyers). The exercise of collective purchasing power can take several forms, including consumer cooperatives, boycotts, and affirmative buying.

Consumer cooperatives, particularly food cooperatives, have a long history in the United States and elsewhere. Radical consumerists advocate the cooperative model as a means not so much of reducing the cost of goods as one of empowering citizens and giving them control over economic institutions at the community level. The Buyers Up program, whereby homeowners and small businesses in a particular city combine their purchasing power to negotiate a lower price for home heating fuel, is intended to have social as well as economic benefits. As Nader has said, "The consequences of homeowners banding together go far beyond saving a few dollars. . . . Buyers' groups can be the early links that bond people together. Then they'll start asking questions about municipal services, the schools, pollution" (quoted in Rowe, 1985, p. 12). The ideal society, according to Nader, would be one composed of small economic units, with manufacturing run by workers and retailing run by consumers. Nader, although he does not romanticize worker-owned enterprises, believes that their power could be effectively balanced by collective buying power (Ignatius, 1976).

Consumer boycotts represent another political use of purchasing power. Boycotts have been applied to achieve practical ends such as lower prices, as in the case of the meat and coffee boycotts called in the 1960s and early 1970s (Edwards, 1977). More often, however, their goal is moral (Friedman, 1985; Garrett, 1987). The issues at stake in such boycotts include exploitation of consumers in other nations (such as the infant milk formula controversy), discrimination against women and racial minorities, mistreatment of workers, and pollution of the environment. Reformists might question whether such issues are the concern of the consumer movement, but radicals readily incorporate them.

If a boycott means deliberately *not* purchasing a particular item, then a "girlcott" might be an appropriate name for the practice of buying certain products for political reasons. In 1985, for example, groups in Australia and the United States announced campaigns to buy products from New Zealand in support of that country's refusal to permit ships carrying nuclear weapons to dock in its ports ("Buycotte . . . ," 1985). Similarly, the Nabolom Bakery in Berkeley, California, urged its patrons to "Buy a Scone for Peace": the bakery would donate the proceeds to support a nonviolent blockade of the Livermore Nuclear Weapons Laboratory.

A more systematic approach to "shopping for a better world" has been advocated by the Council on Economic Priorities, an organization dedicated to enhancing the *social* performance of corporations. As the council defines it, social performance refers to corporate behavior that is undertaken voluntarily with respect to charitable contributions, representation of women and minorities on boards of directors, involvement in South Africa, weapons-related contracting, and disclosure of information to the public. The council publishes comparative ratings of the social performance of food, health and personal care, airline, automobile, hotel, oil, appliance, and household product companies (Lydenberg et al., 1986). Consumers can then buy a camera from a company that, say, stopped selling its merchandise in South Africa, or cook their supper on a kitchen range made by a firm not involved in the manufacture of nuclear weapons.

**Increasing Corporate and Individual Accountability.**   Another proposal of radical consumerists, especially Morton Mintz and Mark Green, is the restucturing of corporations. Specifically, they advocate federal (as opposed to state) chartering, placing public members on corporate boards of directors (Stone, 1976), and making corporate officers criminally responsible for the actions of their firms.

The idea behind federal chartering of corporations is that a basic contract exists between the people, in the form of their government, and the corporation by which the former set the ground rules for the latter. According to radicals, the grant of corporate status should require that a corporation be responsive to well-defined public interests and regularly account for its social performance. State chartering, they say, has turned into a mockery by which states compete to lure companies into their jurisdiction. The states adopt probusiness corporation codes in exchange for collecting incorporation fees. This explains why tiny Delaware is home to about half of the Fortune 500 companies (Green, 1980). The move to federal chartering would give society the opportunity to rewrite its contract with corporations. Essentially, corporations would be granted licenses to operate, and these licenses could be revoked for improper conduct. Federal chartering also could be used to limit a corporation's lines of business. For example, General Motors could be licensed to manufacture cars but not refrigerators. Exxon could be permitted to sell gasoline but not solar power equipment. In short, the radical proposes federal chartering as a means of reversing the trend toward conglomeration and bringing the giant corporation under public control (Mintz and Cohen, 1971; Nader, 1973).

Like federal chartering, placing public members on corporate boards of directors could also increase corporate accountability to the public. These directors would urge large corporations to pay more attention to product quality, the environment, working conditions, racial minorities, and women (Mintz and Cohen, 1976). In addition, the presence of public directors might help restore the influence that has slipped from boards into the hands of top management (Green, 1980).

Federal chartering and public directors essentially impose external pressures on corporate officials. Radicals, holding that corporate accountability must also stem from within, advocate establishing personal accountability of a corporation's leadership. Enlightened conduct would follow through fear of punishment or a desire for the rewards of enlightened social responsibility. Radicals believe that the surest way to deter corporate crime is to treat corporate officials as criminals. Too often, corporations receive a small fine, executives are publicly chided but otherwise unpunished, and patterns of misconduct go on unaffected. Top corporate officials should go to jail when consumers or workers are knowingly and intentionally injured, say radicals.

Radicals believe, too, that employees ought to have the courage to "blow the whistle" on their company when they discover unconscionable acts. To the radical consumerist, whistle-blowers are heroic figures. They risk their job and reputation to point out dangers in a nuclear power plant, to expose laxity in the handling and inspection of chickens in automated processing plants, or to report illegal withholding by oil companies of mineral lease payments that are owed to Native American tribes and state governments. Although unions will often protect whistle-blowers from retaliation by their employers, radical consumerists advocate a federal law that would defend nonunion employees as well (Green, 1980).

Whistle-blowers may expose some of the worst abuses, but a corporation's moral leadership must begin at the top. Consequently, radicals have sought to heighten the consciousness of corporate leaders. One method has been the encouragement of shareholder resolutions whereby controversial issues are raised at annual meetings. For example, a resolution might stipulate that a company hire more women in management, cease trading with the South African government, or stop selling infant milk formula in third world countries. These insurgent shareholder resolutions are never passed, but they often influence corporate policy nevertheless. In exchange for the withdrawal of a resolution, a company may voluntarily alter its policies or at least set up a task force to study the issue at hand (Purcell, 1979).

Ralph Nader's most recent book, *The Big Boys* (Nader and Taylor, 1986) illustrates yet another way of increasing the accountability of corporate executives. The book offers portraits, and not entirely negative ones, of the chief executive officers of seven major U.S. corporations, including Roger Smith of General Motors and Paul Oreffice of Dow Chemical. Some critics of *The Big Boys* charge that the book shows that Ralph has "gone soft." Nader, however, describes his purpose as destroying the anonymity and inaccessibility of the men who exercise such enormous influence over the everyday lives of Americans (Easterbrook, 1986).

In all, radical consumerists see the world in absolute moral terms; it is a world populated by devilish corporations bent on wiping out their unsuspecting customers (De Toledano, 1975). Radicals attribute consumer problems to the blind pursuit of profit by unaccountable individuals. Accordingly, the solution to consumer problems lies in fighting corporate power with collective buying power. Where corporations cannot be controlled through the marketplace, their system of governance should be reorganized and their leaders morally reeducated. Ultimately, consumers must wean themselves from dependence on corporations by, like Nader himself, scaling down their material desires and adopting a "small is beautiful" ethic.

## Ideological Change

Distinguishing between reformists and radicals illuminates the philosophical breadth of the consumer movement as well as the sources of internal ideological strain. Nevertheless, it is important to emphasize that movement participants feel no compulsion to be consistently radical or reformist. They are free to blend ideologies as well as change their philosophy with the passage of time. The evolution of Nader's views has been followed by the press (Ignatius, 1976), but ideological shifts in the movement as a whole are no less interesting.

During the early 1970s, the movement became more radical with respect to its ideological tone and the breadth of the issues it tackled (Mayer, 1981). Beginning in the late 1970s, however, the movement's center of political gravity began to swing back in the reformist direction, partly because President Carter had placed several consumerists in positions of regulatory authority, making it hard to dismiss government agencies as inevitably controlled by business. Also, many consumerists supported the logic of industry-specific deregulation and resorted to the reformist language of efficiency rather than the radical language of equity.

Then, when Ronald Reagan was elected president in 1980, the consumer movement shifted still further in the direction of ideological reformism and refocused its concern on traditional safety and pocketbook issues. Consumerists found themselves fighting to prevent the budgets of consumer protection agencies from being drastically cut and their favorite programs from being dismantled or "deregulated" (Claybrook et al., 1984; Tolchin and Tolchin, 1983; "Warning . . . ," 1982). When proposing new initiatives, consumerists stuck to the safe ground of information disclosure requirements, product efficiency, and safety. Operating in an inhospitable political environment, the consumer movement returned to the basic issues that had fueled its earlier growth and attracted a wide base of support. When political conditions improve, the movement will no doubt have a backlog of additional issues to promote, and radical ideology may again become ascendant.

*Chapter Five*

# Determinants of Political Success and Failure

Battles over consumer policy occur in several government arenas—legislative, regulatory, judicial. Regardless of the arena, most analysts agree that representation of consumer interests typically will be less effective than representation of business interests. Consumers are unlikely to be intensely concerned about a given issue, and they are likely to believe that their personal involvement is unnecessary since there are so many other potential contributors to the cause. In contrast, the effect on businesses of a proposed consumer policy is likely to be substantial and confined to a few firms. As a result, the temptation to be a free rider is much less for a business than it is for a consumer.

Given this constellation of political forces, it is surprising that consumer advocates ever prevail. Yet prevail they have, and with some regularity. What accounts for consumerism's occasional successes in the political arena, and, by extension, when are consumer activists likely to fail?

Success in the political arena is a slippery concept. Is it a success or a failure when a law is passed but not vigorously enforced, as in the case of most laws requiring young children to use special seat restraints? Is it a success or a failure when a case is won in court but the defendant continues to engage in the same illegal behavior, as when a firm goes on dumping toxic substances into a river after having received a minimal fine?

There appear to be at least two components of political success—social and economic. The social component involves establishing new social norms and reaffirming existing ones (Handler, 1978). It typically consists of passing (or blocking) legislation, promulgating (or preventing) a regulation, or winning a court decision. But even when consumerist forces are successful in establishing a new norm, ultimate success depends on how the *economic* welfare of consumers has been affected.

A classic example of a policy that succeeded in social terms but failed in economic terms was one involving the flammability of children's sleepwear. Consumerists supported a 1972 Commerce Department standard that required sleepwear manufacturers to make their pajamas less flammable. Thus, a new social norm was established regarding acceptable exposure to risk among young children. Although several flame-retardant chemicals were available at the time, TRIS was the favorite among manufacturers because of the feel it imparted and its low cost. In relatively short order, TRIS was used in about half of all children's sleepwear. Unfortunately, tests began to reveal that TRIS could cause genetic mutations and might be a carcinogen. The Consumer Product Safety Commission, in charge of enforcing the Flammable Fabrics Act, banned the sale and manufacture of TRIS-treated sleepwear in April of 1977, at considerable cost and inconvenience to consumers and businesses alike. Thus, a policy that was a social success turned out to be an economic failure (Bollier and Claybrook, 1986).

To date, there has been little systematic study of the factors that promote success of the social component of consumer policy. The research that does exist consists almost exclusively of accounts of the battles over particular pieces of legislation, with only an occasional mention of more general factors (Nadel, 1971; Pertschuk, 1986; Vogel and Nadel, 1976). Combining these legislative histories with other relevant research, this chapter provides a more inclusive framework for analyzing the success or failure of consumer policy in the legislative domain. (No attempt is made here to explain the fate of consumerists in the courts.) Analysis of the economic impact of consumer policies will be the subject of the next chapter.

Two general sets of factors determine the degree of success that interest groups have in the legislative process, one largely beyond their control, but the other, their political tactics, determined by them. For example, interest groups have relatively little control (at least in the short term) over governmental rules concerning limits on and disclosure of campaign contributions, but they have a high degree of discretion over which members of Congress receive their campaign contributions and in what amounts. Thus, what can be called *environmental* factors refer to the relatively unchangeable environment in which interest groups operate and over which they have little control, such as the public's mood or the political predispositions of key governmental decision makers. In contrast, *tactical* factors are those over which interest groups have a large measure of control—for instance, the skill with which consumer groups enter into short-term alliances with business groups.

## Environmental Determinants of Legislative Success

Serendipitous events such as scandals and dramatic accidents can have a significant impact on legislative outcomes. Plane crashes, drug tamperings, and accidents at nuclear power plants tend to set the legislative wheels into motion. Unfortunately for consumerists, the timing of these events is beyond their control. Only slightly more subject to prediction and control are the shifts that occur periodically in the mood of the public and in the sympathy of key government figures toward consumerism.

### Public Opinion

Public opinion rarely accomplishes anything by itself, but it does influence key players' actions. For instance, most elected officials follow public opinion, a few lead it, and none want to alienate it. Interest groups attempt to mobilize public sentiment, portray themselves as the public's champions, and put their opponents on the defensive—preferably by accusing them of something hideous like deforming babies or killing motorists (Wilson, 1980).

Public opinion is not completely beyond the control of consumerists, but it is extremely fickle. Political economist Anthony Downs (1972) observes that public opinion goes through a recognizable "issue-attention cycle." During the first stage, the public is unaware or unconcerned about a particular social problem, which is only one of many potential public issues. Then a galvanizing event occurs which allows the problem to break out of the pack and be transformed into a genuine social issue. A stage of "alarmed discovery and euphoric enthusiasm" sets in during which the public believes that the problem can be painlessly solved. It is during this second stage that activists must use public sentiment in support of their goals, for during the third stage the public will come to realize how costly it will be to make significant progress. For example, everyone is "against" smog—unless reducing it means taking the bus to work. A fourth stage quickly follows in which public interest in the issue gradually declines. Finally, the issue moves into "a twilight realm of lesser attention or spasmodic recurrences of interest" (p. 40). If a social movement has been successful, it will have institutionalized societal concern with the problem in the form of new organizations and policies designed to help solve it.

Downs's view of the issue-attention cycle is based on his observation of societal concern about pollution and poverty, but the cycle seems to apply to consumer issues as well. The period prior to 1962 represents the first stage during which some members of Congress attempted to make public issues out of consumer problems like auto and drug safety but met with little success. Then, in 1962, the public was shocked by revelations of the side effects of the drug thalidomide, and President Kennedy delivered the first consumer message to the U.S. Congress. Public interest in consumer issues continued to build until 1966, when one could speak of consumer protection as a full-blown public issue, symbolized by the *Newsweek* cover story that declared Ralph Nader to be the "Consumer Crusader" (Nadel, 1971).

The 1962–72 period, corresponding to Downs's second stage, was characterized by alarmed discovery and public confidence in the government's ability to alleviate consumer problems. Dozens of laws and regulations were enacted to protect the consumer. The third stage of consumerism's issue-attention cycle occurred between 1972 and 1976 and involved public realization of the cost of reform. For example, when gasoline was inexpensive, it didn't matter that safer and less polluting cars consumed more gasoline, but the cost of safety and clean air became more salient after the oil price shocks of 1973–74 and 1978–79.

By 1976, public opinion had shifted, and President Carter was elected on a platform that promised decreased government involvement. Interest in consumer protection waned during the Carter administration (phase 4), although the public remained quite supportive of the goals of the consumer movement (Atlantic Richfield, 1982; Sentry Insurance, 1977; Smith and Bloom, 1986). By 1980, Ronald Reagan had come to represent public hostility to Big Government, and his landslide victory buried consumer protection as a public issue. In line with Downs's model, however, consumer protection had by that time become institutionalized in the form of government agencies and numerous laws and regulations (phase 5). Public opinion had become largely irrelevant to the survival of consumer issues. Thus, the concept of an issue-attention cycle emphasizes how unpredictable public opinion can be and therefore how important it is to exploit it when the opportunity exists.

## Leadership by Government Activists

Even when consumerists have public opinion on their side, it is virtually impossible for them to make political headway without support from within the government. The president is probably the most visible but least important source of support. Presidents Theodore and Franklin Roosevelt supported the measures of their day aimed at ensuring good quality in foods and drugs. More recently, Presidents Kennedy and Johnson sent legislative recommendations to Congress and created new mechanisms of consumer representation within the executive branch. Nevertheless, no American president has made consumer protection one of his top priorities. There are just too many competing areas of concern. Symbolic support is about all that consumerists can hope for from a president.

The greatest source of a president's influence on consumer affairs probably comes indirectly through his appointments to executive and regulatory agencies. Yet, even here, presidential power is limited. Two of the most important consumer protection agencies—the Federal Trade Commission and Consumer Product Safety Commission—are headed by a panel of five commissioners who are appointed to seven-year terms that overlap those of the president. When a president has the opportunity to appoint new commissioners, he is constrained by the fact that no more than three of the five can be members of a given political party.

Few pieces of consumer protection legislation would be passed without vigorous consumer advocacy by members of the U.S. Senate and House. Activism on behalf of consumerism goes far beyond casting votes in favor of consumer legislation. It includes sponsoring legislation, introducing strengthening amendments (or weakening ones on anticonsumer bills), serving as a bill's floor manager, and generating publicity concerning consumer issues (like writing books or articles). Most important, consumer advocacy by a member of Congress involves lobbying one's colleagues and exerting influence within congressional committees.

Consumer advocacy within Congress is not marked by coordinated action, with one or two senators or representatives overseeing action across all consumer issues. Rather, the system is fragmented and marked by a certain degree of rivalry. The activist usually specializes in a few consumer issues, using a position of leadership on a committee or subcommittee to control congressional action. When the public demand for consumer protection is strong members of Congress may even compete with one another for the good publicity that comes from being the consumer's champion (Nadel, 1971).

Most consumer activists within Congress have been Democrats. During the latter half of the 1960s, Democrats Abraham Ribicoff, Philip Hart, Warren Magnuson, and Benjamin Rosenthal ruled the roost of consumer protection from their positions atop the Senate Executive Reorganization Subcommittee, the Senate Antitrust Subcommittee, the Senate Commerce Committee, and the House Government Operations Committee, respectively. During the latter half of the 1980s, Democrats Howard Metzenbaum and Henry Waxman carried on this tradition as chairs of the Senate Subcommittee on Antitrust, Monopolies, and Business Rights and the House Subcommittee on Health and the Environment, respectively.

A consumer protection bill has little chance of passage if it is referred to a committee chaired by someone who opposes the legislation. A chair can simply refuse to let a bill be discussed in committee. Or if public pressure is sufficient to force at least some discussion of the proposed legislation, the chair can engineer a negative committee vote, in which case the bill will never be voted upon by the entire House or Senate. For example, any legislation that would harm the U.S. auto industry has no chance of getting out of the House Energy and Commerce Committee, chaired by John Dingell of Michigan. Similarly, any bill that would discourage cigarette consumption is going to pass only over the dead bodies of tobacco-state senators like Jesse Helms of North Carolina and Wendell Ford of Kentucky (Pertschuk, 1986).

Given the practice of "logrolling" among legislators (trading support for each other's bills), membership on a committee is often enough for someone to exercise considerable influence over a particular bill. In explaining why it took so long to pass legislation requiring full disclosure of interest rates for loans, political scientist Mark Nadel (1971) describes the sticky situation in the Senate Banking and Currency Committee. The most vociferous opponent of the bill in the committee was Senator Wallace Bennett. Not only did the senator own several businesses that relied on credit transactions, but his brother Harold was the president of the National Retail Merchants Association, which strongly opposed truth-in-lending legislation. According to Nadel, conflict of interest also marked the position of another committee member, Senator Edward Long, the president of a major Missouri loan company and two banks.

In sum, consumerists can run into a brick wall when legislative committees contain powerful members who oppose particular bills, whether because of differences of opinion concerning the national interest or because of personal self-interest or the interests of constituents. On occasion, consumerists have changed the minds of powerful opponents or have deftly maneuvered around them. More often, though, the only way to deal with an opponent who exercises strong committee influence is to work toward his or her defeat in the next election.

Conveniently timed tragedies, a public receptivity to reform, and supportive members of government greatly facilitate the job of enacting consumer legislation. If consumer activists had to wait for conducive environmental factors, however, they would be unable to pursue a coherent legislative agenda. As a result, consumerists use a variety of tactics to increase their prospects of political success.

## Tactical Determinants of Legislative Success

The tactical determinants of legislative success can be grouped into three broad categories: (1) choosing the right goals, (2) taking the offensive, and (3) skillfully dealing with the opposition.

### The Choice of Goals
Marketers are fond of saying that products are not bought; they are sold. The same applies to legislative proposals, which must be sold to two crucial markets—the public and political decision makers. Convincing the former helps persuade the latter.

**Appealing to the Public.**    The first step in the political selling process is selecting a "product" with potential mass appeal. In this respect, consumerists have two strong selling points: appeals to fear and to the pocketbook. When it comes to arousing people's fears, not all risks are equal. Research by psychologists and economists has shown that people tend to exaggerate certain risks while downplaying others. We tend to be particularly sensitive to product risks that (1) produce violent accidents rather than prolonged illnesses, (2) affect many people simultaneously rather than the same number of people in isolated incidents, and (3) are not fully known before one engages in an activity (Lowrance, 1976; Slovic, Fischhoff, and Lichtenstein, 1979, 1982). Airline disasters have all the ingredients for arousing public fear, whereas the hundreds of thousands of slow deaths from cigarettes and other carcinogens are ignored or repressed. Consequently, consumerists are faced with the challenge of steering consumer outrage over a few dramatic events into a broader concern with less immediately disturbing safety issues.

Similarly, everyone wants to save money, but hardly anyone wants to take the time and effort to acquire consumer information or comparison shop. As a result, members of the public tend to support proposals to provide consumers with prepurchase information, such as labels describing nutrient content or energy efficiency, although such proposals usually fail to arouse much consumer passion. It is even more difficult for consumerists to excite the public about threats to competition, even though these issues may be vitally important. For example, most consumers are quick to buy beer and soft drinks when they see them marked with a "special low price" tag in the supermarket, but few are interested in stopping bottlers' plans to raise prices by obtaining exclusive territorial distributorships. Few people would argue *against* legislative proposals to provide consumers with information or ensure open competition, but these proposals lack public appeal and so remain difficult to enact.

**Appealing to Legislators.**   Consumerists can boost their chances of legislative success by selecting issues that play into the "career maintenance needs" of legislators (Nadel, 1971). The fact that most members of Congress wish to be reelected helps explain two features of consumer legislation. The first is the tendency to pass bills that potentially benefit all consumers rather than merely a subset. In reviewing consumer protection legislation passed during the 1960s, Mark Nadel discerns an "unmistakable story": legislation that conferred benefits on all consumers was far more common than legislation that disproportionately aided low-income consumers.

The career maintenance needs of legislators help explain a second common feature of consumer protection laws. A member of Congress naturally wants to take as much credit as possible for actions that benefit his or her constituents and minimize personal responsibility for actions that are unpopular. One way of satisfying these two requirements is to pass broadly stated legislation that responds to a pressing public concern and then let a regulatory agency or executive department "sweat the details." The legislation establishing the Consumer Product Safety Commission is a perfect example. It charges the commission with the task of protecting consumers from unreasonable risks of injury associated with products, including the possibility of product misuse by consumers. Who can quarrel with that goal? Yet, the commission, not legislators, gets the political heat when a product needs to be recalled, banned, or made subject to design standards.

In sum, consumerists improve their prospects for success when they promote legislation that corresponds to the needs of the public as well as those of legislators. Members of the consuming public want to be protected from the risks that they *perceive* to be the greatest, not necessarily those that in fact pose the greatest dangers. Similarly, consumers want to save money but without having to devote too much time to acquiring information and comparing alternatives. Legislators, for their part, are eager to support proposals that will earn them political capital but without exposing them to political risk.

It is convenient when consumerist proposals simultaneously fulfill the needs of the public and of politicians. Difficulties arise, however, when a consumer problem does not fire the public's imagination or when its solution requires sacrifice on the part of consumers and exposes legislators to political risk. Consumerists must then use a number of tactics to present their case in the most favorable light.

## *Taking the Offensive*

Beyond selecting an issue with potential appeal to the public and members of Congress, a number of other tactics can further enhance the prospects of success in the legislative arena. One of these is to capitalize on, and sometimes stage, events that receive media coverage. Another is to name a bill in a way that identifies it with unassailable values of truth, justice, and the American way.

**Managing the Media.** It is a sad but compelling fact that a tragedy or crisis is often required to stimulate government (and business) action. In 1982, several people were murdered by a lunatic who placed cyanide inside Tylenol capsules. In a matter of weeks, the federal government issued regulations requiring that medicine bottles be made tamper-proof. Yet, this example is the exception rather than the rule. Only rarely does a dramatic event like the Tylenol poisonings translate directly into legislative action. More typically, consumer groups must be quick to take advantage of the window of opportunity afforded by tragedies and crises. They must, in a sense, manage events.

The passage of drug safety legislation in 1962 is often attributed to public revulsion to thalidomide, the drug that caused children to be born without limbs. The story is more complicated, however. Thalidomide was initially marketed in several European countries. But it was only because of the efforts of a single FDA medical officer, Dr. Frances Kelsey, who insisted on further testing of the drug, that it was never approved for sale in the United States.

Thalidomide's ill effects were known several months before it became a public issue. As Mark Nadel (1971) tells it, there was no public reaction to a small article in the *New York Times* on 11 April covering a speech by Dr. Helen Taussig in which she reported a link between thalidomide and birth defects. In late May, Dr. Taussig reiterated her concerns before a Senate committee investigating drug prices which was chaired by Estes Kefauver. Her remarks received no press coverage, however. In fact, one of Senator Kefauver's staff members, John Blair, didn't want Dr. Taussig to testify at the May hearings, believing that it was too early to spring the story. Finally, when it appeared that a bill too weak for Senator Kefauver's tastes might be reported out of the Judiciary Committee, John Blair alerted the *Washington Post* and *Washington Star* to the fact that the marketing of thalidomide in the United States had been narrowly avoided. The *Post's* consumer reporter Morton Mintz gave the story front page treatment, after which stories appeared throughout the country, accompanied by pictures of curly-headed babies with stubs protruding where their arms and legs should have been.

There is an instructive footnote to the thalidomide episode. The scandal raised the specter of dangerous drugs being all too easily released upon the American public. Yet the legislation that was passed in response to the terrible incident had little to do with ensuring drug safety. Laws had been on the books for several decades that forbade the sale of dangerous drugs. Neither did the resulting legislation address the economic issue of drug prices that had originally concerned Senator Kefauver. Rather, the legislation addressed a third issue—drug effectiveness. Therefore, the episode allowed consumer activists to capitalize on public outrage over thalidomide in order to secure new legislation, but it was not exactly the bill they wanted.

Of course, having to wait for a tragedy or scandal to occur severely limits consumerists' freedom of action. Consequently, consumer organizations also try to create attention-grabbing events. In the late 1960s and early 1970s, Nader's Raiders released a number of investigative reports on federal agencies. The most successful of these charged the Federal Trade Commission with extreme laxity in enforcing consumer protection statutes. The report's findings were immediately branded as a pack of distortions by the FTC's chairman. Nevertheless, the findings were quickly confirmed by a special committee of the American Bar Association, forcing President Nixon to appoint more vigorous leaders at the FTC. The exposé approach used by Nader's Raiders set a pattern for the consumer movement that continues today.

**Properly Christening Your Bill.**    Onomatologers (people who study names) believe that the name given to a child at birth affects his/her entire life prospects. Names also seem to make a difference when it comes to proposed legislation. It is almost essential that the official or abbreviated name of a consumer protection bill include a word like *truth* or *fair*. The words *equality* and *competition* will also do, as in the Competitive Equality Banking Act of 1987. There is truth-in-lending, truth-in-packaging, truth-in-mileage-readings, truth-in-savings, truth-in-airline-scheduling, even truth-in-menus. Similarly, there is the Fair Debt Collection Practices, Fair Credit Reporting Act, and Fair Credit Billing Act.

Not all bills with the word *fair* in their titles are necessarily fair. So-called fair trade laws fix the price at which products may be sold to the public. These laws are fair in the eyes of small retailers, but large discount houses perceive them as grossly *un*fair.

The prolonged search for a politically palatable name is best seen in the attempt to create a consumer protection agency. The primary purpose of the agency was to represent consumer interests before other agencies. Unfortunately, the title Consumer Protection Agency implied that, like the Environmental Protection Agency, the new government entity would have the power to enforce laws and make regulations. The second title, Agency for Consumer Advocacy, was perhaps more accurate, but it only heightened the fears of those who saw the new agency as a permanent mechanism for harassing businesses (Winter, 1972). Eventually, the name Office of Consumer Representation was settled upon. In addition to explicitly referring to the function of representation, an "office" sounded smaller and less threatening than an "agency." Unfortunately, the right name was found only after support for the idea had eroded (Ripley and Franklin, 1984; Schwartz, 1979; Stein, 1979).

## *Dealing with Powerful Opponents*

Even when consumerists have cultivated the mass media, built public awareness for their legislative proposal, and given it an appealing title, a critical task remains—overcoming or at least neutralizing the political clout of the forces lined up in opposition to the proposal. Accomplishing this task often entails three strategies: (1) turning opponent assets into liabilities, (2) exploiting opportunities to gain powerful business allies, and (3) compromising.

**Making the Best of a Bad Situation.** Consumerists aren't going to outmuscle their opponents, for the resources of the consumer movement are typically dwarfed by those of the business or industry that is the target of their legislative proposal. Enlisting the support of the labor and environmental movements is sometimes a feasible strategy for beefing up one's resources. But this strategy can be self-defeating since, by broadening the conflict, it can activate representatives of the business community as a whole, such as the Chamber of Commerce or the National Association of Manufacturers. Thus, to be successful, consumerists must find ways to isolate their opponents and put them on the defensive.

Former FTC chairman Michael Pertschuk provides rich examples of consumerists outmaneuvering more powerful opponents in his ode to public interest lobbying, *Giant Killers* (1986). One of his stories concerns the attempt in 1983 to strengthen the government-mandated warning printed on cigarette packages and in advertising for cigarettes. His account shows the way in which industry arrogance can lead to its defeat. As Pertschuk tells it, Sen. Orrin Hatch of Utah had introduced a cigarette labeling bill, perhaps to please his Mormon constituency. Nevertheless, Hatch was eager for some sort of compromise, since an overly dire cigarette warning would threaten the constituents of his fellow moral majoritarians, Senators Jesse Helms and John East of North Carolina. At first, the tobacco lobby seemed to agree to a compromise that would slightly strengthen the single, existing warning rather than require four rotating warnings (the position advocated by health lobbyists). Instead of "Warning: The surgeon general has determined that cigarette smoking is dangerous to your health," the new message would read "Surgeon general's warning: Cigarette smoking increases your risk of cancer and heart, lung, and other serious diseases."

Then the tobacco lobby misplayed its cards. It tried to build support for the compromise by telling individual members of the Senate Health Committee that all the other members had already agreed to it, thinking that none of the senators or their staff members would compare notes. When the senators discovered the trick that was being played upon them, and when the tobacco industry refused to go on record as supporting the compromise wording, even Orrin Hatch was livid. The senators on the Health Committee reacted by recommending an even stronger warning which read "Warning: Cigarette smoking causes cancer, emphysema, and heart disease; may complicate pregnancy; and is addictive."

There were many other hurdles that needed to be cleared before eventual passage of the Comprehensive Smoking Prevention Education Act in 1984. Throughout, the powerful tobacco lobby engaged in duplicitous conduct and refused to accept any compromise, alienating even its faithful congressional allies and dissipating its enormous reservoir of influence. In contrast, the health lobby, according to Pertschuk, was the picture of reasonableness. It built bridges with Rep. Charles Rose of North Carolina by supporting legislation to ban the import of tobacco treated with forbidden pesticides. The tobacco growers whom Rose represented benefited from reduced foreign competition, while health lobbyists could be comforted by the fact that American smokers would be protected from harmful pesticides. The health lobby was also deft in enlisting the support of Rep. Albert Gore, Jr., of Tennessee (a major tobacco-growing state) in working out a deal with the tobacco lobby. Finally, the health lobby made some painful compromises, including deletion of any reference to the addictive nature of smoking. Still, in winning passage of a labeling bill that required four rotating warnings, the health lobbyists' greatest accomplishment was showing that the tobacco lobby was neither monolithic nor invulnerable.

**Building Consumer–Business Coalitions.**   If an industry targeted by consumer legislation consisted of a single, monopolistic firm, then the lines of battle would be clearly drawn, and consumerists would rarely prevail against the superior political muscle of the threatened firm. In practice, differences of interest exist within and across industries, allowing consumerists to form powerful alliances with businesses. Consumer and business groups can enter into a formal alliance, but more often they lobby independently with the effect of reinforcing each other's efforts. In a few cases, consumer groups can even refrain from lobbying, knowing that a business group will have sufficient incentive to represent their common interests.

Within a competitive market, a consumer protection proposal may provide firms with the opportunity to capitalize upon their own economic advantages or to neutralize those of competitors. For example, manufacturers who use natural ingredients or original components, such as real cheese or virgin wool, have joined consumerists in supporting content disclosure requirements because these standards are a means of fighting off competition from firms using artificial, synthetic, or recycled materials (Pertschuk, 1982).

Service providers as well as manufacturers can enter into consumer-business alliances. In the name of maintaining high levels of client trust and confidence, members of various state-regulated professions, such as doctors, pharmacists, and attorneys, have traditionally forbade advertising. Consumer groups have come to regard such advertising bans as a means of reducing price competition. In their efforts to encourage advertising by professionals, consumer groups are often joined by younger professionals who have recently entered the field and by those who wish to operate high-volume, low-price clinics (and, or course, by the advertising industry itself).

A particularly ironic instance of consumer groups lobbying alongside a giant corporation occurred in 1985 when Chrysler Corporation and consumer organizations joined in opposing a federal rollback of fuel economy standards for 1986 automobile models. General Motors and Ford claimed that a corporate average fuel efficiency standard of 27.5 miles per gallon would force them to lay off thousands of workers in plants that produced large, less fuel-efficient cars. Chrysler, having invested heavily in the development of fuel-efficient cars, complained that it would be penalized if the standard was weakened. Ralph Nader asked the National Highway Safety Administration to call GM and Ford's "massive corporate bluff" ("U.S. Lowers . . .," 1985), but the government relented and lowered the standard to 26 miles per gallon.

Even when all the firms within an industry present a common front against consumerist proposals, consumerists may find business allies outside the targeted industry. Perhaps the classic example of this phenomenon occurred when the National Highway Traffic Safety Administration (NHTSA) decided in 1981 to rescind a proposed automobile safety standard that would have required automatic seat restraints in all new vehicles. State Farm Insurance Company, the National Association of Independent Insurers, and the consumerist Center for Auto Safety teamed up to challenge NHTSA's decision, eventually winning a Supreme Court case in 1983. The insurers took part because it was in their economic self-interest to prevent deaths and injuries; there would be fewer victims to compensate.

Another straightforward illustration involves the enactment of state lemon laws that give owners of new motor vehicles the right to a refund or a replacement under certain fairly stringent circumstances (Nicks, 1986). Automobile manufacturers have generally opposed lemon laws, as one might expect. Dealers have favored them, however, because restitution comes out of the pocket of the vehicle's manufacturer, while the dealer avoids losing the future business of a disgruntled customer.

Sometimes the interest of some businesses in a proconsumer policy has been so strong that consumer groups could sit back and watch, husbanding their scarce political resources for some other battle. One such case concerned unauthorized copying of material from audiocassettes. Record manufacturers and holders of copyrights had proposed a system whereby consumers are taxed either when they buy blank tapes or when they buy a machine capable of recording material. The proceeds would have been distributed according to some formula among the various entities whose material had presumably been pirated. Opposition to this proposal was led by such firms as Minnesota Mining and Manufacturing Company and General Electric, firms that do not wish to see a tax imposed on their products. With corporate heavyweights lined up against the proposal, consumer groups had little need to voice their opposition to the price increases associated with a royalty surcharge on sales of blank tapes and cassette players (Glen, 1985).

Of course, consumerists cannot always count on having a powerful ally within the business community. When the possibility does arise, however, the tactical issue for consumerists is extracting the maximum political advantage without being co-opted or becoming too sensitive to business arguments. Some consumerists argue against negotiating, compromising, and working with business groups (Bradley, 1987), but this position entails forfeiting a major source of political clout. The skillful consumerist knows when to enter coalitions with business groups and when to stay out of them.

**The Art of Compromise.** In any negotiation, one can err either by compromising too readily, by giving up ground that one could have easily won with a little more persistence, or by being too unyielding, with the result that negotiations break down and an opportunity for mutually beneficial exchange is lost. For instance, the failure to establish a consumer protection agency has been blamed on Ralph Nader's rejection of a weakened version of the concept (Schwartz, 1979; Stein, 1979). Mark Green (1978), however, disputes this version of events and supports Nader's logic that a weak agency can be worse than no agency at all. In other situations, uncompromising point men like Nader can strengthen the hand of more moderate consumer organizations that are willing to engage in negotiation.

Compromise is almost always necessary for consumerists since they lack the resources to push for an unequivocal legislative victory. In 1984, consumer activists wanted legislation that would speed the Food and Drug Administration's approval process for generic drugs. They secured passage of the Drug Price Competition Act, but at the price of granting drug manufacturers longer patent protection for their new discoveries. Similarly, in 1986, Congress enacted legislation to provide compensation for families of children injured by the side effects of vaccines for major childhood diseases such as polio. Included in the legislation, however, was a provision that consumerists would have preferred to omit—a limit on the liability of drug companies that manufacture the vaccines.

When the economic, political, and social climate of the nation favors consumer protection, as it did in the late 1960s and early 1970s, consumer advocates can occasionally resist the pressure to compromise. During the 1960s, they held out for tough auto safety regulations, and they won the establishment of a Consumer Product Safety Commission with extensive powers and mechanisms for public participation. In the less hospitable climate of the 1980s, consumerists had to play the legislative game like everyone else, and that meant being willing to compromise.

## Accomplishments

There are several elements in the political environment over which consumerists have little or no control. No one can predict when planes will fall out of the air or when deadly side effects will result from a pharmaceutical product. Nevertheless, a large area for the exercise of tactical skill exists. The passage of so many major pieces of consumer-oriented legislation suggests that the consumer movement has done well in the tactical realm. Below is a partial chronology of the movement's major legislative accomplishments since 1962:

| | |
|---|---|
| 1962 | Drug Amendments to the federal Food, Drug, and Cosmetic Act |
| 1965 | Federal Cigarette Labeling and Advertising Act |
| 1966 | Child Protection Act; Fair Packaging and Labeling Act; National Traffic and Motor Vehicle Safety Act |
| 1968 | Truth-in-Lending |
| 1970 | Credit Card Liability Act; Fair Credit Reporting Act; Poison Prevention Packaging Act |
| 1972 | Consumer Product Safety Act |
| 1974 | Equal Credit Opportunity Act; Fair Credit Billing Act |
| 1975 | Energy Policy and Conservation Act; Magnuson-Moss Warranty and Federal Trade Commission Improvements Act |
| 1976 | Medical Device Amendments to the federal Food, Drug, and Cosmetic Act |
| 1977 | Fair Debt Collection Practices Act |
| 1978 | Electronic Fund Transfer Act |

1980     Infant Milk Formula Act
1984     Drug Price Competition and Patent Restoration Act

In addition to legislative victories, consumer organizations have seen their ideas realized in the form of industrywide rules promulgated by federal agencies like the Federal Trade Commission, Consumer Product Safety Commission, National Highway Traffic Safety Administration, and Food and Drug Administration. Individual states have also passed laws and regulations that establish important consumer rights, including lemon laws covering defective new cars, seatbelt use laws for children or adults, drug price posting requirements, mandatory price marking on all grocery items, record confidentiality and accessibility for medical patients, and rules governing utility shut-offs for nonpayment.

To round out the list of the consumer movement's political successes, one can add successful opposition to legislation and regulation that consumerists have viewed as anticonsumer. For example, defeating a bill that would strip the Federal Trade Commission of its powers to conduct investigations of the insurance industry is no less a victory than passing a law that facilitates comparison of the price of insurance policies. In context, these negative victories are as important as actions that break new ground in consumer protection.

Thus, the consumer movement in the United States has been able to sustain its core organizations, achieve legitimacy in the eyes of the public, and score impressive victories in the legislative and regulatory arenas. Yet the ultimate yardstick by which the movement must be measured is its impact on consumer welfare. To what extent have the government and business initiatives stimulated by consumerists resulted in fewer accidental deaths and injuries, greater value when consumers make purchases, and easier access to remedies when problems occur? The next chapter answers these questions.

*Chapter Six*

# The Economic Impact of the Consumer Movement

Are consumers better off as a result of the consumer activism that has taken place in the United States and elsewhere? How many additional product-related deaths and accidents would have occurred if there had been no movement? How much more money, time, and effort would consumers have expended? How many more times would consumers have found themselves without a remedial course of action in the event of a defective product or a deceptive sales practice? These are the standards by which consumerism should ideally be judged. Unfortunately, we cannot replay history without the influence of the consumer movement in order to separate its effects from all the factors that might have contributed to any observed improvement in the lot of consumers. In practice, the best we can do is conduct modest evaluations of specific policies that can reasonably be considered the result of pressure from the consumer movement.

The purpose of policy evaluation is simple enough: to determine how a particular action affected a particular group of people within a particular period of time. Nevertheless, even seemingly simple evaluations of clearly defined policies can yield deceptive results. Consider what would appear to be two relatively straightforward instances of policy evaluation. One involves assessing the impact of improved factory lighting on worker productivity. The classic Hawthorne studies found that increasing factory illumination was indeed effective in improving productivity—but so was decreasing the level of illumination. It turned out that people worked harder because they knew they were part of an experiment, regardless of whether the lights were turned up or down (Roethlisberger and Dickson, 1939).

A second and more germane example of the difficulty of evaluating policies concerns the effects of mandated automobile safety features, such as collapsible steering wheels, on the rate of motorist injuries. A simple comparison of injury rates before and after the advent of federal regulation suggests that it has been successful in reducing motorist injuries. Yet, Sam Peltzman (1975a) has said that a complete evaluation should include injury rates among pedestrians and bicyclists, too. He argues that safety features have given some motorists a false sense of security, resulting in more reckless driving and increased deaths and injuries among pedestrians and bicyclists, and he presents statistical data that make a plausible case.

If seemingly clearcut evaluations are subject to such major pitfalls, how can one hope to evaluate a more complex consumer policy, the actions of an entire consumer agency, or the consumer movement as a whole? This chapter reviews the attempts to evaluate the impact of consumer policies on consumer welfare. Despite their flaws, these studies represent the best evidence available with which to draw conclusions regarding consumerism's effects on the marketplace and on consumers.

## The Logic of Policy Evaluation

Evaluation studies take many forms. Some focus on small-scale local initiatives—for example, a change in a teacher's curriculum—whereas others assess large-scale federal programs—for example, the early childhood education program Head Start. Evaluation studies can be impressionistic or highly quantitative. They can generalize from a single case study or employ rigorous experimental designs. Some evaluation studies are conducted before a policy has been decided upon and focus on its hypothetical effects; others are carried out only after a policy has been implemented so that actual effects can be observed.

Despite the enormous variation among studies, the crux of evaluation is determining the effects of a social intervention. To evaluate properly the impact of the consumer movement in the United States, two critical issues need to be addressed: (1) whether it is reasonable to equate the consumer movement's effects with those of federal laws and regulations, and (2) whether other factors might be responsible for any effects observed. These two issues will be briefly discussed.

## *Approximating the Consumer Movement's Influence*

Using the effects of federal consumer protection laws and regulations as a proxy measure of consumerism's influence presupposes the movement played a decisive role in the passage of the law or regulation under consideration. Unfortunately, precise estimates of the consumer movement's degree of responsibility for policy outcomes do not exist. Therefore, a conservative strategy is to limit an analysis of the movement's impact to those federal actions that are most commonly associated with the movement's political actions and leave out actions where the movement's impact is more debatable.

Another problem exists in trying to equate the impact of consumerism with the impact of relevant federal laws and regulations. This approach assumes that federal agencies faithfully carry out the intent of a consumer policy. In practice, the effectiveness of federal agencies in pursuing consumer welfare is commonly compromised by a number of factors, including bureaucratic inertia and animosity toward the goal of consumer protection among an agency's leaders. Thus, the failure of government to implement consumer policies aggressively and intelligently exerts a downward bias on an estimate of the movement's accomplishments.

An exclusive focus on the impact of federal laws and regulations underestimates consumerism's impact in other ways also. It assumes that the consumer movement has had no effect on state and local governments when in fact it has spawned a great deal of activity at these levels (for example, lemon laws covering defective automobiles). Similarly, it ignores any impact the movement has had on the consciousness and behavior of American businesses and consumers (for example, the educational influence of comparative product testing by Consumers Union). Finally, examining the effects of a law or regulation only in the nation in which it legally applies fails to account for the policy's possible influence on other countries.

The overall effect of using federal laws and regulations as a surrogate measure of the consumer movement is to downplay the extent of the movement's influence. Nevertheless, the vast majority of existing evaluation studies focus on the impact of a specific federal law or regulation. Unless one wishes to ignore this accumulated knowledge and start from scratch, there is little choice but to equate the impact of consumerism with the impact of consumer legislation and consumer protection agencies. Thus, this chapter concentrates on the movement's impact on American consumers by virtue of the federal actions in has encouraged.

## Ruling Out Other Possible Influences on Consumer Welfare

Suppose that we have decided that a particular law owes its existence to the consumer movement and that consumer welfare has been enhanced in the way intended by the law. How do we know that consumer welfare has been improved by the law per se or by some other factor? For example, the passage of a law setting minimum energy efficiency levels for appliances might be followed by improvements in appliance efficiency, but isn't it possible that businesses would have boosted the energy efficiency of their products without the impetus of a law?

The challenge of evaluation research is to reduce the possibility that a "mystery" factor other than the policy being studied is responsible for any effects observed. There are many candidates for this factor (Phillips and Calder, 1979, 1980). If consumers display greater sensitivity to interest rates after the passage of legislation requiring full disclosure of loan costs, is the law responsible or could it be that tough economic conditions simultaneously forced consumers to pay more attention to interest rates? If highway deaths decline in the years following imposition of a fifty-five-mile-per hour speed limit, could the reduction in mortality reflect a decline in the percentage of teenagers among all drivers? Or if customer complaints about spoiled dairy products decrease in the six months after the August implementation of open dating on packages, is the new information helping consumers select fresher products or could it be that spoilage rates decline automatically between summer and winter months?

There are a number of scientific methods for increasing one's certainty that a causal relationship exists between an action and its apparent effects. The ideal method is an experiment in which units of observation (such as people, cities, states) are randomly assigned to either a treatment or a control group and multiple observations are made before and after the implementation of any policy. Random assignment ensures that the treatment and control groups are similar in all respects except for the policy under investigation.

The testing of new drugs exemplifies the experimental approach. Patients suffering from the same problem are randomly assigned to experimental groups. The treatment group receives the new drug, while the control group receives a pill or injection with no known therapeutic benefits. Neither patients nor personnel administering the drugs and monitoring patient response know which patients are receiving the "real" drug. In addition, both treatment and control groups are subjected to precisely the same round of measurements and observations. When these procedures are followed, any observed differences between the two groups can reasonably be attributed to the drug being tested, since possible confounding factors have been controlled.

For a host of reasons, the use of a true experimental design is rarely possible when evaluating consumer policies. In this event, elimination of competing explanations for a policy's impact is achieved through statistical rather than experimental means. Various techniques are used to see whether the statistical association between a presumed cause and its presumed effect is diminished when other potential causes are taken into account. For example, one might examine the rate of cigarette consumption before and after the imposition of rotating health warnings on packages and in advertisements, controlling for other possible influences on cigarette consumption, including changes in the nation's age structure or in the price of cigarettes. A primary criterion for inclusion in this chapter is the extent to which an evaluation study has attempted to rule out competing explanations of a policy's effects.

## What the Studies Tell Us

Literally hundreds of consumerist-inspired laws and regulations have been enacted with the intention of producing benefits for consumers. Yet, the precise magnitude of these benefits (a policy's effectiveness) has been estimated in only a small percentage of cases. Still smaller is the number of studies that address the relationship between the benefits generated by a policy and the costs imposed by it (a policy's efficiency).

The review of research that follows is confined to studies that have explicitly estimated either policy effectiveness, efficiency, or both, after a policy has been implemented. There are many "regulatory analyses" which attempt to project a contemplated policy's likely economic impact. These studies are excluded from consideration here because they are particularly susceptible to nonscientific sources of bias. An industry might exaggerate costs to avoid a proposed regulation, and a government agency has an incentive to overstate likely benefits to justify the resources it has already expended in formulating a regulation.

Reviewing studies of consumer protection initiatives is not an exercise

Figure 6.1. A Report Card for Consumer Protection Efforts*

| Consumer Issue | Key Studies | Findings |
|---|---|---|
| *Positive* | | |
| Auto safety | Crandall et al., 1986 | $5 billion annual net benefits; little evidence of increase in nonoccupants risk due to offsetting behavior by drivers |
| Consumer Product Safety Commission | Zick, Mayer & Snow, 1986 | Saved approximately 18,000 lives during first ten years; no data on the cost of saving a life |
| Magnuson-Moss Warranty Act | Schmitt et al., 1979 | Warranties have, on balance, improved in coverage, duration, and readability |
| Generic drugs | Lewin, 1987; "The Big . . . ," 1987 | Brand name drugs are 70 percent more expensive than generics without offering therapeutic superiority |
| Regulations on overbooking | Snow & Weisbrod, 1982 | Rules generated net benefits for airline passengers |
| Airline deregulation | Morrison & Winston, 1986; McKenzie & Shughart, 1987 | $6 billion annual savings for consumers; no evidence of decline in safety or profitability due to deregulation |

*Consumer protection efforts are classified as positive, negative, or mixed according to the author's assessment of the evaluation studies available as of 1 January 1988.

## Figure 6.1. (*Continued*)

| Consumer Issue | Key Studies | Findings |
|---|---|---|
| *Positive* | | |
| Trucking deregulation | Delaney, 1987 | $56 billion annual savings for consumers; no evidence of reduced highway safety |
| *Negative* | | |
| Drug efficacy amendments | Peltzman, 1973; Wiggins, 1981 | Net annual loss of $250–$350 million due to reduced flow of new drugs and higher prices for existing drugs |
| Mattress flammability | Linneman, 1980; Viscusi, 1984a | Net annual loss of $2 million for ineffective standard |
| Corporate average fuel economy standards | Crandall et al., 1986 | No impact on fuel consumption while raising cost of large vehicles and delaying new car purchases |
| Miles per gallon estimates | Senauer et al., 1984 | Mileage overestimates led American consumers to spend $500 million in unanticipated costs; also costs of underestimation |

## Figure 6.1. (*Continued*)

| Consumer Issue | Key Studies | Findings |
|---|---|---|
| *Mixed* | | |
| Child-resistant closures | Howe, 1978; Viscusi, 1984b | Howe finds that accidental ingestions declined for regulated products while rising for unregulated ones; Viscusi's study concludes that regulation caused an increase in accidents due to "lulling effect" |
| Crib standards | Consumer Product Safety Commission, 1979; Viscusi, 1984a | CPSC study attributes a 44 percent decline in injuries and one of 33 percent in deaths to standards; Viscusi finds limited evidence of effectiveness and suggests that costs exceed benefits |
| Pajama flammability | Dardis et al., 1978 | Annual net benefits of $15 million, but only if one ignores choice costs and assumes elastic demand |

for the fainthearted. The reason is not so much that these studies can be highly technical, although they often are. Rather, it's because after having slogged through the technical portions of the studies, one finds that the conclusions are likely to be equivocal and subject to criticism by other researchers. The primitive state of evaluation research regarding consumer policy makes it impossible to deliver a precise estimate of consumerism's total economic impact on consumers. Instead, this chapter will place consumer policies into three categories depending on whether the available scientific evidence shows a policy's effects to be primarily positive, negative, or subject to conflicting evaluations.

This review will point out major limitations or weaknesses of particular studies. This emphasis on the shortcomings of policy evaluations, combined with the fact that two rigorous studies can sometimes contradict each other, may give the impression that policy evaluation is either hopelessly inexact or completely determined by a researcher's preconceived ideas. Such an impression might be partly warranted, but the critical response that awaits any evaluation study serves as a check on the publication of excessively flawed or biased research.

## Positive Results

**Auto Safety.**    For more than two decades, consumerists have played the issue of automobile safety like a drum to enlist and sustain public support. As a result, the federal government has implemented many costly standards for the safer manufacture of new cars. It is therefore fair to ask whether the increased price of new cars that is due to auto safety regulations—estimated to be as high as $2,000 per vehicle—has been justified in terms of the lives saved and injuries averted.

In 1975, economist Sam Peltzman (1975a, 1975b) leveled a potentially devastating criticism against the federal government's efforts to improve automobile safety. He claimed that government standards had indeed reduced occupant deaths and injuries but at the expense of increased risk to nonoccupants such as pedestrians, motorcyclists, and bicyclists. By making drivers feel safer, the government had encouraged reckless driving behavior which resulted in increased deaths among nonoccupants. The *net* safety effect of government regulation, Peltzman contended, was essentially zero. Moreover, he had data to back up his argument.

If Peltzman intended to be provocative, he succeeded. His study stimulated a number of efforts to rebut or refine his results (Cantu, 1980; Crandall et al. 1986; Joksch, 1976; Robertson, 1977). Most subsequent assessments of government safety programs have found that occupant fatalities and injuries have been reduced by the regulations, with little apparent effect on nonoccupants. The most recent effort to compare costs and benefits of auto safety regulation was conducted by Crandall and his associates (1986). In an analysis that attempted to overcome criticisms of past studies, they estimated the impact of auto regulation on automobile prices as well as the safety of occupants and nonoccupants. (They did not, however, attempt to quantify any of the alleged negative effects of regulation on innovativeness and international competitiveness of the American auto industry.) The analysis performed by Crandall and his colleagues was highly sophisticated and, as a result, did not yield a single measure of either costs or benefits of automobile safety regulation. Among the many strengths of their study was their attempt to establish the extent to which the greater safety of car occupants is offset by increased fatalities among nonoccupants. They found the size of the "Peltzman effect" to be minimal. They also presented estimates of the net benefits of auto regulation under several alternative assumptions, allowing the reader to select the most reasonable. In particular, what is the economic value, in dollars, of avoiding a highway fatality—$100,000, $500,000, $1 million, $10 million (Shodell, 1985)? Should a bumper standard be counted as a safety feature even though its primary purpose is to reduce repair costs? To what extent do manufacturers figure out less costly ways of complying with a regulation as time passes?

Crandall and his coauthors found that, except under the most pessimistic assumptions, the benefits of automobile safety regulation exceed its costs. Assigning a value of $300,000 to the prevention of a premature death, excluding the costs of complying with the bumper standard, and assuming that manufacturers learn over a period of years how to reduce the costs of meeting standards, the net benefits of government-mandated automobile safety measures are in the neighborhood of $5 billion annually. (In contrast, the authors were much less sanguine about the economic wisdom of auto emission and fuel economy standards.)

Whereas the research by Crandall and his associates probably represents the best available estimate of the effectiveness and efficiency of the first decade of federal automobile safety regulation, information is only beginning to trickle in regarding mandatory seatbelt-use laws and child-restraint laws. Some of the first reports were surprising. In New Jersey, for instance, auto-related fatalities actually rose in the first six months after passage of a mandatory seatbelt-use law (Wilson, 1986). Another study reaches a far more favorable conclusion by using a longer time frame and examining the first eight states to pass mandatory seat-

Figure 6.2. Recalls: The Most Extreme Form of Auto Safety Regulation

belt-use laws ("Belt-Use Laws . . .," 1987). The study finds a 8.7 percent reduction in the number of drivers and front-seat passengers killed in traffic crashes since the implementation of the laws. Moreover, fatality rates for rear-seat passengers, who are not covered by the laws, have remained unchanged, thereby increasing the likelihood that the improvement for front-seat passengers is attributable to the law rather than other factors.

Very little data on the effectiveness of child-restraint laws have so far been disseminated. To date, most studies show that child-restraint laws have reduced the number of children *injured* in crashes but have failed to reduce the number of children *killed* (Wagenaar, Webster, and Maybee, 1987). The lack of a statistically significant effect with respect to fatalities may be the result of the fortunate fact that relatively few children die in automobile accidents. In all, the two most significant automobile safety initiatives of the 1980s—mandatory seatbelt-use laws for adults and child-restraint laws—appear to be creating their intended results, but their exact long-term impact remains to be determined.

**The Consumer Product Safety Commission.** The Consumer Product Safety Commission (CPSC) was established with a great deal of fanfare in 1973. It was supposed to represent a new breed of regulatory agency. Unlike its sister safety agencies, the National Highway Traffic Safety Administration and the Food and Drug Administration, it was an independent agency rather than a subunit within an executive branch department. In addition, it included a special petitioning mechanism to promote public access, and it enjoyed broad powers to recall dangerous products and issue industrywide regulations. (The CPSC should not be confused with the Consumer Protection Agency that was proposed but never established and was designed to represent consumer perspectives within other federal agencies.)

Children draw a large portion of the CPSC's attention and resources. It has set standards regarding the flammability of children's sleepwear, the packaging of pharmaceutical products so as to prevent accidental ingestions, and the design of baby cribs, rattles, bicycles, and swimming pool slides. The CPSC is concerned about the safety of adult consumers, too. Its mattress flammability standard is intended to benefit cigarette smokers, the majority of whom are presumably adults. Similarly, the CPSC's design specifications for walk-behind power lawn mowers are aimed mainly at keeping arms, legs, fingers, and toes attached to their adult owners.

The CPSC is required to analyze the economic implications of its *proposed* actions, but it is not compelled to gather information on the actual effects of its policies once they take effect. Consequently, there are relatively few retrospective assessments of the CPSC's regulations. Conducting standard-specific analyses of CPSC actions is discouraged also by several scientific difficulties. Accident rates are rarely collected for the precise product class that has been the subject of a commission action. For example, the CPSC has regulated the flammability of mattresses, but its data on deaths from home fires may not separate out mattress-related fires. And even if one had relatively precise data regarding a specific category of injury, difficulties would remain. The number of accidents related to a particular product are often very low, usually a few per hundred thousand users; it is difficult to know whether a small change is due to a government action or to a statistical blip.

A final problem in evaluating specific product safety standards involves interpreting changes in accident rates over time. Comparing accident rates before and after a regulation is issued would seem to measure a standard's impact, but this procedure can yield misleading results. On the one hand, manufacturers often change their production techniques in anticipation of a government-mandated standard. On the other hand, it takes years, sometimes decades, before people replace their preregulation products with safer regulated ones.

For all these reasons, policy evaluators have shied away from analyzing the specific effects of CPSC actions. Among the few studies that have been conducted of individual standards, the majority have given the CPSC mixed or negative reviews. (These studies are discussed in succeeding sections.) Yet, even if the negative assessments are justified, it should be remembered that product standards represent only a small portion of the commission's total activities; other activities involve bans, recalls, consumer education, and the encouragement of voluntary industry action.

To escape from the limits and methodological problems of standard-specific studies, several authors have tried to render an overall evaluation of the CPSC. The most flattering but least sophisticated attempt was conducted by the Consumer Federation of America (Lower, Averyt, and Greenberg, 1983). This study simply compared national rates for accidental home injuries and deaths before and after the establishment of the commission in 1973. The CFA study reported that, although overall accidental deaths and injuries in the home were on the decline even before the CPSC began its operations, the rate of decline was two and a half times faster after the CPSC was established. The CFA study concludes on the basis of this difference that the commission saved nearly forty thousand lives during its first nine years. Unfortunately, the accelerated decline of the accidental death rate after 1973 is not necessarily attributable to the CPSC. Other factors could account for the change in rates— for example a possible decline in the number of young children (the group most susceptible to home injuries) during the 1970s and early 1980s.

Research by Viscusi (1984a) considered alternative explanations of the CPSC's apparent effectiveness and reached a very different conclusion from that of the CFA. Using national household accident rates as his yardstick, Viscusi compared the pre- and post-CPSC periods while controlling for other variables such as real per capita consumption and the age composition of the population. The estimates obtained showed that the CPSC had no statistically significant effect on home accident rates.

A study published in 1986 by Zick, Mayer, and Snow reaches an intermediate conclusion. It applauds Viscusi's attempt to control for other factors that could have affected the accidental injury rate but criticizes the specifics of his approach. Most important, Viscusi includes the "lagged" household accident rate in the prior year (for example, for 1980 when predicting 1981) in order to account for the fact that consumers are continuously replacing older and less safe models with newer and safer ones. Unfortunately, the household accident rate in the prior year is so strongly correlated with the rate in the current year that it overwhelms the possible influence of other factors. Moreover, the lagged value of the accident rate measures much more than the increasing safety of the consumer's stock of goods.

Zick and her coauthors offer their own estimate of the CPSC's effectiveness. Instead of national injury rates, they examine annual accidental home deaths on a state-by-state basis over a twenty-three-year period spanning the establishment of the CPSC. An approach different than Viscusi's is used to take account of the fact that consumers gradually deplete their stock of goods and replace them with newer, safer models. Zick and her coauthors conclude that, in the absence of the CPSC, 17,941 people would have died accidentally in their homes during the commission's first ten years of operation. This figure is less than half of the CFA's estimate but, in contrast to Viscusi, is a clear vote in favor of CPSC's effectiveness. (Efficiency may be another matter. None of the three studies was designed to assess whether the CPSC had chosen the least costly means of reducing product accidents nor whether resources spent by the CPSC and complying industries might have been better spent on, for example, automobile safety or early cancer detection programs.)

**Information Disclosure.**    Policies to ensure the consumer's right to safety are matched by those that pursue the consumer's right to information. These information policies frequently take the form of government-imposed disclosure requirements that fall into eight categories: (1) product identity (for example, a garment's country of origin); (2) ingredients (sodium content in food); (3) product life or perishability (expiration dates for drug potency); (4) comparative performance or efficiency (energy efficiency of appliances); (5) comparative prices (annual percentage interest rate on loans); (6) terms of sale (cooling-off rights in door-to-door sales); (7) proper use (washing instructions for clothing); and (8) warnings (health hazards of cigarette smoking).

Studies of the effects of information disclosure requirements typically confine themselves to measuring consumer awareness, comprehension, liking, and reported use of information as well as satisfaction with the purchase decision (Brandt, Day, and Deutscher, 1975; Day and Brandt, 1974; Friedman, 1972; Lenahan et al., 1973; McElroy and Aaker, 1979; Scardino, Birch, and Vitale, 1976). Using these measures, most information requirements appear to be public policy "successes." Very few studies, however, attempt to quantify the *impact* of information on either the shopping process or consumer decisions. In the rare instances in which an outcome measure has been included, the impact of information disclosure requirements seems to be minimal. For example, Day and Brandt (1973) found that consumer knowledge of truth-in-lending information was unrelated to the choice of a credit source or the decision to use cash or credit.

In the case of at least one information disclosure requirement, the potential benefits for consumers can be measured in terms of easily observable action on the part of manufacturers. This case involves the warranty disclosure provisions of the Magnuson-Moss Warranty Act of 1975. In response to evidence of consumer confusion regarding the terms of product warranties, the act requires that warranties be available for consumer inspection prior to purchase. In addition, the act sets out conditions that manufacturers must meet if they want to use the term *full warranty,* including the requirement that the product be replaced or bought back if it cannot be repaired within a reasonable amount of time. All other warranties have to be described as *limited.*

In lobbying against the Magnuson-Moss Warranty Act, some manufacturers claimed that if they chose not to meet the stringent requirements of a full warranty, they would offer the weakest possible limited warranty. Thus, they claimed, the act would provide consumers with less rather than more warranty coverage. The Federal Trade Commission attempted to assess the impact of the act by comparing the content of warranties of forty products before and after its passage (1974 compared to 1977). Contrary to the fears raised by some manufacturers, the act appeared to have had a positive effect on warranty coverage (Arthur Young & Co., 1979; Schmitt, Kanter, and Miller, 1979). The average duration, scope, and remedies in a 1977 warranty were as good or better than in 1974. Furthermore, exclusions and limitations of buyers' rights were found less frequently in 1977, and the average level of warranty readability improved slightly. In this instance, then, a consumer information policy appears to have had a documentable beneficial effect on consumer well-being.

**Are Generic Drugs a Good Buy?**   Federal and state action to promote the use of generic drugs has been sought by consumer groups and representatives of the elderly as a means of reducing medical costs. At the federal level, the passage of the Drug Price Competition and Patent Term Restoration Act in 1984 gave a major push to the sale of generic prescription drugs by speeding up the process by which they are approved by the Food and Drug Administration. For their part, state laws typically allow pharmacists to substitute generic drugs when a doctor has prescribed a brand-name version. In some states, a doctor must specifically write "dispense as written" if he or she wants to prescribe a brand-name product.

Ignoring the possibility of quality differences between generic and brand-name drugs, one can obtain a rough estimate of the consumer savings from generics. *Consumer Reports* examined the prices of the eleven most frequently prescribed drugs and found that, on average, brand names were 70 percent more expensive than generics ("The Big Lie . . .," 1987). Assuming that is a reasonably accurate average for all generic versus brand-name comparison, one might conclude that, since sales of generics amounted to $5.1 billion in 1986 (Lewin, 1987), consumers saved $3.57 billion. If this figure is even remotely accurate, generics provide very substantial economic savings to consumers.

**Air Travel.**   In 1972, little did Allegheny Airlines realize the consequences of bumping Ralph Nader from one of its flights. At that time, customers holding confirmed reservations on overbooked flights had no recourse when they arrived at a gate only to find an airplane filled to capacity. Nader sued Allegheny Airlines and helped prod the Civil Aeronautics Board into issuing several regulations, including rules governing compensation for bumped passengers.

In his lawsuit, Nader sought the complete elimination of overbooking and bumping. It is difficult to know whether he was really serious about such an extreme solution to the problem, since an outright ban on over-

Figure 6.3  Public Perception of Airline Deregulation

booking would likely have resulted in higher ticket prices and loss of consumer choice—for example, airlines would have had to deny requests for reservations on flights that eventually took off with empty seats. In an analysis of the economic aspects of overbooking regulation, Snow and Weisbrod (1982) conclude that the CAB's rules regarding overbooking clearly increased consumer welfare, although the rules disproportionately benefited passengers who, like Nader, tend to arrive at the terminal only a short time before a flight's scheduled departure.

The consumer movement also played an important part in the enactment of a far more encompassing policy affecting airlines—elimination of the economic aspects of airline regulation. Although Nader and other consumerists are often associated with calls for *more* government regulation, they have championed deregulation when it comes to setting prices and choosing whether to enter a line of business (Green and Nader, 1973). The Airline Deregulation Act of 1978 established a timetable for undoing the policies that had governed the economic aspects of airline industry for forty years. No longer would airlines have to seek government approval to change their fares or offer service to a particular community. Furthermore, airlines would be allowed to pursue freely the efficiencies of a hub-and-spoke system wherein travelers are fed by spoke routes in and out of major airports (hubs) for flights between major airports. In all, consumers could expect lower prices and more options (everything from no-frills to luxury service).

The major airlines and their employees generally opposed deregulation, seeing in it a threat to their profits and wages. Three additional fears were expressed that could affect the welfare of consumers: (1) service to small communities might be abandoned, (2) flight frequency might decrease, and (3) safety might be compromised in the rush to compete with respect to price.

Studies of deregulation's effects conclude that, until recently at least, the anticipated benefits of deregulation had been achieved with few if any of the alleged negative consequences. Studying fares in the 1979–84 period, Schwieterman (1985) found that prices dropped for all classes of travelers in all types of markets. Among consumers, business travelers enjoyed a disproportionate share of the gains compared with pleasure travelers. An even more comprehensive and sophisticated assessment of airline deregulation was conducted by Morrison and Winston (1986) using data from 1977 and 1983. Their conclusions were uniformly glowing. They found not only that travelers had benefited to the tune of $6 billion annually (computed in 1977 dollars), but that industry profits were $2.5 billion higher than they would have been without deregulation. In addition, the authors found no evidence of deregulation's purported disadvantages: decreased service to small communities, decreased flight frequency, or decreased safety levels.

The two studies that returned such positive verdicts on airline deregulation were based on data through 1984. Since that time, there has been a rising chorus of negative comments, possibly indicating that future studies will be more critical of airline deregulation. Fare increases have been kept in check by deregulation, but air travelers are increasingly frustrated by lost bags, late arrivals, and overbooking (McGinley, 1987b). Perhaps more important, the fear that deregulation has compromised airline safety has been fueled by an upsurge of airline accidents and near collisions, despite recent studies that underscore that safety has not deteriorated under deregulation, and that, in fact, it may have even improved (McKenzie and Shugart, 1987; Morrison and Winston, 1988). Although editorial cartoonists have had a field day emphasizing the deregulation-induced perils of flying, the most serious reservation about deregulation has been the trend toward "reoligopolization" whereby price competition can decline in an industry composed of a few major carriers, each of which dominates traffic in and out of a particular hub (Adams and Brock, 1987; Kahn, 1988; Kilman, 1987; "The Big Trouble . . .," 1988).

Until new studies are completed that draw contrary conclusions, however, airline deregulation seems to have lived up to its billing as a means of benefiting consumers. Fares are below what they would have been without deregulation. Were airport capacity not so constrained and the number of experienced air traffic controllers not so limited, airline deregulation might well have brought improvements in service quality in addition to lower fares. Thus, within the constraints under which it has operated, airline deregulation must be considered a success.

**Consumerism at the Truck Stop.**    Although individuals are unlikely to perceive the effect of trucking deregulation on their lives, the fact is that the cost of transportation by truck is reflected in the price of virtually every consumer good—from watermelons to washing machines. Hence, legislation designed to promote competition in the trucking industry has had enormous implications for consumers.

The Motor Carrier Act of 1980 relaxed restrictions on entry into the industry and gave carriers flexibility in setting their own rates. This deregulation seems to have had its intended effects. The number of new carriers applying for operating authority increased 322 percent between 1980 and 1982 (Foppiano and Pozdena, 1983), and as one would expect from greater competition, rates have come down significantly. One study conservatively estimates the consumer benefits of trucking deregulation in 1985 at $56 billion—$250 in savings for every man, woman, and child in America (Delaney, 1987).

Several of the alleged negative effects of trucking deregulation have failed to materialize. Small communities have felt no adverse effects in terms of either the availability or quality of service (Foppiano and Pozdena, 1983). Moreover, the number of injuries and fatalities involving trucks on a per-mile basis have gone down, not up, since 1980 (Americans . . ., 1987). As one might expect, the group that has suffered as a result of trucking deregulation has been employees in the industry; they can no longer count on wage levels propped up by supracompetitive rates.

**Banking on Consumerism.**   The consumer movement has been responsible, to varying degrees, for a number of important laws and regulations governing the banking industry. One of the earliest of these laws was the 1966 truth-in-lending legislation which required full disclosure of the terms of consumer loans. Two decades later, in 1987, Congress passed legislation limiting the period during which a bank can hold a check before crediting it to a customer's account. In between, the Depository Institutions Deregulation and Monetary Control Act of 1980 and the Garn–St. Germain Act of 1982 unleashed fundamental changes in the banking industry. For example, regulations governing the pricing of banking services, such as interest rates on checking and savings accounts, were largely eliminated.

Despite the enormity of banking deregulation, very little precise information exists concerning its effects on consumers. We do know that consumers shifted in droves from checking accounts that failed to earn interest to NOW (Negotiable Order of Withdrawal) accounts that did. These interest-bearing checking accounts yielded consumers over $10 billion in 1986 (Zimmerman and Keeley, 1986). Similarly, consumers have shifted their savings deposits from accounts with interest ceilings (usually below 6 percent) to higher-paying money market deposit accounts.

There have been some negative aspects to banking deregulation, but they do not appear to have counterbalanced its significant financial advantages. For example, banks have initiated or increased charges for many services that appeared to be virtually "free" under regulation (for example, charges for maintaining savings accounts with small balances; high minimum balances on checking accounts to avoid a monthly service fee). These new charges have fallen most heavily on elderly and low-income consumers (Cooper, 1985), but banks have responded to consumerist pressure by instituting a number of special programs to serve these groups (Diamond, 1985). Another purported negative side effect of bank deregulation has been the increase in the number of failures of financial institutions. It is difficult, however, to separate the influence of deregulation from the effect of other changes in the economy, such as the rapid decline in the price of oil.

In all, the definitive study of the impact of banking deregulation on consumers remains to be conducted. In addition, little is known about the economic effects of legislation that has increased consumers' awareness with regard to banking transactions (for example, truth-in-lending, Real Estate Settlement Practices Act), that has lessened discrimination in financial transactions (Equal Credit Opportunity Act), or that has shielded consumers from abuse or honest mistakes by creditors (Fair Credit Billing Act, Fair Debt Collection Practices Act, Fair Credit Reporting Act).

There appears to be a large number of cases in which the best available evidence points to the apparent success of consumer policy initiatives. In many instances, the estimates of gross or net consumer benefits range into the billions of dollars. The greatest amount of scholarly attention has been directed at evaluating consumer safety policies, whereas the impact of information disclosure and deregulatory policies remains more speculative. Still, regardless of the type of consumer policy, the positive assessments tend to be based on policy effectiveness, or gross benefits generated; these policies may or may not be efficient. As we turn next to evaluations that return unfavorable verdicts on consumerist initiatives, a finding of policy ineffectiveness by definition renders that policy inefficient as well.

## Negative Results

**The Effectiveness of the Drug Effectiveness Amendment.** The 1962 Kefauver-Harris Amendments to the federal Food, Drug, and Cosmetic Act require proof of a new drug's effectiveness before it can be sold to the public. Prior to this legislation, a new drug had to be safe but not necessarily efficacious. Although passage of the 1962 Drug Amendments was facilitated by the fears aroused by the thalidomide episode, the amendments were primarily designed to save dollars, not lives. Specifically, they were intended to help consumers save the money that might otherwise by wasted on useless drugs.

At the time of the passage of the 1962 Drug Amendments, the number of ineffective drugs appeared to be high. For example, a National Academy of Sciences study found that only 41 percent of 4,300 FDA-approved drugs on the market between 1938 and 1962 could demonstrate effectiveness for at least one of its health claims (Simmons, 1973). One study placed the economic loss to consumers resulting from the purchase of ineffective drugs in 1966 at $300 million (Jondrow, 1972). Seven years after passage of the amendments, a report of the Department of Health, Education, and Welfare estimated that as much as 25 percent of drug therapy was still ineffective (Green and Waitzman, 1979). In 1983, Public Citizen's Health Research Group devoted an entire book to over-the-counter "pills that don't work," including Anacin, Listerine mouthwash, Robitussin cough syrup, and Preparation H (Kaufman et al., 1983).

Ineffective drugs not only rob consumers of their dollars but sometimes threaten consumer health by using up precious time. In the extreme case, a person may not turn to an effective drug until after a disease is beyond control. In addition, consumers may have adverse reactions to a supposedly safe but ineffective drug. Thus, improved consumer health is likely to be among the benefits of a prohibition against ineffective drugs.

Economist Sam Peltzman (1973) turns this argument about the benefits of the 1962 Drug Amendments on its head, claiming that the amendments may have reduced consumer health and resulted in an annual economic loss to consumers of over $400 million. Peltzman's analysis of the effects of the amendments is bold and ingenious. Essentially, he believes that the proof of efficacy requirement raised the costs of developing new pharmaceutical products. This, in turn, dampened pharmaceutical innovation and reduced consumer access to new and more effective drug therapies—thus costing some consumers their lives. Peltzman further contends that the effectiveness requirement raised consumer prices by reducing competition in the pharmaceutical industry. All this might have been worth it, says Peltzman, if the amendments had removed large numbers of ineffective drugs from the marketplace, but in his view, drug manufacturers had adequate incentive prior to 1962 to market effective products. In any event, he finds that the amendments had little impact on the level of drug efficacy. Peltzman concludes that, failing to meet the minimal criterion of policy effectiveness, the amendments fail any test of efficiency as well.

One of the key elements in Peltzman's analysis—and the target of subsequent criticism—is his method of measuring trends in drug innovation and drug effectiveness. To measure change in the rate of introduction of new drugs, he compares the pre- and post-1962 periods and finds a substantial decline in new drugs. His negative interpretation of this downward trend appears to be supported by the finding that, in the post-1962 period, several important new drugs were introduced in Europe before they were in the United States (Wardell and Lasagna, 1975).

One obvious weakness of a before-after comparison such as Peltzman's is the possibility that the observed decline in new drugs was due to factors other than the amendments (and the other variables that Peltzman includes in his model). More important, a reduction in new drug introductions is not necessarily bad if ineffective drugs are the ones being held off the market (although Wiggins [1981] found that the amendments had no less a dampening effect on important pharmaceutical innovations than on ones that represented minimal therapeutic advances). And if drug regulation is overly restrictive in the United States, how does one account for the dangerous drugs that have still fallen through the safety net (Metzenbaum, 1986)?

Despite numerous criticisms of Peltzman's analysis (Bollier and Claybrook, 1986; Green and Waitzman, 1979; McGuire, 1975), no one has come up with better cost-and-benefit estimates. Peltzman is probably correct that a trade-off exists between greater certainty about drug effectiveness and the rate at which valuable new drugs are introduced on the market. At some point, increased certainty becomes detrimental to consumers; the question is whether we have reached that point yet ("TPA . . .," 1987).

**CAFE and MPG.**   Until the energy crises of the 1970s, the energy efficiency of a person's car was pretty much a personal prerogative. The Energy Policy and Conservation Act, passed in 1975, signaled a philosophic change in which gasoline consumption became everyone's business. Energy consumption was seen as directly related to the United States' balance of payments and its vulnerability to the political whims of oil-exporting nations. The act imposed corporate average fuel economy (CAFE) standards on automobile manufacturers. The standards began at 18 miles per gallon in 1978 and gradually increased to 27.5 for the 1985 model year. In addition, the act required that labels be attached to new cars to allow potential buyers to compare the fuel efficiency of vehicles.

Judging from evaluations conducted to date, neither provision of the Energy Policy and Conservation Act has been effective in achieving its objectives. The CAFE standards did little to reduce energy consumption, and the fuel efficiency labels failed to help consumers make more informed decisions. If anything, these two measures may have been harmful to consumers.

Regarding the CAFE standards, one might argue that they violate the consumer's freedom of choice, (Henderson, 1985). Supporters of the standards would respond that there is an overriding national interest in fuel conservation. If so, did the CAFE standards reduce energy consumption? Crandall and his colleagues (1986) reach the conclusion that increases in fuel economy after 1973 were almost wholly the result of the voluntary response of automobile manufacturers and consumers to rising prices for motor fuel; CAFE standards had virtually no impact. They did not impose a binding constraint on automobile manufacturers until 1981, at which point gasoline prices started falling and consumers started demanding larger cars. Crandall and his colleagues suggest that meeting the CAFE standards significantly increased the cost of large vehicles. Although these higher prices may have encouraged some buyers to purchase smaller, less expensive cars, other buyers may have simply postponed their purchase—leaving them with cars that were less safe, less fuel efficient, and more polluting than the new vehicle they would have purchased.

The standards have been subject to attack for additional reasons (Henderson, 1985). American automobile manufacturers have a comparative advantage in producing large cars and face relatively little competition in this market. Ideally, American manufacturers would like to focus their attention on the production of larger cars and import smaller vehicles from abroad or enter into joint ventures. The CAFE standards force U.S. manufacturers into making small cars, however, because they are not allowed to count their foreign production when computing the average fuel consumption of their fleet of cars. In short, American producers are required to manufacture cars that they are ill-prepared to produce and that American consumers do not want.

The lifting of trade restrictions on Japanese vehicles intensified the pressure on American manufacturers of small cars. As sales of their small cars decreased, American manufacturers found it still more difficult to meet the CAFE standards for their entire fleet. It is not surprising, then, that the Department of Transportation responded favorably to the request by Ford and GM to lower the CAFE standards for 1986 cars.

What about the requirement to post fuel efficiency ratings on all new cars? Overly optimistic mileage estimates from ratings obtained under ideal driving conditions can distort expenditures and harm consumers (Senauer, Kinsey, and Roe, 1984). When consumers *over*estimate the fuel economy of a new car, they will be willing to buy a more expensive car then they would otherwise have. The result is that consumers eventually need to economize in some other area of spending—say, dental care—in which they could have obtained more utility per dollar than buying an expensive automobile. In a minority of cases, mileage estimates inaccurately *under*estimate the fuel economy of a vehicle. When this occurs, consumers may choose to do without a feature they really could have afforded. Senauer and his coauthors estimate that in 1982 American consumers incurred unanticipated fuel expenditures of about $500 million that were due to the inaccuracy of miles-per-gallon ratings.

The CAFE standards and mileage estimate labels are only two of several government measures designed to help consumers get more for their money when purchasing a car. Others include disclosure of information regarding tires (treadwear, temperature resistance, traction) and warranty coverage of used cars. Little is known about the economic impact of these measures. Nevertheless, the overall pattern in the area of automobile regulation seems to be that safety measures are reasonably effective whereas quality standards (exemplified by energy efficiency requirements) and information disclosure policies are not.

The number of studies that state unequivocally that a consumer policy has been ineffective is relatively small. Yet several important themes run through most of these negative assessments. First, the authors often conclude that market forces were sufficient for the generation of consumer benefits; additional government action was unneeded. Second, even an apparently benign policy such as the 1962 Drug Amendments can have serious side effects. A final lesson is that consumers react to policies in ways that may reduce their effectiveness. Taken together, say the critics of consumer policy, there are ample grounds for regulatory humility. In the words of FTC chairman Daniel Oliver, "The free market does not have to work perfectly to work better than government regulation (FTC . . .," 1988, p. 1).

## Mixed Results

A careful review of existing studies can still leave the impact of a consumer policy in doubt. Two equally competent (or equally flawed) studies may suggest opposite conclusions, as is the case for child-resistant closures and crib design regulations. Uncertainty as to whether the effects of a policy were positive or negative can also occur when a single study's conclusions depend on which of several explicit sets of assumptions are considered most reasonable.

**Should Child-Resistant Closures Be Resisted?**     In 1970, the U.S. Congress passed the Poison Prevention Packaging Act. The act's goal was to protect young children from dangerous substances commonly found in homes. With enforcement being carried out by first the Food and Drug Administration and later the Consumer Product Safety Commission, eleven regulations were issued between 1972 and 1974. Aspirin, prescription drugs, turpentine, drain cleaners, lighter fluid, and furniture polish were among the targeted products.

In 1978, the commission published a brief study purporting to document the effectiveness of child-resistant packages (Howe, 1978). Changes over time in the number of ingestions associated with regulated products was compared to changes in the number of ingestions associated with unregulated or partially regulated products, thus partially controlling for nonregulatory factors that might influence accidental poisonings. The data were collected from a sample of over a hundred hospital emergency rooms during fiscal years 1973–76 and covered children up to four years of age. Over the three-year period examined, accidental ingestions for the unregulated product group increased by 20 percent. In contrast, ingestion experience in the partially regulated and fully regulated product groups declined by 33 and 38 percent, respectively. The conclusion drawn was that all ingestions would have increased by 20 percent in the absence of child-resistant packaging, resulting in approximately twenty thousand additional emergency room injuries to young children.

Despite its clever research design, the CPSC study can be criticized. There may be important differences in the nature of the products found in the unregulated, partially regulated, and fully regulated groups. In particular, no data were presented on the ingestion trends for the three classes prior to the passage of product packaging standards. To the extent that the CPSC was using good sense in its selection of initial products to be regulated, it presumably imposed standards on those products where improvements in safety could be achieved most readily. Thus, a differential rate of change across the three basic product classes would have been expected.

The most fundamental criticism of the CPSC study's results, however, was leveled by W. Kip Viscusi (1984b, 1985). He makes two points. First, because protective caps are so difficult to open, people leave bottles open, thereby making it easier for children to gain access to their contents. Second, he posits a "lulling effect" by which consumers become less cautious because they believe the products have been made less dangerous. In addition, Viscusi believes that consumers do not necessarily differentiate their treatment of regulated and unregulated products. For example, people may store medicines with and without child-resistant caps in the same bathroom cabinet. As a result of this "indivisibility" of regulated and unregulated products, children's exposure to the risks of unregulated products could actually increase by virtue of greater parental confidence in the safety of regulated products.

Viscusi draws attention to the fact that rates of ingestion for unregulated products rose (instead of remaining steady) at the same time that the rate for regulated products declined. He interprets these trends as showing that government regulation may have *caused* an increase in the injury rate associated with unregulated products, thereby invalidating it as a baseline from which to measure the benefits of regulation. He attempts to bolster his case through an empirical analysis of poisonings involving analgesics. Aspirin was covered by a child-resistant closure standard starting in 1972, but other analgesics like acetaminophen (used in Tylenol) were not covered until 1980. As a result, the decline in the number of accidental deaths involving aspirin poisoning could have been partially attributable to a consumer shift from aspirin to acetaminophen preparations. In addition, Viscusi asserts that the rising number of accidental deaths associated with unregulated analgesic products is above and beyond what one might expect from increasing consumption, thereby suggesting the existence of a lulling effect. With respect to analgesic products, at least, Viscusi concludes that child-resistant packaging has probably increased rather than decreased the number of accidental poisonings.

It is possible to argue with Viscusi's statistical model, especially the way in which his inclusion of the lagged value of the dependent variable (in this case, the accidental poisoning rate) tends to overwhelm the possible influence of other independent variables. Nevertheless, he raises an important and inescapable basis for discounting estimates of the benefits of child-resistant packaging. It is plausible that regulations will lead to some decline in consumer caution, to some misperception that "child-resistant" closures are "child-proof," and to some increased exposure to unregulated products. The size of these counterproductive effects is not clear, but they should be included in a proper assessment of the effectiveness of child-resistant packaging.

Differences in theory and methods appear to account for the conflicting conclusions drawn by the Viscusi and CPSC studies. Viscusi's analysis is driven by a theory in which people offset government action designed to make them safer by engaging in riskier activity. It is essentially the same theory presented by Peltzman when he asserts that motorists drive more recklessly when their cars are equipped with safety features. In contrast, the CPSC does not test a behavioral theory. If anything, it is driven by the need to make the CPSC look good.

With respect to methodology, Viscusi focuses primarily on analgesics, examines trends in both adult and child accidental poisonings between 1971 and 1980, and bases his conclusions on comparisons across time (while attempting to control for nonregulatory factors that might have influenced poisoning rates). The CPSC study examines all products covered by child-resistant packaging regulations, confines its analysis to accidental poisonings of young children, refers to only the 1973–76 period, and compares across products (fully regulated versus partially regulated versus unregulated) rather than across time.

Given these theoretical and methodological differences, it is perhaps not surprising that the studies' conclusions are so contradictory. Research that draws on the strengths of each will be needed for a fair assessment of the government's efforts to protect young children from accidental poisonings.

**Making Cribs Safer.**  Between 1970 and 1973, the Food and Drug Administration received death certificates for 133 children whose deaths were related to problems in the structure of their cribs. The majority of these deaths involved strangulation or suffocation caused by the child becoming wedged between the mattress and the crib frame or by slipping feet first through the vertical slats and then being caught by the head (*Federal Register,* 1973). In addition, the FDA estimated that 150 to 200 infants die annually in the United States and about 50,000 more incur nonfatal injuries in crib-associated incidents. (The majority of incidents are falls and are probably not directly attributable to flaws in crib design.)

The FDA determined that design requirements in the manufacture of cribs could reasonably be expected to reduce accidental injuries and deaths to infants. For example, strangulation incidents might be reduced by setting minimal distance standards between slats or other crib components. Similarly, minimum requirements regarding rail height might prevent children from readily falling out of their cribs. These and other standards were issued in late 1973 by the Consumer Product Safety Commission, which had taken over administration of the Federal Hazardous Substances Act.

According to a CPSC report (1979), crib-related injuries declined by 44 percent and deaths by 33 percent after implementation of the standard. Viscusi (1984a) challenges this favorable evaluation. He points out that the total number of crib deaths was erratic in the post-1973 period. A better measure, the crib injury *rate,* declined only slightly between 1973 and 1980. Further, in 1981, the injury rate shot up to a level higher than in 1973. Even Viscusi grants that the crib safety standard must have been effective in saving a few lives and avoiding some injuries, but he raises an important question: has the standard's effectiveness been sufficient to justify the costs of redesign and extra materials imposed on manufacturers and consumers? Put differently, one might ask whether the resources devoted to making safer cribs saved more lives and averted more injuries than would have been the case if, say, free children's car seats had been distributed to low-income families.

**Making Children's Sleepwear Safer.**     The Flammable Fabrics Act (and its amendments) made possible the setting of flammability standards for children's sleepwear. Developed by the Department of Commerce, the standards became official in July 1972. A few months later, authority for enforcing them passed to the newly created Consumer Product Safety Commission. Eventually, consumer economists at the University of Maryland produced, under contract with the National Science Foundation, a detailed analysis of the costs and benefits to consumers of the new standards (Dardis, Aaronson, and Lin, 1978; Department of Textiles . . . , 1978; Smith and Dardis, 1977).

The researchers used two models for estimating the costs. The first examined only the increased prices resulting from the standard. Using catalog prices from Sears, Roebuck, and Company and Montgomery Ward, the authors attributed a 30 percent price increase to the standard (controlling for inflation). To derive an estimate of the total price-related costs of the standard, this price increase was multiplied by per capita expenditures on children's sleepwear prior to the standard. The second model took account of the fact that consumers not only paid higher prices but also lost certain choices. In particular, untreated cotton pajamas virtually disappeared from the market as a result of the standard. Including the loss of consumer choice greatly inflated the estimate of the total costs.

The benefits of the standard were based on the estimated number of deaths and injuries it prevented. For children who would have been injured but not killed in the absence of the standard, the primary benefits were measured in terms of the hospitalization costs avoided. For children who would have died in the absence of the standard, benefit estimates were based on their potential lifetime earnings (discounted to current values). Lacking firm data on the number of deaths and injuries avoided by the standard, the authors presented two sets of benefit estimates based on the assumption that the effectiveness of the standard was either high or moderate. The analysis explicitly excluded any estimate of the benefits of sparing victims and their families the pain and suffering associated with a burn injury or death.

Comparing the costs and benefits of the standard, the researchers found that the benefits exceeded the costs if one ignored the consumer costs associated with loss of choice. The net benefits of the standard were roughly on the order of $15 million. When the costs of reduced consumer choice were included, the cost-benefit ratio became unfavorable, especially when it was assumed that consumer demand is relatively insensitive to prices. Thus, even if one accepts that the sleepwear flammability standard has reduced deaths and injuries to children, one can still challenge the standard's efficiency. Depending on the assumptions that one wishes to make, the children's sleepwear flammability standard either passes, comes close to passing, or fails a test of its economic efficiency.

## Conclusion

The consumer laws and regulations for which evaluations have been conducted represent only a portion, surely less than half, of all policies intended to improve the economic well-being of consumers. Evaluations have been most common and most precise where the potential gains and losses to consumers have been the highest. Major initiatives regarding the safety of automobiles, pharmaceutical products, and household products have been subjected to a sophisticated level of analysis. Significant progress has also been made in understanding the economic impact of industry deregulation, especially with regard to air and truck transportation. The most room for improvement lies in the area of policies that attempt to increase consumer information. Evaluations of these policies often document consumer awareness of information or their reported intention to use it, but they frequently stop short of demonstrating that consumers actually use the information and that their welfare is improved as a result.

On the positive side, a reasonably efficient allocation of resources for conducting evaluations has taken place, with the federal policies with the greatest potential impact on consumers receiving the most attention. On the negative side, however, it is evident that the vast majority of evaluations have focused on the theme of policy effectiveness without addressing the broader question of policy efficiency.

From the point of view of deriving an overall assessment of the consumer movement's impact, the greatest impediment may not be the small number of evaluations of federal policies but rather the virtual absence of evaluations of policies implemented by state government and private organizations. For example, we have absolutely no sense of the extent to which consumer welfare has been affected by Consumers Union's fifty-two years of operation nor the Better Business Bureau's seventy-six years. By the same token, we lack even the grossest measures of the impact of the many state laws that govern aspects of retailing—such as advertising, availability of goods, and rights of rescission—or aspects of service delivery—such as the licensing of various occupations.

Confining oneself to the federal consumer policies that have been subjected to evaluation in economic terms, it is possible to construct a favorable assessment of consumerism's impact by focusing on the following policies: airline deregulation, trucking deregulation, automobile safety standards, the overall operations of the Consumer Product Safety Commission, and policies that encourage the purchase of generic drugs. Together, these policies appear to generate benefits that range in the tens of billions of dollars annually. On the other side of the coin, some policies have been seen as being negligible or dubious in their effects. These include the 1962 Drug Amendments and corporate average fuel economy standards for automobiles. Additional policies have been ridiculed for being too extreme—for example, the Delaney Clause's ban on all carcinogenic substances regardless of their benefits—or for being too trivial— as in the case of the CPSC standard for the placement of striking surfaces on matchbooks.

The ocean of conflicting claims, caveats, and qualifications provided by evaluation studies shows that economic evaluation, as economists readily admit, can take one only so far. It is a decision tool, not a decision substitute. Ultimately, values other than effectiveness and efficiency do and should affect public policy.

# Chapter Seven

# Global Aspects of Consumerism

The achievements of the consumer movement in the United States do not begin to approximate the achievements of consumerism worldwide. Consumerism, in one shape or another, exists in virtually every market-oriented economy, including those of less developed countries. Although the United States has been a leader in some areas of consumer affairs, it is a laggard in others. The purpose of this chapter is to compare American consumerism with consumerism in other countries and to explore their interrelations.

## A Consumerist's Dream

Imagine Ralph Nader returning to his sparsely furnished apartment, tired from a long day of jousting with cunning business lobbyists, providing secret information about corporate wrongdoing to friendly journalists, and testifying at a congressional hearing. As he flops into a padded armchair, he begins to relax and sink into a dreamlike state.

Because Nader is still wearing one of the twelve pairs of shoes he bought when he left the U.S. Army in 1959, he is not quite comfortable enough to be transported to a fantasyland of consumer-owned cooperatives and worker-owned businesses. But his mind takes him to an only slightly less utopian world in which governments have gone to great lengths to protect consumers—from greedy businesses and from themselves. This consumer paradise has the following features:

- The government funds not only a national product testing organization but consumer advisory, lobbying, and research organizations as well.

- Consumers can go to government-supported neighborhood centers when they need information about a purchase or advice on how to file a complaint.

- The government appoints a high-level ombudsman to serve as watchdog of the marketplace by negotiating directly with businesses or, when necessary, filing legal actions on behalf of consumers.

- Consumer groups are given free access to television during prime-time to discuss consumer issues and ways of avoiding marketplace rip-offs.

- No advertising whatsoever, including political advertising, is allowed on television.

- Consumer education courses are obligatory for all schoolchildren.

- A nationwide law requires all automobile occupants to wear seatbelts.

- A combination of private and public funds supports a team of trained safety experts who visit individual homes and search out potential safety hazards.

- Cigarettes, although not banned, carry warnings such as "Smoking kills."

- The manufacture or sale of toys involving war themes is banned.

- There are more than enough government scientists to review new drug applications because their agency's budget is augmented by charges levied on companies seeking approval for their products.

Nader's reverie is not as fanciful as it appears, for each of these policies is already in place in at least one country outside the United States.

## Consumerism's Common Features

Some form of consumerism exists wherever a moderate degree of market-based economics is combined with a democratic political system. Despite important differences among countries, reflecting unique economic and political conditions, there is a great deal of homogeneity in the consumerism found in highly industrialized nations. Similarly, consumerism in less developed nations exhibits a general pattern as well. This chapter examines consumerism within industrialized nations and then within industrializing countries as well as the relationships between the two.

## Commonalities across Industrialized Countries

Among the many commonalities in the character of consumerism in industrialized, market-oriented countries, three stand out. First, regardless of the nation, the dominant ideology of consumerism has been reformist rather than radical (see chapter 4). This reformist bent has meant that consumer activists have focused primarily on ridding the marketplace of hazardous products and deceptive sales practices rather than, say, challenging the power of oligopolistic firms and highly concentrated industries. By the same token, the reformist ideology that dominates consumerism in most nations has brought with it an emphasis on solving consumer problems through government regulation of business conduct, such as imposing product design specifications and information disclosure requirements, rather than the use of direct economic pressure on firms through boycotts, collective consumer buying, and selective investment in ethical firms.

A second common feature is the importance of product testing organizations in the consumer movements of various countries. In terms of total membership, the most successful of these organizations are Consumers Union in the United States, the Consumers' Association in Great Britain, and Stiftung Warentest in West Germany. The magazines published by these organizations arm consumers with practical knowledge about products as well as information about more general developments affecting consumers. In addition to this basic function, product testing organizations provide funding, legitimacy, and coordination for other consumerist activities in their countries. For example, Consumers Union has provided funds to help establish other consumer organizations, and it continues to hold conferences that help consumer advocates identify issues and set priorities.

A third common thread running through consumerism in industrialized, market-oriented nations is the consumer movement's close ties to other social movements, especially to the labor and environmental movements. In the United States, these social movements often form strategic alliances around common concerns. In other nations, the line between consumer organizations and other types of social movement organizations is much less sharp. Consumer groups are often spawned by trade unions, as in France; housewives' associations, as in Japan; and consumer cooperatives, as in the Scandinavian countries. Further evidence of this blurred division is the way appointments are made to regulatory bodies. For instance, the nine-member Market Court in Sweden has three members representing business and three members representing *either* labor or consumers. Similarly, the "consumer" representatives on the governing board of Sweden's National Board for Consumer Policies are typically drawn from the Cooperative Union, the Confederation of Trade Unions, and the Central Organization of Salaried Employees (Boddewyn, 1985).

## *Reasons for the Convergence among Industrialized Nations*

The common features that characterize consumerism in most industrialized nations stem from several sources. Most important, consumers in all these nations face many of the same conditions of production and consumption. In addition, there has been a diffusion process by which policies have been both deliberately exported and informally transferred from one country to another.

**The Global Marketplace.** Consumerism has raised many of the same issues in different countries in part because consumers worldwide encounter many of the same firms and technologies. Multinational corporations (headquartered, more often than not, outside the United States) peddle their products throughout the world ("The World's Largest . . . ," 1986). There is probably no better testimony to the global nature of distribution than the $156 billion trade deficit the United States rang up in 1986 (Jones, 1987), but even consumers in protectionist Japan enjoy products from around the world.

Consumers in different countries are not only united through being offered the same products; consumers also appear to want many of the same things. Families in virtually all developed nations aspire to own first a car and then a house or apartment. Countries also resemble each other in the rates of ownership of household appliances, and the United States is not always the clear leader. Per capita, more Italians own washing machines than do Americans, more Belgians own food processors, just as many Danes own vacuum cleaners, and almost as many Finns—despite the natural coolness of the Finnish climate—own refrigerators (*Major Appliance . . .* , 1987; *European Marketing Data . . .* , 1985). Consumers in the United States are more likely than their foreign counterparts to own dishwashers, microwave ovens, and video cassette recorders, but the lead may be only temporary.

The similarity in the supply and demand conditions experienced by consumers worldwide translates into a similarity in the kinds of consumer problems encountered. When a new drug turns out to have a negative side effect, an automobile is found to have a design defect, or an electrical appliance tends to break down soon after the expiration of the warranty, the product's global distribution means that consumers in different countries share the same misery.

As opposed to products, services like medical care, banking, and home repairs tend to be offered to consumers within a single country only. Nevertheless, consumers in one country may still experience the same problems as their counterparts in other nations. Life insurance provides an interesting example of a service decision that apparently confounds consumers worldwide. Americans are not the world's heaviest purchasers of life insurance; the Swiss and Japanese buy more per capita. But consumers in all three countries find it difficult to compare the values of different policies and make a wise decision (Committee on Consumer Policy, 1986).

In short, one reason consumerism has followed similar avenues in different countries is that consumer discontent is fueled by the same factors worldwide. The proliferation of new and complex products, the use of increasingly sophisticated marketing techniques, and the difficulty of obtaining speedy and satisfactory resolution of complaints have contributed to the emergence of consumerism in many countries (Committee on Consumer Policy, 1983).

**Diffusion of Consumerism.** The similarities in the consumerism of industrialized, market-oriented nations are attributable to a second factor—organizations that have been explicitly established to promote sharing of resources and coordination among consumerists in various nations. These organizations include the Consumer Policy Committee of the Organization for Economic Co-operation and Development and the European Consumer Product Safety Association. Even more important in spreading and managing consumerist activity in several countries are the International Organization of Consumers Unions (IOCU) and the Bureau Européen des Unions de Consommateurs (BEUC).

As its name suggests, IOCU is a federation of consumer organizations in thirty-two nations, with corresponding members in another nineteen countries (*IOCU . . .*, 1986). Established in 1960, the group engages primarily in three types of activity: providing technical support for its member organizations, including sharing of testing methods and results; encouraging the formation of consumer groups where they are weak or nonexistent; and advocating for consumers, especially those in developing countries. Its headquarters are in The Hague, but its commitment to third world consumers has been expressed by the opening of regional offices in Penang, Malaysia, and Montevideo, Uruguay as well as its successful campaign for the adoption of the United Nations Guidelines for Consumer Protection (Harland, 1987; Peterson, 1987). With that victory in 1985, IOCU turned its attention at the UN to adopting a code of conduct for multinational corporations.

Equally characteristic of IOCU's advocacy activities are its efforts to establish and support a number of international coalitions, each of which addresses a single type of consumer issue. In 1980, for instance, IOCU was a cofounder of Health Action International (HAI), an organization dedicated to the safe, rational, and economic use of drugs worldwide. HAI's programs are designed to inform consumers regarding the risks of pharmaceutical products, prevent the sale of dangerous drugs, and promote the proper use of drugs, such as antibiotics, whose therapeutic value can be diminished by overuse. Closely related to HAI is Consumer Interpol, an international network of organizations whose purpose is to alert its members to dumping—the exportation of products too dangerous for sale in the domestic market (such as defective medical devices, contaminated foods, banned pesticides). Consumer Interpol was initially funded by the Dutch government in 1981, with IOCU providing it with technical assistance. It is essentially an early warning alert system run by the potential victims of dumping (Abraham and Asher, 1986).

The IOCU is an important member of a number of other international networks: the Pesticide Action Network; the International Baby Food Action Network, established in response to marketing of breastmilk substitutes in developing countries; Action Groups to Halt Advertising and Sponsorship of Tobacco; and the "No-More-Bhopals" Network, dedicated to adequate compensation for Bhopal's victims and increased public control of hazardous technologies.

The mission of the European Bureau of Consumers Unions (BEUC) is only slightly less ambitious than that of IOCU. The BEUC attempts to coordinate consumer policy among the twelve member countries of the European Economic Community (EEC, or the Common Market). The countries range from highly industrialized West Germany and France to substantially less industrialized Greece and Portugal. The task of finding common ground for consumer policy within the EEC is complicated by this diversity. For example, consumer representatives from more developed nations might criticize a proposed safety standard because it is weaker than the one that already exists in their country, whereas representatives from less industrialized countries may perceive even a relatively weak safety standard as burdening their export industry.

The BEUC also faces a difficult job in trying to reduce prices that have been inflated by long-standing national subsidies (especially regarding textiles and agricultural products) or state-owned monopoly enterprises. The bureau criticizes the large price differences that often exist between two bordering countries, arguing that the lower price should prevail throughout the Common Market. Similarly, BEUC has been an advocate of airline deregulation, a position that has been resisted by the state-owned airlines.

Despite powerful sources of resistance, BEUC does score an occasional victory. In 1985, a rare convergence of interests resulted in the EEC's decision to ban hormones in the fattening of livestock on the grounds of both health and flavor. More important, producers finally became convinced that restricting hormone use would reduce the amount of meat available for sale, thereby solving chronic overproduction. As a result, beginning in 1988, all hormones were banned in domestically produced and imported livestock, making the EEC countries the world leaders in this area of consumer policy.

The diffusion of consumerist policies among developed nations is not only the result of deliberate attempts to spread the word. Much of the diffusion occurs much more informally. One country may be the first to experience a particular consumer problem; other nations observe and learn from its attempts to solve it. The United States is often regarded as the cradle of consumerism, but Sweden has frequently been the "bellwether of the rest of the world" in the area of consumer protection (Cetron and O'Toole, 1982). Sweden was the first nation to require seatbelts and padded dashboards, mandate the listing of product ingredients, mount "a long-term, all-out coordinated program for combatting smoking" (Molitor, 1979), and promote low tar and nicotine cigarettes. Still other countries have led the way in individual areas of consumer policy. In 1972, Australia was the site of the world's first mandatory seatbelt-use law, from where the idea passed to New Zealand, France, Puerto Rico, Sweden, Belgium, the Netherlands, Finland, Israel, and Norway in less than four years (*Federal Register,* 1984).

In sum, the common consumerist tendencies found in highly industrialized, market-oriented countries are the result of both deliberate attempts at exporting consumerism as well as an unstructured process by which some countries learn from the successes and failures of others. Some consumer policies, however, even successful ones, remain characteristic of a single country or cluster of countries.

# Differences between the United States and other Developed Nations

Most of the differences between consumerism in the United States and consumerism in other highly industrialized countries are attributable to the relative degree of government intervention in a given economy. Outside the United States, where government intervention is typically more formal and extensive, governments have been more willing to promote consumerism directly and less hesitant to infringe on individual freedom of choice and expression in the name of the social good. By the reverse logic, a greater separation of government and the economy has made consumerism in the United States the pacesetter in providing consumers with avenues for pursuing postpurchase grievances as well as exploring the possibilities of industry deregulation as a means of improving consumer welfare. In addition, because of the greater latitude allowed advertisers in the United States, certain unique methods of maximizing the benefits and minimizing the costs associated with advertising can be found in this country.

## Distinctive Features of Consumerism outside the United States

**Consumer Representation.** A rough continuum exists along which industrialized, market-oriented countries can be placed in terms of the primary means by which consumers are represented in the political arena (Forbes, 1987; Rose, 1981). At one end of the continuum are nations that resemble the United States in terms of the vitality of nongovernmental consumer groups. It is in these nations—the United States, Canada, and Australia—that it is most appropriate to speak of consumerism as a grass-roots social movement. At the other end of the continuum are nations in which the interests of consumers are formally represented by distinct governmental entities. This end of the spectrum is best represented by the Scandinavian countries, but elements of government support of consumer representation can be found in virtually every European nation. In some instances, governmental bodies are specialized with jurisdiction in narrowly defined areas of consumer protection; in other cases, a ministry may have authority over a broad range of consumer issues.

The consumer ombudsmen found in Sweden, Norway, Denmark, and Finland are perhaps the most visible example of high-level government institutionalization of consumer representation. An ombudsman is some-one, usually a government official, charged with investigating and resolving complaints. The existence of a government ombudsman dates back to 1809 in Sweden (Forbes, 1987), but a special ombudsman for consumers is a more recent phenomenon. There is some variation among the four Nordic countries, but the basic functions of their consumer ombudsmen are to extract voluntary compliance by businesses with consumer protection laws and, when necessary, bring legal actions against offending firms (Graver, 1986). The powers of the ombudsmen are usually confined to the economic aspects of marketplace transactions—for example, advertising, sales practices, and contract terms—to the exclusion of safety considerations (with Sweden being an exception). Although the ombudsmen receive complaints from individual consumers, they rarely become involved in seeking restitution for a single person, being more concerned with stimulating policies that will benefit groups of consumers (Boddewyn, 1985). Finally, in a sign that consumerism may someday spread to socialist countries, the Polish parliament appointed a law professor specializing in consumer rights to the position of citizens' ombudsman in November 1987 ("Ewa Letowska . . . ," 1988).

Government-assisted consumer representation takes other forms outside the Nordic countries. In the United Kingdom, for instance, the National Consumer Council serves as a consumer advocate within the national government, using a combination of lobbying and research to press its position. More common is the use of a consumer advisory council to represent consumers' views within a national ministry of economic affairs. In the Netherlands, private consumer organizations are compensated when they are consulted by the government or asked to participate on national or international committees ("Consumer Policy . . . ," 1986). As a final example of government support of consumer representation, the Australian government helped create the Australian Federation of Consumer Organizations (AFCO) to coordinate the activities of some fifty consumer and community groups. In addition to representing the views of its constituent organizations, AFCO also serves as a source for appointees to government and private organizations dealing with consumer matters (Committee on Consumer Policy, 1983).

**Consumer Information and Education.**    The existence of government institutions to represent the consumer viewpoint is based on the assumption that collectively consumers are politically weak (Johansson, 1976). A similar premise, that individual consumers are ignorant of important product features, justifies government subsidization of product testing organizations as well as other programs to assist individual consumers. With the exception of the United Kingdom, most governments in western Europe financially support a product testing organization (Thorelli and Thorelli, 1977). In Norway, a government-sponsored product testing magazine reaches 20 percent of all households (Committee on Consumer Policy, 1983), a percentage that dwarfs the 3 to 4 percent of American households that subscribe to *Consumer Reports.*

Government efforts to promote well-informed consumer decisions extend beyond subsidizing product testing organizations. In Norway, consumer education in the schools is mandatory (Thorelli and Thorelli, 1977). In France, the National Institute of Consumption (INC), whose activities are heavily subsidized by the national government, is allocated a weekly total of twenty-four minutes of prime-time television to educate consumers. The national government in Great Britain supports a network of citizens' advice bureaus to which consumers can turn. Local governments there have also established, often with national funding, more specialized consumer advice centers to dispense prepurchase advice as well as assistance in dealing with postpurchase complaints (Prentice, 1978). One of the advantages of the government-assisted programs in countries like Norway and Great Britain is their potential to reach beyond the affluent elite of information seekers who purchase product testing reports (Thorelli, Becker, and Engledow, 1975) and help people in all social classes.

**Restriction of Individual and Business Freedoms.** When freedom from a specified harm conflicts with freedom to place a product on the market, nations with more collectivist traditions than the United States tend to resolve the conflict in favor of the former. The problem of automobile-related fatalities and injuries provides a vivid illustration of how the concept of freedom is applied differently in other countries than it is in the United States. Laws requiring automobile occupants to wear seatbelts have been in place for years in virtually every other Western nation, including Anglo-Saxon countries such as Canada, Australia, and Great Britain. In contrast, mandatory seatbelt-use laws were only recently enacted and in only parts of the United States, and then largely in response to a looming federal requirement for expensive automatic seat restraints.

Foreign governments are also more willing to restrict businesses in the name of the public interest. Nowhere is this better exemplified than in the many limitations that apply to television advertising in other nations. Denmark allows no advertising on television whatsoever. Norway prohibits the advertising of alcohol and tobacco as well as advertising that portrays women as sex objects or exploits the female body as a means of selling a product (Graver, 1986). For a while, the Canadian province of Quebec banned television advertising directed at children. Almost all European countries restrict television advertising to certain times of day and require that it be shown in blocks, or "magazines," allowing consumers to avoid commercial messages if they wish. In the United States, however, proposals to restrict television advertising have been effectively countered with the battle cries of "freedom of speech" and "self-regulation." The only exception is the legislative ban on the advertising of cigarettes, a restriction that has been partially offset by increased advertising in other media.

A final example of a freedom-limiting consumer policy outside the United States involves the banning of an entire class of products on non-safety grounds. Many parents worldwide bemoan the fixation of children with guns. First Sweden (1977) and later Finland (1987) simply banned "war toys." In outlawing these products, the Swedish and Finnish governments denied consumers the freedom to purchase war toys and businesses the freedom to sell them.

## Distinctive Features of Consumerism in the United States

The comparatively socialist nations of Western Europe have been the pioneers with respect to consumer policies that enhance consumer representation and informed consumer choice. In addition, these governments have shown a greater willingness than the United States to prohibit activities on the part of producers or consumers. The United States, on the other hand, has been the world leader in developing means of consumer redress, attempting to serve consumers better through competition rather than government regulation, and finding ways to encourage but still control the expression of advertisers.

**Consumer Redress.** Several means of allowing consumers to pursue postpurchase grievances were first or most extensively developed in the United States: cooling-off periods on door-to-door sales, lemon laws, strict liability as a basis for product liability claims, and class action suits. The Federal Trade Commission's cooling-off rule, promulgated in 1972, allows buyers to cancel a contract up to three days after the sale.

The rule originally applied only to door-to-door sales but was later extended to any transaction that occurs away from a seller's regular place of business—for example, at conventions. The cooling-off period was eventually adopted by several European nations, in some cases extending the rescission period to a full week.

Lemon laws constitute a more recent and more dramatic example of an innovation in the consumer's ability to obtain redress. First enacted in Connecticut in 1980, lemon laws are designed to help consumers when a new car has serious defects that cannot be readily repaired. With some minor variation among states, the thrust of the law is that a consumer is entitled to a refund or a new car if a serious defect has not been repaired within four attempts or if the vehicle is out of service for repairs for a total of thirty days for miscellaneous repairs under the original warranty. In practice, lemon laws are less than a godsend. Despite revisions and improvement by some states, a dissatisfied new car owner may still have to bring a private legal action to enforce a lemon law (Nicks, 1986). Nevertheless, these laws represent an important step in establishing the consumer's right to a product that functions in a reasonable manner, and they have spawned several state laws covering warranties on used cars.

The doctrine of strict liability as it applies to product liability cases constitutes another mechanism of consumer redress that has seen its strongest expression in the United States. Traditionally, a plaintiff had to show that a product's manufacturer had been negligent, but beginning in 1963 with the establishment of strict liability, the manufacturer could be found liable even without evidence of negligence. The principle behind strict liability is that the manufacturer is better able to bear the economic costs of an accidental injury than is the individual consumer; in addition, the manufacturer can create an "insurance policy" for its customers by slightly raising the price of its product to cover injury claims (Hammer, 1980).

The net effect of a shift from a negligence standard to a strict liability standard has been to improve the consumer's prospects of being compensated in the event of a product-related injury. Nevertheless, the so-called liability crisis of the mid-1980s has led to the charge that the doctrine of strict liability can harm consumers. Egged on by greedy attorneys, the insurance industry argues, the courts have become swamped with product liability suits, resulting directly in excessive court awards and indirectly in escalating insurance rates. Although changes in U.S. product liability law are still the topic of hot debate, the experience of the United States remains of great interest to other countries trying to find the optimal balance in assigning liability for product-related injuries (Reich, 1986).

Class action suits are another area in which the United States has been an innovator. In principle, class action allows a group of aggrieved consumers, no one of whom would have sufficient economic means or incentive to take a private legal action, to bring suit as a single party or in the name of a still larger group of individuals—for example, a group of consumers who were all harmed by a single pharmaceutical product. Even antitrust violations such as price fixing can be challenged by class action suits.

Like lemon laws, class action suits are more impressive in principle than in practice, for there are substantial barriers to their effective use. To bring a federal class action suit in the United States one must show that neither individual legal action nor joint suits by small groups of individuals who allege harm are practical, and there must be questions of law and fact common to the entire class. If, for example, an intrauterine device causes sterility among some users but unintended pregnancies among others it may not be possible to bring a single class action on behalf of all injured consumers. Finally, any awards may be eaten up by legal fees, with little compensation actually reaching consumers. Nevertheless, the concept of class action remains an important one to consumers and is being examined by some European countries (Committee on Consumer Policy, 1983).

**Industry Deregulation.**   Beginning with banking and railroads in the nineteenth century, a number of industries in the United States have come under federal regulation for the purpose of promoting orderly competition and stable, if not low, price levels. Until recently, this type of economic regulation applied to most of the nation's infrastructural industries: transportation, communication, agriculture, energy, and financial services. In many European countries, government ownership, often with monopoly control, was viewed as a substitute for this type of industrywide regulation.

During the 1970s, economic regulation in the United States came under considerable fire from both economists and consumerists. It was described as obsolete at best and a government-sanctioned form of price fixing at worst. As a result, a substantial degree of deregulation has occurred. Although results of deregulatory policies vary from industry to industry (see chapter 6), European consumer groups have begun to explore the idea that deregulation can serve the consumer's best interests, especially in the transportation and communication industries.

**Advertising Encouragement and Regulation.** No industrialized country matches the United States in terms of the amount of money spent on advertising. Expenditures per capita in the United States are twice those in Canada, four times those in Great Britain, and six times those in France (*World Advertising Expenditures,* 1986). Advertisers in the United States also enjoy greater media access and freedom with respect to ad content than in other countries. Consistent with this latitude, the U.S. government has simultaneously encouraged advertising when its absence is likely to harm consumers and controlled it when its effects are potentially harmful.

To encourage advertising that might benefit consumers, the federal government has overturned traditional bans on comparative advertising and advertising by professionals. Comparative ads are those in which one company makes a direct and specific comparison between its product and that of a competitor. For example, a Ford advertisement might claim that Ford's LTD sedan has faster acceleration, more trunk space, and a much lower price than a Mercedes with similar features. In 1972, the Federal Trade Commission ended bans on comparative advertising, determining that, though comparisons might not be exhaustive, some consumer information was better than none. Comparative advertising remains rare, however, outside the United States.

The justification for allowing advertisements by professionals like doctors, dentists, and lawyers was even more compelling than that regarding comparative ads. Codes of ethics and, in many cases, state laws had traditionally banned advertising by professionals on the grounds that it degraded the profession's image and undermined confidence in the practitioner. These restrictions also served to limit price competition. In removing the barriers to advertising by professionals, the federal government successfully argued that consumers would receive more information and that price competition would be stimulated. As a result, advertising by professionals has become a major fixture of the American scene, while European countries remain cautious about its use.

Complementing policies that unleash advertising to stimulate competition are policies to police advertising that is misleading or deceptive. Regulatory methods include advertising substantiation rules, mandatory disclosure (such as health warnings in cigarette ads), provisions for corrective advertising in the case of deceptive ads (Scammon and Semenik,

1982; Wilkie, McNeill, and Mazis, 1984), and counteradvertising to balance the effects of controversial commercial messages (such as the antismoking messages of the 1960s and the later proposal to air good-nutrition messages for children). Mandatory disclosure, corrective advertising, and counteradvertising are all considered drastic mechanisms and are rarely invoked. As other nations liberalize their rules regarding advertising, however, they may choose to adapt the regulatory mechanisms established in the United States.

## Consumerism in Developing Nations

Consumerism in developing countries is shaped by two broad types of factors. On the one hand, there are the relatively indigenous characteristics of markets and consumers in these nations. On the other hand, developing nations import goods, visions of "the good life," and consumer policies from more developed nations.

### Internal Influences on Third World Consumerism

Much of what we know about consumerism in developing nations has come from research done by Hans Thorelli of Indiana University. Beginning with studies focused on consumer information in Western European nations (Thorelli and Thorelli, 1974, 1977; Thorelli, Becker, and Engledow, 1975), Thorelli and his colleagues have since turned their attention to consumerism in less developed countries (LDCs), notably Thailand, Kenya, and the People's Republic of China (Thorelli, 1982; Thorelli and Sentell, 1982; Waruingi, 1980).

After analyzing markets and consumers in LDCs, Thorelli concluded that the priorities for consumer policy should be exactly the inverse of those in more developed countries (MDCs). In the MDCs, Thorelli asserts, consumer information programs are most appropriate, followed by consumer education. Consumer protection measures by government are the least pressing, since many are already in place, especially regarding health and safety. Furthermore, the ability of individuals in MDCs to make consumer decisions for themselves is supported both by market conditions (for example, truthful advertising and constant quality across different specimens of the same product) and consumer characteristics (for example, high levels of educational attainment).

In LDCs, in contrast, basic consumer protection measures are often lacking, and neither the market conditions nor the consumer characteristics necessary for self-protection are widespread. According to Thorelli, there are three dominant features of markets in LDCs. First, a majority of products are manufactured locally but without adequate levels of quality control. Second, transportation and storage facilities are inadequate for the task of preserving fresh foods. Third, sellers place little importance on consumer satisfaction and may willingly sell adulterated goods or cheat with respect to weights and measures. For their part, consumers are often poor and uneducated. Although consumers in LDCs are motivated to obtain information, whatever they can learn is often ephemeral and unreliable. Thus, it is unrealistic to suppose that providing consumers in LDCs with information will seriously change their "position of eternal underdog" (Thorelli, 1983, p. 148.)

Thorelli recommends that the first priority of consumer policy in LDCs be consumer protection. This means more than ensuring that products are reasonably free from risk; consumer protection should also involve replacing the random and ephemeral elements of the marketplace with standards of product integrity and quality. According to Thorelli, consumer education should be the second priority in the area of consumer policy, if for no other reason than it is a prerequisite for the effectiveness of consumer information programs. Moreover, education includes much more than simply how to use consumer information; it involves becoming knowledgeable about market processes, budgeting, decision making, asserting consumer rights, and accepting consumer responsibilities.

## External Influences on Third World Consumerism

Thorelli's analysis of consumerism in less developed countries is based primarily on the relatively indigenous characteristics of markets and consumers in these nations. As a result, he emphasizes the differences between LDCs and MDCs. For example, he tends to equate third world consumers with low-income people buying domestically produced goods, ignoring the growing middle-class consumers who increasingly purchase goods from abroad. It is important to complement Thorelli's research by considering the ways in which consumerism in developing countries is affected by events beyond their borders. Specifically, developed nations export goods, consumption standards, and aspirations, as well as conceptions of consumer policy to developing countries.

*Foreign Goods.* In an increasingly global marketplace, it is inevitable that consumers in LDCs will have access to goods produced in MDCs. This has both positive and negative aspects. On the positive side, firms based in MDCs are sensitized to the ethic that consumer satisfaction and repeat purchases are of paramount importance. This is likely to mean that levels of quality control will be high and that mechanisms will exist for dealing with consumer problems. This enlightened approach to marketing directly benefits third world consumers who purchase goods from first world manufacturers; it also has the potential effect of promoting a similar ethic among third world producers.

The negative side of exports from developed to developing countries is the practice of using the latter as a testing ground for new products and a dumping ground for abandoned ones. Depo-Provera, an injectable contraceptive, provides a powerful example (Dowie, 1979; Minkin, 1981). It has been used for more than a decade outside the United States, primarily in developing nations with burgeoning populations, but it has failed to receive approval from the U.S. Food and Drug Administration (Boffey, 1984; Sun, 1982), owing to its apparent carcinogenicity when tested on beagles and monkeys. Advocates of Depo-Provera's use in developing nations claim that its benefits far outweigh its risks and that it is safer than oral contraceptives ("Panel . . . ," 1983).

Whereas Depo-Provera represents a potentially dangerous product that was widely distributed outside an exporting country but never used within it, other products are exported after they have been pulled from the domestic market because of concerns about their safety. Products that have been dumped in this way include baby pacifiers, baby cribs, children's pajamas, drugs, medical devices, pesticides, and fungicides (Dowie, 1979; "Exporting Hazardous Products," 1984). Dumping is by no means confined to American firms, but it does typically involve exports from a developed to a developing country.

Dumping can also involve leaving a product in third world markets long after it has been removed from markets in developed nations. One example concerns the Dalkon Shield, the intrauterine device that caused many problems. Under intense pressure, the Dalkon Shield's manufacturer "voluntarily" halted sales of its product in the United States in 1974, but sales were not terminated in developing countries until almost a year later. In fact, the Dalkon Shield was implanted in women as late as 1980, with doctors telling their patients, "This is from the United States and it's very good" (Mintz, 1985).

Even when products imported by developing nations are safe by the standards of a developed nation, they may still present dangers when consumed in the context of a less developed country. Nowhere is this better exemplified than in the scandal involving infant milk formula. In several third world countries, hospital personnel gave new mothers free tins of powdered milk formula and encouraged them to give up breastfeeding. The problems arose when mothers returned home from the hospital. They lacked several things that had been present in the hospital setting: clean water with which to mix the formula, sufficient fuel to sterilize their one bottle and nipple, a refrigerator to store any unused milk, and, above all, enough money to continue obtaining enough formula. Thus mothers gave their babies diluted amounts of formula under unsanitary conditions, resulting in malnutrition and its related diseases, including mental retardation and death (Garson, 1977). More than a decade after these problems were first publicized, the practice persisted. In 1983, a panel headed by former U.S. senator and secretary of state Edmund Muskie audited the Nestlé Company's compliance with a code of conduct it had pledged to uphold. The panel found substantial merit to many of the complaints lodged by the International Nestlé Boycott Committee (organized to stop the practice) and called for corrective action by the company ("Nestlé Audit . . . ," 1983). In 1986, the United Nations estimated that one million infants die annually because they are fed from bottles rather than breastfed (Gaschott, 1986).

The sale of infant milk formula in developing countries is not, strictly speaking, dumping because the product itself is deemed safe in the domestic markets of the exporting countries. The case, rather, points to a problem far greater in its potential importance than dumping. Products that are safe and valuable when consumed by affluent people in developed countries can do damage when consumed in the context of developing countries.

**Consumption Standards and Aspirations.** Not just the products but the consumption standards and aspirations of developed countries find their way to developing countries—often via tourists whose affluent consumption styles are displayed. Sometimes relatively inexpensive objects from first world countries can be imbued with great importance by third world consumers. For example, Arnould and Wilk (1984) describe Peruvian Indians who carry rocks painted to look like transistor radios and Ethiopian tribesmen who pay large sums to look through a children's slide viewer at one of Pluto's adventures. Belk (1988) recounts Papua New Guinea tribesmen who wear bright Western ties around their collarless necks and place Chivas Regal wrappers around the middle of their traditional snakeskin drums.

Consumption standards and aspirations are also transmitted to third world consumers through the mass media, especially advertising, movies, and television programs. When a cigarette advertisement is printed or broadcast in a developing country, it serves to publicize not only a particular brand but the lifestyle of the portrayed smoker as well. Some people in MDCs find it objectionable that firms can pay to have their particular brands embedded in a movie or television show (for example, Reece's Pieces in the film *ET*), but for third world consumers, all the products displayed in the mass media are potential objects of desire.

The exportation of Western consumption styles and aspirations is often a good thing. Few people would dispute that Western standards of sanitation have enhanced the quality of life in developing nations. It could also be argued that a certain degree of material acquisitiveness stimulates work effort and economic development (Blair, 1965). Nevertheless, there is some evidence that the introduction of Western consumption aspirations causes problems as well, especially when luxury goods are obtained at the expense of necessities. In a study of the diffusion of durable goods in Brazil, Wells (1977) found that a primary means by which less affluent households obtained goods like radios, refrigerators, and televisions was reducing consumption of necessities such as food.

In reviewing evidence from a number of countries, James and Stewart (1981) attempted to identify the conditions under which the introduction of new products into third world countries increases or decreases consumer welfare. Although they allowed for both positive and negative outcomes, most of their examples involve what they believe are decreases in consumer welfare. They write of Kenya importing soap that is more expensive and functionally inferior to local varieties, and of consumers in other developing countries substituting processed food for more nutritious and less expensive alternatives: refined for unrefined sugar, sliced wrapped bread for locally baked bread, imported breakfast cereals for traditional breakfast foods. Although there is nothing wrong with consumers genuinely valuing characteristics like appearance, convenience, or a product's country of origin, James and Stewart believe that consumer preferences in developing countries are artificially determined by the promotional efforts of foreign companies.

Even when the poorest consumers in developing countries simply cannot afford to substitute more expensive, less nutritious food for local varieties, they are nevertheless not totally immune to the influence of consumption aspirations imported from abroad. Lauterbach (1972) notes that in a South American slum, sanitary conditions might be deplorable and electric service intermittent, yet a fair number of the poorly constructed shacks will have television antennas, not always with a set attached, and refrigerators, not necessarily containing a decent supply of food. At a broader level of analysis, one might speculate that consumption standards imported from the developed world not only shift the priorities of individuals but also skew social investment toward the provision of private goods at the expense of public goods (like garbage collection, education, or public housing).

**Consumer Organizations and Policies.** If the bad news is that goods and consumption standards of MDCs can have negative effects when exported to LDCs, then the good news is that these negative effects can be mitigated by importing consumer policies from the same source. We have already noted the efforts of the International Organization of Consumers Unions in fostering the growth of product testing organizations in third world countries. These organizations often serve as the nucleus of the fledgling consumer movements found in developing countries.

Comparative product testing is not the only area in which developing nations can draw upon the experiences of developed nations in formulating consumer policies. For instance, the consumer advice centers found in Great Britain have been copied in Hong Kong and Portugal ("Consumer Movement," 1986; "Consumer Training," 1986). And nations like Bangladesh, India, and Malaysia are following the lead of more developed countries in their attempts to discourage cigarette smoking through limiting cigarette advertising and requiring health warnings ("Smoking," 1986).

In another effort to transfer consumer policy from developed to developing countries, the UN has sought to establish a single, worldwide set of rules to protect consumers. After long negotiations, the General Assembly unanimously adopted its Guidelines on Consumer Protection on 9 April 1985. The guidelines attempt to replace the moral double standard that sometimes exists in international trade (as in the case of dumping) with minimum international standards regarding the safety and quality of products, the distribution of goods, and the obtaining of redress for consumer problems. The guidelines are largely symbolic until adopted by law in individual nations, but, according to Peterson (1985), "they are . . . expressions of support for the kind of consumer protection we in the United States . . . have been enjoying for decades, indeed for generations" (p. 307).

Yet consumer groups in the third world do not wish to merely imitate their sister organizations in the first world. As Mary Mananzan, a nun and founder of the Manila-based Citizen's Alliance for Consumer Protection, has said, "We won't tackle the quality of toilet paper or bacon. We must choose to deal with issues that affect the majority of our people—the poor" (quoted in Sim, 1985). Similarly, when a consumer group in Bombay opened a stand at one of the city's busiest markets, it was supplied not with sophisticated product testing data but with two pieces of basic equipment: a correctly calibrated scale to detect fraudulent weights and with bottles of common chemicals to detect adulterants added to spices.

When consumer organizations open their doors in third world countries, the result can be far-reaching. With a legacy of feudalism, kowtowing to colonial masters, and religious traditions that encourage fatalism, third world consumers are often passive, lacking in self-confidence, and overly respectful of social superiors. In such a situation, getting a person to come forward with a consumer problem can be a major victory. According to the head of an Indonesian consumer group, "Whenever we help someone win a case who has never before dared to fight those in power, we observe that suddenly he or she has new confidence. It is empowering work we are doing" (Sim, 1985).

As consumer organizations from developed nations come into greater contact with those from developing countries, the traditional direction of influence from the former to the latter may be altered. In the process of helping third world nations set up product testing organizations and consumer education programs, groups from first world nations may become sensitized to the fundamental problems of developing countries: economic development and the uneven distribution of wealth.

*Chapter Eight*

# The Future of Consumerism

Throughout its long history, consumer activism has been subjected to frequent, and often contradictory, attacks by those who have predicted its rapid demise. Some critics have accused the consumer movement of being too radical and unappreciative of the ways in which capitalism serves the best interests of consumers; others have assailed the movement for being too reformist and for not challenging the basic premises of the capitalist mode of production. Similarly, by stressing only the functional aspects of goods and services and by suggesting that consumers be constantly concerned with wringing every last penny of purchasing power out of their incomes, consumerists have been criticized for taking all the fun out of consuming. Yet, consumerism is just as often condemned for being too materialistic and for failing to promote life-styles that are compatible with the planet's biological and resource limits.

Despite being criticized from all points on the political spectrum, consumerism has demonstrated remarkable staying power. It has survived two world wars, during which consumer concerns were necessarily subordinated to national survival, as well as presidential administrations (like Reagan's) hostile to governmental consumer protection efforts. Since the late nineteenth century, consumerism has continually evolved, adapting its goals and methods to the times.

Given the movement's success in eliminating the most egregious cases of consumer abuse and its high level of institutionalization in government and private organizations, one might well ask whether there is much need for further consumer activism. When a social movement becomes skilled

155

at negotiation and compromise, does it lose its ability to arouse the passion of the public? Will there continue to be new waves of activism, or has consumerism achieved a routinized steady state?

## Conditions Underlying the Emergence of Consumerism

One can propose that, based on the three waves of U.S. consumerism, organized consumerist activity is most likely to occur when two conditions come together: (1) a social climate marked by a progressive social ethos, and (2) a set of specific consumer problems connected to rapid change in the mode of producing and/or distributing goods. Generally, a progressive social climate challenges existing authorities in the name of social justice, democracy, and broad societal interests, but progressivism stops short of seeking drastic change in social and political arrangements, choosing gradual reform instead. The Progressive Era of the last few years of the nineteenth century and the first two decades of the twentieth, the New Deal period of the 1930s, and the Great Society of the 1960s were all dominated by a similar progressive political ideology. The three eras of U.S. consumerism were embedded in these progressive periods, drawing their supporters from participants in the larger social movement while at the same time adding strength and everyday relevance to it.

A progressive social climate is in itself insufficient for the generation of a consumer movement, however. The social category "consumer" is certainly consistent with the progressive appeal to broad-based societal interests, but so are the categories "voter," "taxpayer," and "worker." Therefore, specific consumer problems must exist if the progressive impulse for social reform is to be steered in the direction of consumer activism.

The problems that served to catalyze consumer movements have typically been related to rapid changes in the techniques of production and distribution, and hence patterns of consumption. The turn-of-the-century Progressive Era was characterized by the emergence of advertised and branded products sold on a national scale, especially food, drugs, and personal hygiene items. The second era of consumerism during the 1930s corresponded to the electrification of the American home, the diffusion of new household appliances, and more intensive use of advertising as a sales method. The third wave that took place starting in the 1960s correlated with an explosion of new products and new methods of distribution. The products, first made available to consumers in the 1950s, included color televisions, tape recorders, power lawn mowers, central air-conditioning, and V-8 engines. The revolution in distribution entailed the building of shopping malls, the issuing of credit cards, and the selling of standardized fast food.

The emergence of consumerism outside the United States has followed a slightly different pattern, being largely confined to the post–World War II period. Nevertheless, consumerism in other nations largely confirms the association between progressivism and consumerism. For example, consumerism took root earlier in the Scandinavian countries than in their less progressive European neighbors. In nations like France, West Germany, and the United Kingdom, which are subject to wider swings in their dominant political orientation than are Nordic countries, consumerism has flourished most readily under reformist, social democratic regimes.

Thus, a fourth wave of consumerism in the United States or a surge of activism worldwide would appear to await the confluence of a progressive political climate and specific consumer problems associated with new patterns of consumption. When is the next round of progressive social reform likely to occur? Noted historian Arthur M. Schlesinger, Jr. (1986), believes that periods of political reform and public concern occur in thirty-year cycles in the United States, with the next wave due in the 1990s. If Schlesinger is correct, a number of consumer problems may be waiting in the wings to take advantage of the revival of progressive spirit. What are these issues?

## Emerging Consumer Issues

Like previous waves of consumerism, changes in the production, distribution, and consumption of goods are likely to generate the consumer issues of the future. To these basic developments in the economy, one can also add a few demographic factors that may influence the pattern of issue emergence. Although the United States is the basis of the speculative analysis that follows, the arguments may apply to other countries, too. The United States is frequently a bellwether nation when it comes to consumerism, and both consumption and consumerism are increasingly global in character. Thus events in this country are likely to reflect broader international developments.

## *Economic Forces*

Despite the dictum that consumers are sovereign, consumer problems arise when methods of production and distribution reflect the priorities of sellers rather than those of buyers. The analysis of emerging consumer problems begins, then, with important trends in production and distribution, and then proceeds to changing patterns of consumption.

**Production.**   Numerous trends in the production of goods appear to have important ramifications for the possible emergence of consumer issues. A large and increasing proportion of the goods consumed in the United States is produced abroad. This does not necessarily mean that consumers will suffer at the hands of absentee sellers. There is no a priori reason to believe that Japanese or Swedish companies are any less concerned about satisfying their American customers than are domestic firms. Nevertheless, standards of product safety and performance vary from nation to nation, especially between more developed and less developed countries. As a result, products may be imported into the United States that fall below American standards. This possibility is only exacerbated by the increased flow of counterfeit goods, which are often inferior in quality to products they imitate. When a consumer purchases counterfeit brakes for a car or a doctor installs a counterfeit pacemaker in a patient's chest, serious consequences can ensue (O'Donnell et al., 1985). The problem of importing inferior products can be thought of as an ironic twist on the practice of dumping onto the markets of second and third world nations products that have been deemed unsafe for use in first world countries.

The increased presence of foreign-made goods in the United States raises the possibility of an additional consumer issue—protectionism for domestic producers, a trend that spells bad news for consumers. According to one estimate, American consumers paid $71 billion in higher prices in 1983 as a result of trade restrictions (Weidenbaum and Munger, 1983), and this during a presidential administration that largely resisted protectionist pressures! In another response to successful foreign products, American firms (such as makers of computer equipment) have begun to ask for a more liberal reading of antitrust statutes so that they can pool their resources and compete more effectively against foreign competition. Relaxation of antitrust laws, especially if combined with trade restrictions, could leave consumers at the mercy of only one or a few firms.

Another set of potential consumer problems could result from the trend to deregulate various industries. Deregulation has the potential to benefit consumers greatly, but it must be accompanied by vigorous antitrust enforcement and a commitment to ensure a minimum degree of access to certain categories of consumers. In the case of airline deregulation, some of its advocates now see a danger of particular cities being dominated by a single carrier (like Pittsburgh by USAir, Minneapolis by Northwest). They feel that the government has allowed too many mergers and buyouts and that airport capacity must be expanded if airline deregulation is to yield its expected benefits.

Deregulation can also create problems of access for certain types of consumers. Once deregulated, firms are likely to concentrate their efforts on the most profitable markets. In the case of banking, this means customers with large accounts; in the case of airline travel, it means urban areas that support a great deal of air traffic. The negative side of this process is that banks might choose not to serve low-income customers, and airlines might abandon small cities. To date, a variety of government-imposed and voluntary policies have largely mitigated this potential problem of consumer access. Yet, the inexorable logic of deregulation is that business decisions will be dictated by considerations of efficiency and profit rather than fairness and access to basic services.

Food production techniques, especially the heavy use of pesticides and drugs, constitute another trend that is arousing consumer alarm. Despite assurances from government officials and industry representatives that the American food supply is safe (Shabecoff, 1987), average consumers as well as consumer activists are unconvinced ("Pesticide Problems Mount," 1988; Sachs, Blair, and Richter, 1987). In 1987, consumer attention was drawn to the connection between salmonella infections and poultry processing. A report by the National Academy of Sciences described how feces and stomach contents were spread in poultry plants when high-speed, mechanical processing equipment ripped open the birds' intestines (Anthan, 1987). At least one consumer group, the Community Nutrition Institute, urged consumers to boycott poultry until the industry and the Department of Agriculture took additional steps to safeguard the poultry supply. Unfortunately, a consumer who was boycotting poultry products might face equal dangers eating seafood or beef. Evidence is growing that industrial chemicals dumped into coastal waters are contaminating fish and shellfish ("Report Urges FDA . . . ," 1987). Similarly, the beef industry has been accused of indiscriminately using hormones, antibiotics, and other drugs. A 1986 report issued by the U.S. House Government Operations Committee charged the FDA with failing to test and approve 90 percent of the drugs given to animals by farmers and veterinarians (Henderson, 1986).

Pesticides may pose the greatest threat to the food supply, however. A 1987 National Academy of Sciences report raised the possibility that pesticides on food may be responsible for twenty thousand cancers a year in the United States ("Pesticide Regulation," 1987). And banning a particular pesticide in this country is not necessarily the solution; the dangerous substance often comes into the United States on imported food. For example, officials from the FDA admitted under congressional questioning that not a single pineapple imported from the Philippines had been inspected despite the fact that the pineapples had been treated with heptachlor, a chemical banned since 1978 as a carcinogen (Shabecoff, 1987).

**Distribution.** Consumer issues of the future may also be related to trends in the distribution of goods. Unlike the realm of production, however, methods of distribution often reflect the interests of both buyers and sellers. As a result, the same techniques that generate substantial benefits for consumers can also pose problems. The trend toward one-stop shopping in megastores illustrates this conflict. Time-pressed customers appreciate the convenience of being able to buy food, clothing, motor oil, and life insurance all in one place. But in saving time, consumers restrict their consideration of alternatives and may easily end up with an item that represents a poor combination of price and quality. Disappointed consumers are not going to remember that they saved time in the purchasing process when they realize they could have gotten more for their money at another establishment. This discontent, well founded or not, could result in support for laws that allow consumers to change their minds and cancel purchases, as is currently the case with items sold door-to-door.

A second trend in distribution with the potential to cause consumer discontent is the increasing use of remote shopping, whether by mail, television, or home computer. Again, the popularity of this mode of shopping stems from its convenience, and the continued success of mail-order firms such as L. L. Bean is testimony to the compatibility of high levels of consumer satisfaction with remote shopping. Nevertheless, the practice inherently courts consumer dissatisfaction because people cannot inspect a product before purchasing it. Even the most liberal return policies cannot entirely erase the annoyance of receiving an item that has to be sent back. The more high-tech forms of remote shopping raise additional issues. It doesn't take long for television viewers using the home shopping channels to find out that price savings are less than they expected. A study conducted by the Better Business Bureau found that store prices are almost always lower than a television shopping service's "claimed retail price" and lower than the shopping service's actual selling price 37 percent of the time ("Home Shopping Services," 1987). Similarly, ordering goods via home computer raises a number of potential consumer protection issues: defining a valid contract, properly matching goods ordered with goods received, impulse buying, unauthorized purchases, and assigning responsibility when problems occur (Mayer, 1988; Shapiro, 1986).

The prospect of the cashless society is a final example of how trends in distribution could create the consumer issues of tomorrow. Already, only a quarter of all consumer purchases are paid for in cash (MasterCard International, 1987). The trend is toward highly automated transactions involving rapid data transmission and remote data storage. Even discounting the nightmarish visions of computer theft and unauthorized access to personal information, one can easily imagine the more mundane possibilities of mistakes and breakdowns. A transaction conducted by a computer takes on an air of infallibility; challenging an error becomes an intimidating task. Moreover, the instantaneous nature of computer transactions makes it more likely that damage will be done before errors are discovered. Finally, the very process by which technological innovations raise customer expectations regarding speed and efficiency also heightens customer irritation and impatience when malfunctions occur.

To sum up, it is easy to imagine several ways in which current trends in the production and distribution of consumer goods could pose problems in the future. Under the right social conditions, these problems could be transformed into public policy issues and serve as catalyzing agents for a new wave of consumerism activism.

**Consumption.** An additional list of potential consumer issues can be generated by examining contemporary consumption patterns. What can you say about a nation in which last year's technological breakthrough becomes this year's household necessity and next year's garage sale item? What does it mean for consumers when there are over a thousand introductions of new supermarket and drugstore products per month ("New Product Debut . . .," 1987)? If the consumer activism of the 1930s was fueled by consumer bewilderment in the face of new products, then how much more likely is it that today's dizzying pace of change will ignite a new wave of consumer activism?

A rapidly expanding set of new products offers consumers certain undeniable benefits. Yet, for many of the same reasons as in the 1930s, contemporary consumers may define product proliferation and innovation as a mixed blessing. The rapid introduction of new products, brands, and models can induce discontent through its impact on the decision-making process. In a period when purchase alternatives were less numerous and change slower, a consumer had a reasonable chance of making a truly informed decision. Not only was the task of information gathering relatively simple, but knowledge based on a person's past experience with a product might still be relevant to the current decision. Today, when a consumer goes to replace a household appliance after ten years of satisfactory service, the company that manufactured the existing model probably has been bought out by another company, has moved its factories overseas, uses entirely new production technologies, and offers a dazzling new array of features. The consumer is back at square one, with a long way to go before being able to make an informed choice. Thus, even if all the new alternatives are superior in value to the one being replaced, consumers may still experience a nagging sense that the world has somehow passed out of their control.

The technological sophistication and complexity of new products may also present problems for consumers. Although manufacturers have strived mightily to make new product technologies user friendly, the "opaqueness" of these products is apparent when consumers try to maintain and repair them. For example, how many people dare do the repair work on their car today, and what do you check if your microwave oven goes on the fritz? True, some appliances have become so inexpensive they can be thrown out and replaced when a malfunction occurs, but again this solution can cause feelings of helplessness and exacerbate the issues associated with a throw-away society—mounting disposal problems, environmental pollution, and shrinking resources.

The large array of new products that characterizes today's marketplace forces sellers to find new ways to be heard above the competitive din. Food companies may make unfounded claims about the nutritional value of their product; car manufacturers may rely more heavily on sexual innuendo; beer and cigarette commercials may subtly target children. In the process, advertisers can alienate various segments of the public. Thus, to the extent that a constantly expanding array of new products leads to more aggressive sales techniques, advertising practices may become a third focus of consumer criticism.

There is a final way in which the rapid introduction of new products could fuel a new wave of consumer activism. The promotion of new products frequently relies on the equation of newness and goodness. The implicit message is that people who hold onto a product or style too long are slipping behind their neighbors in the competition for social status. This learned restiveness is, according to historian Colin Campbell (1987), the very essence of the modern consumption ethic. Unfortunately, the quest for status through the acquisition of novel goods is an unwinnable proposition: just as a new good is acquired, an even newer one becomes available. In short, consumers may eventually revolt against the never-ending treadmill onto which modern merchandising has encouraged them to step.

## Demographic Forces

Demographic trends are another factor likely to affect consumer issues of the future. In particular, consumer health issues will probably play a central role, for the overall aging of the U.S. population, as well as the health-related needs of the baby boom generation, will intensify the public's interest in this area.

The graying of America has already influenced the agenda of the consumer movement in the United States. The National Consumers League has described health care as "the next great consumer issue" and has made it a top concern ("Health Care . . .," 1984). The league is directing its primary efforts at ensuring access to basic medical care for all citizens, regardless of income, and finding innovative solutions to the problem of financing long-term care for the elderly. The high cost of current methods affects far more than just the elderly. Increasingly, their children are elderly themselves or are still paying for their own children's college expenses. In either situation, the large amount of money needed to support long-term care of an ailing parent may not be available.

The members of the baby boom generation, by and large, have not yet been asked to help bear the costs of their parents' medical care. Rather, the first members of the generation have reached their forties and are discovering their mortality. As a result, this large and influential segment of the U.S. population is expressing its health consciousness in any number of ways, from a demand for more nutritious foods to an intolerance of smoking in public places. The baby boomers are also moving into positions of influence within major social institutions, including the government and the mass media. Accordingly, it can be expected that consumer health issues will be highly salient for at least the next decade.

Still other demographic factors are harbingers of future consumer issues. Several indicators reveal the financial precariousness of many American households—a high level of consumer indebtedness and low level of saving, the widespread need for two incomes to maintain an average standard of living, and an increasing number of households headed by women. If economic conditions deteriorate, a practical brand of consumerism could emerge that stresses efficiency in consumption, or a more radical brand could appear that asserts consumer rights to minimal levels of food, shelter, and clothing. Beyond a certain point, though, the deterioration of economic conditions could have the effect of subordinating consumerism to efforts to restart the economy.

Consumer problems by themselves are insufficient for launching a new stage of consumer activism. There must also be a supportive social climate that validates reformist attempts to fine-tune society. If this progressive social climate should develop, economic and demographic developments could serve as the seed crystals for a revival of consumerism in the United States and elsewhere.

## Paths for the Consumer Movement

What strategies are available to the consumer movement to hurry the arrival of the fourth wave of consumer activism? And will radical or reformist ideology predominate?

### Equality and Efficiency

The tension between the goals of equality and efficiency runs deep in Western industrialized societies. The democratic political institutions in these nations provide universally distributed rights and privileges, such as equal protection under the law and universal suffrage, that proclaim the equality of all citizens. At the same time, capitalist economic institutions are built on the principle that inequality in income and other sources of material welfare aids in the pursuit of efficiency. Much of the conflict in democratic capitalist societies concerns the proper boundary between the domain of rights and the domain of dollars (Okun, 1975). It might be efficient for individuals to sell their vote to the highest bidder at election time, but this practice would cause affront to our notions of equality. Conversely, taxes are not made more progressive for fear that the motivation to work and invest might be reduced to the point where economic efficiency would suffer. Efforts to increase equality often threaten to reduce efficiency, and vice versa.

Most social movements begin as calls for greater equality, even if it means a sacrifice in efficiency. When Progressive Era reformers demanded an end to child labor and sweatshop conditions, employers warned that these reforms would drive up consumer prices. More recently, advocates for the physically handicapped have argued that they should have access to bus and subway systems, regardless of the cost involved.

Over time, several social movements have been able to layer the pursuit of efficiency on top of their basic goal of equality or fairness. For example, ending job discrimination on the basis of sex and race is not only fair; it also promotes efficiency by allowing everyone's skills to be fully utilized. And environmentalists not only regard pollution as unfair in the way it involuntarily imposes costs on people who are downwind or downstream from the polluters; they also view it as inefficient in that air or water has more valuable uses than being the dumping ground for wastes. Much the same combination of concern for equity and efficiency can be found in the today's consumer movement.

## *The Reformist Evolution*

The consumer movement began as a protest against inequities in the marketplace but gradually has been able to join the issues of equality and efficiency. The first wave of U.S. consumerism was driven by a desire for fairness and equality in dealings between sellers and buyers. Certain practices, such as adulterating food and fixing prices, were challenged on the ground that they were unconscionable. The importance of fairness and equality to the first generation of consumer activists is also illustrated by the primary goal of the National Consumers League: it used the power of consumer boycotts not to reduce prices or raise product quality but to improve working conditions.

By the time of the second era of American consumerism, the movement was concerned with efficiency as well as unfair exposure of consumers to hazardous products and deceptive advertising. The consumerist classic, *Your Money's Worth*, written by a certified public accountant and a mechanical engineer, deplored the sheer wastefulness of production, distribution, and consumption in the United States. The combined goals of equality and efficiency that inspired the second era of American consumerism were further exemplified by the establishment of the product testing organization Consumers Union in 1936. In contrast to its forerunner, Consumers' Research, Consumers Union wanted to take social conditions such as wages and factory conditions into account when rating products and to operate according to the principles of co-operation and socialism. During its first year, the entire staff of Consumers Union, from the editors to the secretaries, received the same weekly salary. Although this experiment in equality soon gave way to the goal of increasing the organization's technical and scientific credibility, to this day Consumers Union attempts to strike a balance between efficiency and equality, between testing and protesting (Silber, 1983).

The third wave of consumerism that took place during the 1960s and 1970s drew its first converts with a call to equality and fairness. It was based on a vision of restoring some balance in the relationship between buyer and seller. Advertisers manipulated consumers by playing upon their deepest fantasies, fears, and anxieties (Packard, 1957). Merchants charged usurious interest rates to the poor living in ghetto areas (Caplovitz, 1963). Undertakers lied through their teeth when dealing with their bereaved clients (Mitford, 1963). Automakers, despite their vast budgets for research and development, routinely placed unsafe products on the market (Nader, 1965). It seemed that consumers had awakened just in time to avoid having their last pennies stolen by greedy and immoral businesses.

Eventually, the rhetoric cooled and the goal of efficiency became an increasingly important part of the consumer movement's message. The mandatory disclosure of product information on labels, packages, and store shelves was justified not so much by the consumer's right to know but by the idea that informed consumers are necessary for the proper functioning of a competitive market. A concern with efficiency was also manifest in laws setting minimal standards of energy consumption by automobiles and appliances as well as in rules that forbade lenders from determining creditworthiness on the basis of functionally irrelevant characteristics such as sex, race, and marital status.

The consumer movement's acceptance of the goal of efficiency reached its peak when it embraced the deregulation of the airline, banking, trucking, and telecommunications industries. Industry deregulation represents the triumph of efficiency over equality because, by driving prices toward the cost of providing service, deregulation eliminates subsidies for "needy" consumers. Under airline deregulation, citizens of small communities may find that their previously subsidized air service has been reduced; under banking deregulation, holders of small checking and savings accounts may face higher service charges.

As subsidies to low-income and rural customers disappeared under deregulation, however, consumerists reasserted the importance of equity. They have sought new mechanisms for ensuring the availability of services to consumers who might be ignored by the economics of the marketplace. For instance, consumerists have supported the adoption of lifeline telephone rates to prevent low-income consumers from being priced out of the system.

What explains the transition from radical to reformist ideology in the American consumer movement? To some extent, radical ideology has been the victim of its own success. The outrageous instances of injustice to consumers upon which radicals drew to bolster their credibility have been largely rectified. The problems that remain are less black and white; their complex nature requires the technical expertise of a reformist. For example, almost everyone agrees that it is unfair to market a pharmaceutical product that causes birth defects on a frequent basis. It is much more difficult to reach consensus, though, on how long new drugs ought to be tested before they are released on the market. The latter question requires a delicate balancing of the costs and benefits of various amounts of testing and is a matter of efficiency rather than equity.

The shift from radicalism to reformism also has been driven by the fact that greater equity, fairness, and social justice is more difficult to achieve than is greater efficiency. Increasing equity is politically painful because it involves reducing the rights and privileges of one group to enhance those of another group. Improving efficiency, in contrast, does not necessarily have to be achieved at someone's expense; it often involves making everyone better off. Given that the pursuit of equity constantly requires the reformer to do battle with vested interests, it is tempting to substitute the goal of efficiency for the goal of equity.

The transition from radical to reformist ideology is also abetted by participation in existing political structures. As the members of a social movement gain legitimacy, they are often invited to advise and consult with public policymakers. In a few rare instances, activists may attain positions of authority within corporations and government agencies. During the Carter presidency in particular, consumerists were appointed to high-level positions within key consumer protection agencies. In the process of working through existing channels on behalf of consumers, consumerists begin to understand, if not totally appreciate, the arguments of their adversaries. As they begin to see both sides of an issue, activists substitute negotiation and compromise for confrontation.

Within the United States as well as other developed nations, the consumer movement still seems headed in an increasingly reformist direction. The Reagan administration hastened this development by clearly shutting down any possibility for more radical change. If consumerists wanted to participate at all in public policy, they had to adopt the tools of economic and legal analysis. And so they did. Led by the Consumer Federation of America, consumerists dueled with the hired guns of industry on such esoteric issues as exclusive franchises for beer wholesalers, railroad shipping rates, general aviation tort reform, telephone company rate structures and return on equity, and health care cost containment.

Reformists in the United States have steered the consumer movement in the direction of sophisticated representation by a professional core of activists who shuttle in and out of government positions depending on the political inclinations of the president. To the extent that grass-roots consumer groups exist, they are quite independent of the movement's leadership in Washington, D.C. With reformists at its head, the movement has pressed for bread-and-butter consumer issues such as safe products, competitive prices, and responsive mechanisms of consumer redress. Issues pertaining to workers' rights and environmental protection remain on the consumerist agenda, but clearly in a position of secondary importance. In terms of broader social goals, the movement tacitly supports the conventional objectives of economic growth and equality of opportunity, but not the more radical objective of income redistribution. In short, efficiency has taken precedence over equality; rationality and scientific expertise have been substituted for passion and moral outrage.

## Conclusion

Given the ascendancy of reformist ideology within the consumer movement, the question arises of whether the movement is entering a new period of still greater effectiveness or whether, on the contrary, its very survival is in question. To date, consumerism's dual emphasis on efficiency and fairness has served it well. In particular, the emphasis on efficiency has made the movement more productive and less confrontational than most social movements. It permits consumer activists and businesses to solve problems in ways that benefit both groups. In addition, the goal of efficiency has provided the consumer movement with a way of rechanneling its energies during periods when the political climate has been hostile to calls for greater social justice.

Despite the advantages of pursuing efficiency, however, it is unlikely that a social movement can survive without simultaneously pursuing humanitarian goals. One reason is that radicals and reformists need each other. The extreme demands of radicals for equality and fairness have helped clear the way for the acceptance of more modest reformist proposals. Conversely, the practical accomplishments of the reformists in promoting market efficiency have provided the radicals with a measure of legitimacy when they are under attack.

An exclusive focus on efficiency also weakens a social movement because political strength does not automatically follow from having economic common sense on your side. Even if one rejects the view that government decision making is automatically biased in favor of the interests of the rich and powerful, it is clear that political outcomes reflect a number of noneconomic criteria. Some of these criteria probably work to the detriment of the political process, as when a decision maker is concerned only about being reelected or promoted. But other noneconomic criteria are absolutely central to the purpose of politics. Economics is the science of allocating scarce resources, but politics is much broader. It is the art of reconciling differences of values and setting social priorities. As such, it is meant to include criteria other than economic efficiency, including justice, fairness, and compassion.

A social movement must lay claim to the moral high ground. Without a shield constructed from ethical imperatives, public interest movements are doomed to defeat in political combat. In the case of the consumer movement, new inputs of moral outrage are needed so that a balance between efficiency and equity can be achieved. Accidents, tragedies, and scandals have always been a source of consumer outrage, but they are too ephemeral and unpredictable to serve as the moral foundation for the consumer movement. Nor would the collapse of national economies or a worldwide depression be likely to stimulate humanitarian concern for the welfare of all consumers; such a catastrophe would more likely drive individuals deeper into a selfish preoccupation with their own economic well-being.

Previous eras of consumer activism have focused on the plight of the workers who produce goods, consumers unable to obtain even rudimentary amounts of impartial information, children manipulated by advertisements, ethnic minorities unfamiliar with the urban marketplace, and elderly people being robbed of their savings by con artists and high-pressure door-to-door vendors. Who will be the objects of moral concern in any future waves of consumer activism?

There is much debate regarding whether skilled jobs are being exported from developed to developing nations, with the result that the middle class is "disappearing." In the United States, for example, wealth seems to be increasingly polarized. Real wages declined for much of the 1970s, and families managed to maintain or improve their standard of living only by working more (Easterlin, 1987; Levy, 1987). Similarly, poverty rates rose throughout most of the 1980s and have once again been defined as a pressing social issue (Moynihan, 1987). The existence of an embattled middle class and a seemingly permanent underclass could give rise to a call for greater consumer rights. One likely direction would be an expansion of programs that provide consumption subsidies for "essential" goods and service, such as banking, telephone, electricity, and heat). Concern with low- and middle-income consumers could also take the form of new disclosure requirements regarding, for instance, credit card interest rates, food and drug prices, and used cars.

The consumerism of developed countries may also be morally recharged through its contact with third world nations. In their efforts to transplant consumerism from developed to developing countries, organizations like the International Organization of Consumers Unions are being exposed to a version of consumerism in which the satisfaction of basic human needs is defined as the ultimate consumer problem. These needs include inexpensive nutritious food, proper sanitation, a minimal degree of access to medical care, and decent housing. Conventional consumer goals, such as safe products, truthful consumer information, and realistic avenues for lodging complaints, although important, are viewed as subordinate to satisfying the subsistence needs of all citizens.

The radical consumerists of the third world embrace a perspective in which consumer problems can be traced to the activities of transnational corporations and the dynamics of international trade. For solutions to these problems, these radical consumerists place their faith in self-help networks, decentralization, coalitions of the marginalized and dispossessed (labor, environmentalists, women's groups, religious organizations, native peoples, gays), and the diffusion of new worldviews. Thus, in contrast to the reformist brand of consumerism that currently predominates in developed countries, the radical variety emanating from developing nations is full of passion and rhetoric. As long as the basic human needs of a significant number of people go unfulfilled, this sense of urgency will persist. In addition, radicals view consumer problems not in isolation but rather as connected to broader social issues: emancipation of women, protection of the natural environment, citizen empowerment, adoption of appropriate technology, and preservation of indigenous cultures against the onslaught of commercial values (Fazal, 1984; Peng, 1980).

Some of the same ideological elements that inform the radical consumerism found in the third world can be found in developed countries in "New Age" groups such as the Greens. The Greens have become a highly visible political force in several European countries and are a budding political movement in the United States. Their often-quoted slogan, "Neither right, nor left, but green," expresses their rejection of both capitalism and socialism in favor of a new set of assumptions about power, progress, and technology. The centerpieces of their political ideology are preservation of the earth's ecological integrity and decentralization of politics. The major obstacle to a blending of New Age politics and consumerism is the former's tendency to subordinate or even reject the consumer aspirations and problems of the great masses of people. The Greens are deeply suspicious of materialist values. They accept the importance of satisfying human needs, but "mere" desires are viewed as frivolous stumbling blocks to true human fulfillment.

The consumer movement will have to develop its own moral vision for the 1990s and beyond. Consistent with the Greens and the more radical consumerists in developing countries, this new vision can incorporate criticisms of the technocratic, centralist, and militarist biases of traditional politics, but it must also validate some materialistic desires, especially those of people who have not yet experienced the benefits of affluence. The new consumerist vision must seek to link consumer issues—but without subordinating them—to the long list of progressive issues involving civil rights, demilitarization, gay rights, feminism, and employment security. Finally, a compelling consumerist view for the future must address consumer problems that are increasingly global in nature.

For the short term at least, consumerism in the United States and other developed nations is likely to retain its reformist character. In developing countries, radical ideology is likely to slowly give way to more reformist perspectives. Reformists in both types of nations will accept and encourage radicals, for the latter represent consumerism's historical roots and sustain its self-image as a social movement that enjoys grassroots support.

The movement has already shown that it can deliver the goods. It has prevented unsafe products from being marketed; ensured that consumers have access to timely and accurate information; guarded against anticompetitive practices that raise prices and lower quality; and guaranteed that consumers have somewhere to turn when a new car is a lemon, a household appliance starts a fire, creditors make harassing phone calls in the middle of the night, or fraudulent investment schemes rob senior citizens of their life's savings. Its next challenge is to preserve this ability to solve everyday consumer problems while building a new moral basis for the future movement.

# References Cited

Aaker, David A., and George S. Day. 1982. "A Guide to Consumerism." In *Consumerism: Search for the Consumer Interest,* 4th ed., ed. David A. Aaker and George S. Day, 2–20. New York: Free Press.

Abraham, Martin, and Allan Asher. 1986. "Dangerous Products: Consumer Interpol." In *Consumers, Transnational Corporations and Development,* ed. Ted Wheelwright, 263–75. Sydney, Australia: Transnational Corporations Research Project, University of Sydney.

Adams, Walter, and James W. Brock. 1987. "Why Flying Is Unpleasant." *New York Times,* 6 August, A27.

Americans for Safe and Competitive Trucking. 1987. "Trucking Safety on the Rise." *Consumers' Research* 70 (May):32.

Anthan, George. 1987. "Improved Chicken Processing Urged." *USA Today,* 13 May, 6A.

Arnould, Eric J., and Richard R. Wilk. 1984. "Why Do the Natives Wear Adidas?" *Advances in Consumer Research,* vol. 11, ed. Thomas Kinnear, 648–752. Provo, Utah: Association for Consumer Research.

Aronowitz, Stanley. 1974. *Food, Shelter and the American Dream.* New York: Seabury Press.

Arthur Young & Company. 1979. *Warranties Rules Warranty Content Analysis.* Washington, D.C.: Federal Trade Commission.

Atlantic Richfield Company. 1982. *Consumerism in the Eighties.* Los Angeles.

"Audi, Told of Sudden Accelerations, Recalls 5000s, But Will Part Help?" 1987. *Salt Lake Tribune,* 16 January, F1.

"Audi's 'Runaway' Recall Draws Swift Challenges." 1986. *Automotive News,* 2 June, 6.

Auletta, Ken. 1983. "Ralph Nader, Public Eye." *Esquire* (December):480–87.

Barksdale, Hiram C., and William R. Darden. 1972. "Consumer Attitudes toward Marketing and Consumerism." *Journal of Marketing* 36 (October): 28–35.

Barrett, Paul M. 1988. "For Many Dalkon Shield Claimants Settlement Won't End the Trauma." *Wall Street Journal,* 9 March, 27.

Belk, Russell W. 1988. "Third World Consumer Culture." In *Marketing and De-*

*velopment,* ed. Erdogan Kumcu and A. Fuat Firat. Greenwich, Conn.: JAI Press.

Belkin, Lisa. 1985. "Consumerism and Business Learn Together." *New York Times,* 13 April, 48.

"Belt-Use Laws Cut Deaths, Study Finds." 1987. *Automotive News,* 10 August, 40.

Bennett, James T., and Thomas J. DiLorenzo. 1985. *Destroying Democracy: How Government Funds Partisan Politics.* Washington, D.C.: Cato Institute.

Berger, Eric Stephen. 1988. "The FDA-Simplesse Scramble." *Wall Street Journal,* 6 February, 32.

Bergner, Douglas J. 1986. *Public Interest Profiles,* 5th ed. Washington, D.C.: Foundation for Public Affairs.

Berry, Jeffrey M. 1977. *Lobbying for the People.* Princeton: Princeton University Press.

"The Big Lie about Generic Drugs." 1987. *Consumer Reports* 52 (August):480–85.

"The Big Trouble with Air Travel." 1988. *Consumer Reports* 54 (June):362–67.

Blair, Thomas L. V. 1965. *Africa: A Market Profile.* New York: Praeger.

Bloom, Paul N. 1978. "The Cereal Companies: Monopolists or Super Marketers?" *Michigan State University Business Topics* 26 (Summer):41–49.

Bloom, Paul N., and Stephen A. Greyser. 1981. "The Maturing of Consumerism." *Harvard Business Review* 59 (November-December):130–39.

Blumer, Herbert. 1951. "Collective Behavior." In *New Outline of the Principles of Sociology,* ed. A. M. Lee, 167–222. New York: Barnes & Noble.

Boddewyn, J. J. 1985. "The Swedish Consumer Ombudsman System and Advertising Self-Regulation." *Journal of Consumer Affairs* 19 (Summer):140–162.

Boffey, Philip. 1984. "Panel Advises against Sale of Contraceptive." *New York Times,* 27 October, 8.

Bollier, David, and Joan Claybrook. 1986. *Freedom from Harm.* Washington, D.C.: Public Citizen and Democracy Project.

Bolt, John A. 1987. "Delta Denies Pulling Ads off the Air Because of On-Air Jokes." *Salt Lake Tribune,* 13 August, 7E.

Bradley, Barbara. 1987. "Consumerists in Pin Stripes Scan Goals." *Christian Science Monitor,* 2 March, 16, 18.

Brandt, William K., George S. Day, and Terry Deutscher. 1975. "Information Disclosure and Consumer Credit Knowledge: A Longitudinal Analysis." *Journal of Consumer Affairs* 9 (Summer):15–32.

Broom, Leonard, and Philip Selznick. 1975. *Essentials of Sociology.* New York: Harper and Row.

Brown, Sharon Hanes. 1987. "Capitalizing on Customer Complaints." *Sky* (March):118–22.

Buckhorn, Robert F. 1972. *Nader: The People's Lawyer.* Englewood Cliffs, N.J.: Prentice-Hall.

Burt, Dan M. 1982. *Abuse of Trust: A Report on Ralph Nader's Network.* Chicago: Regnery Gateway.

"Business Lobbying: Threat to the Consumer Interest." 1978. *Consumer Reports* 43 (September):526–31.

"Buycott . . . and Girlcott." 1985. *Building Economic Alternatives* (Summer):7.

Campbell, Colin. 1987. *The Romantic Ethic and the Spirit of Modern Consumerism.* New York: Basil Blackwell.

Cantu, Oscar R. 1980. "An Updated Regression Analysis on the Effects of the Regulation of Auto Safety." Working paper 15. New Haven, Conn.: Yale School of Management.

Caplovitz, David. 1963. *The Poor Pay More.* New York: Free Press of Glencoe.

Carson, Rachel. 1962. *The Silent Spring.* Boston: Houghton Mifflin.

Cetron, Marvin, and Thomas O'Toole. 1982. *Encounters with the Future.* New York: McGraw-Hill.

Chase, Stuart, and Frederick J. Schlink. 1927. *Your Money's Worth.* New York: Macmillan.

Clark, Peter B., and James Q. Wilson. 1961. "Incentive Systems: A Theory of Organizations." *Administrative Science Quarterly* 6 (September):129–66.

Claybrook, Joan. 1986. "White-Collar Crime." *Trial* (April):35–36.

Claybrook, Joan, and the Staff of Public Citizen. 1984. *Retreat from Safety: Reagan's Attack on America's Health.* New York: Pantheon.

Committee on Consumer Policy. 1983. *Consumer Policy during the Past Ten Years: Main Developments and Prospects.* Paris: Organisation for Economic Co-operation and Development.

———. 1986. "Consumers and Life Insurance." Draft report. Paris: Organisation for Economic Co-operation and Development.

Consumer Federation of America. 1987. *1987 Directory of State and Local Consumer Organizations.* Washington, D.C.

"Consumer Group Criticizes Ford Agreement, Contemplates Suit to Have It Overturned." 1981. *Product Safety and Liability Reporter,* 9 January, 34.

"Consumer Movement." 1986. *IOCU Newsletter,* no. 151 (March):5.

"Consumer Policy in the Netherlands." 1986. Unpublished document provided by Jan Koopman, Consumer Policy Director of the Netherlands Ministry of Economic Affairs, dated 26 June.

Consumer Product Safety Commission. 1979. "Importance of Crib Safety Activities on Injuries and Deaths Associated with Cribs." Washington, D.C.: Office of Strategic Planning.

"Consumer Training." 1986. *IOCU Newsletter,* no. 155 (July-August):6.

Consumers Union. 1984. *America at Risk.* Film. Mount Vernon, N.Y.: Consumers Union.

Cooper, Ann. 1985. "Low-Income Customers Discover Down Sides of Phone, Banking Deregulation." *National Journal,* 26 January, 204–5.

Cowan, Ruth Schwartz. 1983. *More Work for Mother.* New York: Basic Books.

Crandall, Robert W., Howard K. Gruenspecht, Theodore E. Keeler, and Lester

B. Lave. 1986. *Regulating the Automobile.* Washington, D.C.: Brookings Institution.

Creighton, Lucy Black. 1976. *Pretenders to the Throne.* Lexington, Mass.: D. C. Heath.

Dardis, Rachel, Susan Aaronson, and Ying-Nan Lin. 1978. "Cost Benefit Analysis of Flammability Standards." *American Journal of Agricultural Economics* 60 (November):695–700.

Day, George S., and William K. Brandt. 1973. *A Study of Consumer Credit Decisions: Implication for Present and Prospective Legislation.* National Commission on Consumer Finance, Report no. 2. Washington, D.C.: U.S. Government Printing Office.

———. 1974. "Consumer Research and the Evaluation of Information Disclosure Requirements: The Case of Truth in Lending." *Journal of Consumer Research* 1 (June):21–32.

Delaney, Robert V. 1987. "Saving on Trucking Costs." *Consumers' Research* 70 (May):31–33.

Denman, Scott, and Ken Bossong. 1979. "Big Business and Renewable Energy Sources." In *Solar Compendium,* vol. 2, ed. Ken Bossong, 3–25. Washington, D.C.: Citizens' Energy Project.

Department of Textiles and Consumer Economics, University of Maryland. 1978. *Cost-Benefit Analysis of Consumer Product Safety Programs.* Final report to the National Science Foundation's Advanced Productivity Research and Technology Division. Washington, D.C.: National Technical Information Service, February.

De Toledano, Ralph. 1975. *Hit and Run.* New Rochelle, N.Y.: Arlington House.

Diamond, S. J. 1985. "Consumer Groups Push Banks Back to 'Basics.'" *Los Angeles Times,* 19 August, sec. IV, 1.

Dowie, Mark. 1977. "Pinto Madness." *Mother Jones* 2 (September/October):18–23.

———. 1979. "The Corporate Crime of the Century." *Mother Jones* 4 (November):22–25, 37, 38, 49.

Downs, Anthony. 1972. "Up and Down with Ecology—The 'Issue-Attention Cycle.'" *Public Interest* 28 (Summer):38–50.

Drucker, Peter. 1969. "Consumerism: The Opportunity of Marketing." Address before the Marketing Committee of the National Association of Manufacturers, 10 April. Reprinted. *Consumerism: Viewpoints from Business, Government, and the Public Interest,* ed. Ralph M. Gaedeke, and Warren W. Etcheson, 252–58. San Francisco: Canfield Press.

Easterbrook, Gregg. 1986. "Saint Ralph's New Crusade." *Best of Business Quarterly* 8 (Winter):9–15.

Easterlin, Richard. 1987. *Birth and Fortune,* 2 ed. Chicago: University of Chicago Press.

Edwards, Audrey. 1977. "Consumer Movement Grew Out of 'Rights' Activism." *Supermarket News* 24 October, sec. 2, 12–3,44–45.

Ellis, Clyde T. 1982. "The Triumph of Rural Electric Cooperatives." In *Consumer Activists: They Made a Difference,* ed. Erma Angevine, 55–81. Mount Vernon, N.Y.: Consumers Union Foundation.

Emshwiller, John R., and Charles B. Camp. 1988. "On and on Grinds Fight over Old Fords that Slip into Reverse." *Wall Street Journal,* 14 April, 1, 18.

Engelmayer, Sheldon, and Robert Wagman. 1985. *Lord's Justice.* New York: Anchor Books/Doubleday.

*European Marketing Data and Statistics 1985.* 1985. London: Euromonitor Publications.

"Ewa Letowska, the East Block's First Government Ombudsman." 1988. *International Herald Tribune,* 8 January, 5.

"Exporting Hazardous Products." 1984. *Consumer Reports* 49 (February):104–5.

Fazal, Anwar. 1984. "Managing the Impact of Technology on Human Welfare." Address at the World Congress of the International Federation of Home Economy, Oslo, 22–27 July.

*Federal Register.* 1973. "Baby Cribs: Proposed Classification as Banned Hazardous Substance." Vol. 38, no. 71, Friday, 13 April, 9312–13.

———. 1984. "Federal Motor Vehicle Safety Standard; Occupant Crash Protection." Vol. 49, no. 138, Tuesday, 17 July, 28993—94.

Feldman, Laurence P. 1976. *Consumer Protection: Problems and Prospects.* St. Paul, Minn.: West Publishing.

———. 1980. *Consumer Protection: Problems and Prospects,* 2d ed. St. Paul, Minn.: West Publishing.

Fichter, George. 1986. "Birth of a Notion." *United Airlines Magazine* (October):87–96.

Foppiano, Elaine, and Randall Pozdena. 1983. "Three for the Economists." *Federal Reserve Board of San Francisco Weekly Letter,* 6 May, 3.

Forbes, J. D. 1985. "Organizational and Political Dimensions of Consumer Pressure Groups." *Journal of Consumer Policy* 8 (June):105–31.

———. 1987. *The Consumer Interest: Dimensions and Policy Implications.* London: Croom Helm.

"Ford Lists $1.2 Billion in Lawsuits." 1986. *Salt Lake Tribune,* 12 May, D1.

Fornell, Claus. 1978. "The Corporate Consumer Affairs Function—A Communication Perspective." *Journal of Consumer Policy* 2 (December):289–302.

Foss, Daniel A., and Ralph Larkin. 1986. *Beyond Revolution: A New Theory of Social Movements.* South Hadley, Mass.: Bergin and Garvey.

Fox, Stephen. 1984. *The Mirror Makers.* New York: William Morrow.

Friedman, Milton, and Rose Friedman. 1979. *Free to Choose.* New York: Harcourt Brace Jovanovich.

Friedman, Monroe. 1972. "Consumer Responses to Unit Pricing, Open Dating and Nutrient Labeling." In *Proceedings of the Association for Consumer Research,* ed. M. Venkatesan, 361–69. Chicago: Association for Consumer Research.

————. 1985. "Consumer Boycotts in the United States, 1970–1980: Contemporary Events in Historical Perspective." *Journal of Consumer Affairs* 19 (Summer):96–117.

"Fruit, Fish, and Gamma Rays." 1986. *New York Times,* 24 September, A30.

"FTC Votes to Amend Food Store Advertising Rule." 1988. *FTC News Notes* 88 (2 May):1

Galbraith, John Kenneth. 1958. *The Affluent Society.* Boston: Houghton Mifflin.

Gallup, George H. 1972. *The Gallup Poll: Public Opinion 1935–1971.* Vol. 3, *1959–1973.* New York: Random House.

————. 1978. *The Gallup Poll: Public Opinion 1972–1977.* Vol. 1, *1972–1975.* Wilmington, Del.: Scholarly Resources.

Gamson, William. 1975. *The Strategy of Social Protest.* Homewood, Ill.: Dorsey.

Garrett, Dennis E. 1987. "The Effectiveness of Marketing Policy Boycotts: Environmental Opposition to Marketing." *Journal of Marketing* 51 (April):46–57.

Garson, Barbara. 1977. "The Bottle Baby Scandal." *Mother Jones* 11 (December):32–40, 60–62.

Gaschott, Nancy. 1986. "Babies at Risk: Infant Formula Still Takes Its Toll." *Multinational Monitor* (October):11–13.

Gerlach, L., and V. Hine. 1970. *People, Power, Change.* Indianapolis: Bobbs-Merrill.

Glen, Maxwell. 1985. "The Latest Chapter in the Home Audio Taping Battle Unfolds in Congress." *National Journal,* 2 November, 2483–86.

Gold, Philip. 1987. *Advertising, Politics and American Culture.* New York: Paragon House.

Gorey, Hays. 1975. *Nader and the Power of Everyman.* New York: Grosset & Dunlap.

Graver, Kjersti. 1986. "A Study of the Consumer Ombudsman Institution in Norway with Some References to the Other Nordic Countries, I: Background and Description." *Journal of Consumer Policy* 9 (March):1–24.

Green, Mark. 1977. "Overview: The Disappointing 95th Congress." in *Public Citizen Congressional Voting Index.* Washington, D.C.: Public Citizen Congress Watch, 3, 4, 23.

————. 1978. "Who Killed the Consumer Protection Agency?" *Newsday,* 16 February, 73.

————. 1980. "The Case for Corporate Democracy." *Regulation* 4 (May-June):20–25.

Green, Mark, and John S. Berry. 1985a. *The Challenge of Hidden Profits.* New York: William Morrow.

————. 1985b. "White-Collar Crime Is Big Business." *Nation,* 8 June, 697, 704–7.

Green, Mark, and Ralph Nader. 1973. "Economic Regulation vs. Competition: Uncle Sam, the Monopoly Man." *Yale Law Journal* 82 (April):871–89.

Green, Mark, and Norman Waitzman. 1979. *Business War on the Law: An Analysis of the Benefits of Federal Health/Safety Enforcement.* Washington, D.C.: Corporate Accountability Research Group.

———. 1980. "Cost, Benefit, and Class." *Working Papers for a New Society* 7 (May–June):39–51.

Griffin, Kelley. 1987. *More Action for a Change.* New York: Dembner Books.

Gross, Susan. 1975. "The Nader Network." *Business and Society Review* 13 (Spring):5–15.

Haddon, William, Jr. 1970. Testimony given before the Senate Subcommittee on Antitrust and Monopoly, 17 March. In *The Consumer and Corporate Accountability,* ed. Ralph Nader. New York: Harcourt Brace Jovanovich, 1973, 159–64.

Hammer, Willie. 1980. *Product Safety Management and Engineering.* Englewood Cliffs, N.J.: Prentice-Hall.

Handler, Joel F. 1978. *Social Movements and the Legal System.* New York: Academic Press.

Harland, David. 1987. "The United Nations Guidelines for Consumer Protection." *Journal of Consumer Policy* 10 (September):245–66.

"Health Care: The Next Great Consumer Issue." 1984. *NCL Bulletin* 46 (November):1, 8.

Henderson, David. 1985. "The Economics of Fuel Economy Standards." *Regulation* 9 (January-February):45–48.

Henderson, Keith. 1986. "Drugs in Meat: Views on Congressional Findings." *Christian Science Monitor,* 27 January, 25–26.

Herrmann, Robert O. 1970a. "The Consumer Movement in Historical Perspective." Paper no. 88, Department of Agricultural Economics and Rural Sociology. Pennsylvania State University, February.

———. 1970b. "Consumerism: Its Goals, Organizations and Future." *Journal of Marketing* 34 (October):55–60.

———. 1980. "Consumer Protection: Yesterday, Today, and Tomorrow." *Current History* 78 (May):193–96, 226–27.

Herrmann, Robert O., Edward J. Walsh, and Rex H. Warland. 1988. "The Organizations of the Consumer Movement: A Comparative Perspective." In *The Frontier of Research in the Consumer Interest,* ed. E. Scott Maynes, 469–94. Columbia, Mo.: American Council on Consumer Interests.

Herrmann, Robert O., and Rex H. Warland. 1976. "Nader's Support: Its Sources and Concerns." *Journal of Consumer Affairs* 10 (Summer):1–18.

"Hertz's Reparations May Fall Short." 1988. *Wall Street Journal,* 19 February, 17.

Hills, Stuart L., ed. 1987. *Corporate Violence: Injury and Death for Profit.* Totawa, N.J.: Rowman and Littlefield.

Holsworth, Robert. 1980. *Public Interest Liberalism and the Crisis of Affluence.* Boston: G.K. Hall & Co.

"Home Shopping Services." 1987. Internal document of the Council of Better Business Bureaus, Arlington, Va., December.

Hornsby-Smith, Michael P. 1986. "The Structural Weaknesses of the Consumer Movement." *Journal of Consumer Studies and Home Economics* 9 (September):291–306.

Horowitz, Daniel. 1985. *The Morality of Spending.* Baltimore: Johns Hopkins Press.

Howe, David R. 1978. "An Evaluation of the Effectiveness of Child-Resistant Packaging." Washington, D.C. U.S. Consumer Product Safety Commission Office of Strategic Planning, 1 April.

Hughes, Kathleen. 1983. *Return to the Jungle.* Washington, D.C.: Center for the Study of Responsive Law.

Hunter, J. Robert. 1986. "No Demonstration of Need to Impose Liability Judgment Caps." *At Home with Consumers* 7 (June):3, 6.

Ignatius, David. 1976. "Stages of Nader." *New York Times Magazine,* 18 January. 8–9, 44–45, 51–52, 54.

*IOCU Annual Report 1985.* 1986. The Hague, Holland: International Organization of Consumers Unions.

James, Jeffrey, and Frances Stewart. 1981. "New Products: A Discussion of the Welfare Effects of the Introduction of New Products in Developing Countries." *Oxford Economic Papers,* 33 (March):81–107.

Janssen, Wallace F. 1981. "The Story of the Laws behind the Labels." *FDA Consumer* 15 (June):32–45.

Jenkins, J. Craig. 1983. "Resource Mobilization Theory and the Study of Social Movements." *Annual Review of Sociology* 9:527–53.

Johansson, J. K. 1976. "The Theory and Practice of Swedish Consumer Policy." *Journal of Consumer Affairs* 10 (Summer):19–32.

Joksch, H. C. 1976. "Critique of Sam Peltzman's Study." *Accident Analysis and Prevention* 8 (June):131.

Jondrow, J. M. 1972. "A Measure of the Monetary Benefits and Costs to Consumers of the Regulation of Prescription Drug Effectiveness." Ph.D. diss., University of Wisconsin.

Jones, Randall S. 1987. "The U.S.-Japan Economic Problem." *Economic Outlook USA* (Summer):7–10.

Kahn, Alfred E. 1988. "Surprises of Airline Deregulation." *American Economic Review* 78 (May):316–22.

Karpatkin, Rhoda H. 1986. "Changing Issues, Changing Agendas: Winning for the Consumer in the Next 50 Years." In *Proceedings of the 32nd Annual Conference,* ed. Karen P. Schnittgrund, 1–7. Columbia, Mo.: American Council on Consumer Interests.

Karr, Albert R. 1982. "U.S. Move to Scrap Air Bags in New Cars Is Overturned by a Federal Appeals Court." *Wall Street Journal* 2 June, 2.

Kaufman, Joel, Linda Rabinowitz-Dagi, Joan Levin, Phyllis McCarthy, Sidney Wolfe, Eve Bargmann, and Public Citizen Health Research Group. 1983. *Over the Counter Pills that Don't Work.* Washington, D.C.: Public Citizen Health Research Group.

Kilman, Scott. 1987. "An Unexpected Result of Airline Decontrol Is Return to Monopolies." *Wall Street Journal,* 20 July, 1.

Klein, Joe. 1975. "Ralph Nader: The Man in the Class Action Suit." *Rolling Stone,* 20 November, 54–60.

Knauer, Virginia H. 1970. "Federal Role in Consumer Affairs." In *Consumerism: Viewpoint from Business, Government, and the Public Interest,* ed. Ralph M. Gaedeke and Warren W. Etcheson, 227–33. San Francisco: Canfield Press.

Kohn, Alfie. 1984. "Citizen Utility Boards: People Power vs. Power Companies." *Nation,* 29 December, 710–12.

Lafayette, Jon. 1987. "Upbeat for 1988." *Advertising Age,* 14 December, 3.

Lampman, Robert J. 1988. "JFK's Four Consumer Rights: A Retrospective View." In *The Frontier of Research in the Consumer Interest,* ed. E. Scott Maynes, 19–33. Columbia, Mo.: American Council on Consumer Interests.

Lane, Sylvia. 1983. "The Rationale for Government Intervention in Seller-Consumer Relationships." *Policy Studies Review* 2 (February):419–28.

Langway, Lynn. 1983. "Showdown on Smoking." *Newsweek,* 6 June, 60–67.

Lauterbach, Albert. 1972. "The Social Setting of Consumer Behavior in Latin America." In *Human Behavior in Economic Affairs: Essays in Honor of George Katona,* ed. Burkhard Strumpel, James N. Morgan, and Ernest Zahn, 261–85. San Francisco: Jossey-Bass.

Lee, Stewart M., and Mel J. Zelenak. 1982. *Economics for Consumers.* Belmont, Calif.: Wadsworth.

Lenahan, R. J., J. A. Thomas, D. A. Taylor, D. L. Call, and D. I. Padberg. 1973. "Consumer Reaction to Nutritional Labels on Food Products." *Journal of Consumer Affairs* 7 (Summer):1–12.

Lenard, Thomas M., and Michael P. Mazur. 1985. "Harvest of Waste: The Marketing Order Program." *Regulation* 9 (May-June):19–26.

Leuchtenburg, William E. 1973. *A Troubled Feast.* Boston: Little, Brown.

Levy, Frank. 1987. *Dollars and Dreams.* New York: Russell Sage Foundation.

Lewin, Tamar. 1987. "Drug Makers Fighting Back against Advance of Generics." *New York Times,* 28 July, A1.

Lower, A. K., A. Averyt, and D. Greenberg. 1983. "On the Safe Track: Deaths and Injuries before and after the Consumer Product Safety Commission." Unpublished report. Washington, D.C.: Consumer Federation of America.

Lowrance, William W. 1976. *Of Acceptable Risk.* Los Altos, Calif.: William Kaufmann.

Lydenberg, Steven D., Alice Tepper Marlin, Sean O'Brien Strub, and the Council on Economic Priorities. 1986. *Rating America's Corporate Conscience.* Reading, Mass.: Addison-Wesley.

Magnuson, Warren G. 1972. "Consumerism and the Emerging Goals of a New Society." In *Consumerism: Viewpoints from Business, Government, and the Public Interest,* ed. Ralph M. Gaedeke and Warren W. Etcheson, 3–7. San Francisco: Canfield Press.

*Major Appliance Industry Facts Book.* 1987. Chicago: Association of Home Appliance Manufacturers.

Malech, Arlene. 1987. "The Changing Complaint Handling Environment: Implications for the Consumer." In *Proceedings of the 33rd Annual Conference,* ed. Vickie Hampton, 1–7. Columbia, Mo.: American Council on Consumer Interests.

Marchand, Roland. 1985. *Advertising the American Dream.* Berkeley, Calif.: University of California Press.

MasterCard International. 1987. Cited in "Harper's Index." *Harper's,* March, 15.

Mayer, Robert N. 1976. "The Socially Conscious Consumer—Another Look at the Data." *Journal of Consumer Research* 3 (September):113–15.

———. 1981. "Consumerism in the 70s: The Emergence of New Issues." *Journal of Consumer Affairs* 15 (Winter):375–91.

———. 1984. "The Consumer Politics of Trade Restrictions: The Case of Domestic Content Requirements." *Journal of Consumer Affairs* 18 (Winter):343–54.

———. 1988. "The Growth of the French Videotex System and Its Implications for Consumers." *Journal of Consumer Policy* 11 (March):55–83.

Mayer, Robert N., and Debra L. Scammon. 1983. "Intervenor Funding at the FTC: Biopsy or Autopsy." *Policy Studies Review* 2 (February): 506–15.

Maynes, E. Scott. 1976. *Decision-Making for Consumers.* New York: Macmillan.

———. 1979. "Consumer Protection: The Issues." *Journal of Consumer Policy* 3 (Spring):97–109.

McCarthy, John D., and Mayer N. Zald. 1973. *The Trend of Social Movements in America: Professionalization and Resource Mobilization.* Morristown, N.J.: General Learning Press.

———. 1977. "Resource Mobilization and Social Movements: A Partial Theory." *American Journal of Sociology* 82 (May):1212–41.

McCraw, Thomas. 1984. *Prophets of Regulation.* Cambridge, Mass.: Harvard University Press.

McElroy, Bruce F., and David A. Aaker. 1979. "Unit Pricing Six Years after Introduction." *Journal of Retailing* 55 (Fall):44–56.

McGinley, Laurie. 1987a. "Airline Anti-Smoking Drive Gains but Still Faces Strong Opposition." *Wall Street Journal,* 7 August, 25.

———. 1987b. "Bad Air Service Prompts Call for Changes." *Wall Street Journal,* 9 November, 27.

McGinley, Laurie, and Jonathan Dahl. 1987. "Delay Data: Airlines' Figures Hold Surprises—and Spark Controversy," *Wall Street Journal,* 11 November, 27.

McGuire, Thomas. 1975. "An Evaluation of Consumer Protection Legislation: The 1962 Amendments: A Comment." *Journal of Political Economy* 83 (September-October):655–61.

McKenzie, Richard B. 1978. *Caution: Consumer Protection May Be Hazardous to Your Health.* Los Angeles: International Institute for Economic Research.

McKenzie, Richard B., and William F. Shugart. 1987. "Deregulation and Air Travel Safety." *Regulation* 11 (December):42–47.

McKenzie, Richard B., and Gordon Tullock. 1978. *Political Economy: An Introduction to Economics.* New York: McGraw-Hill.

Metzenbaum, Howard M. 1986. "Is Government Protecting Consumers?" *Trial,* (April, 22–27.

Miller, Annetta. 1987. "A Sizzling Food Fight." *Newsweek,* 20 April, 56.

Minkin, Stephen. 1981. "This Is Science?" *Mother Jones* 6 (November): 34–39, 50, 54.

Mintz, Morton. 1985. *At Any Cost.* New York: Pantheon.

Mintz, Morton, and Jerry S. Cohen. 1971. *America, Inc.* New York: Dial Press.
———. 1976. *Power, Inc.* New York: Viking.

Mitchell, Robert Cameron. 1985. "Consumerism and Environmentalism in the 1980s: Competitive or Companionable Social Movements?" In *The Future of Consumerism,* ed. Paul N. Bloom and Ruth Belk Smith, 23–36. Lexington, Mass.: Lexington Books.

Mitford, Jessica. 1963. *The American Way of Death.* New York: Simon and Schuster.

Molitor, Graham T. T. 1979. "Swedish Tobacco Controls—Precedent Setting 'Negative Marketing' Approach." In *Critical Food Issues of the Eighties,* ed. Marilyn Chon and David P. Harmon, 80–90. Elmsford, N.Y.: Pergamon Press.

"Monopoly on the Cereal Shelves?" 1981. *Consumer Reports* 46 (February):76–80.

Moriarty, Erin. 1987. "Lessons of a Consumer Reporter." Address at the 33rd Annual Conference of the American Council of Consumer Interests, Chicago, 3 April.

Morrison, Steven, and Clifford Winston. 1986. *The Economic Effects of Airline Deregulation.* Washington, D.C.: Brookings Institution.
———. 1988. "Air Safety, Deregulation, and Public Policy." *Brookings Review* 6 (Winter):10–15.

Morse, Richard L. D. 1981. "The Consumer Movement: A Middle Class Movement." In *Proceedings of the 27th Annual Conference,* ed. Carol B. Meeks, 160–64. Columbia, Mo.: American Council on Consumer Interests.

Moynihan, Daniel P. 1987. *Family and Nation.* San Diego: Harcourt Brace Jovanovich.

"Mr. Nader's New Year's Wish." 1974. *Wall Street Journal,* 10 April, 16.

Nadel, Mark V. 1971. *The Politics of Consumer Protection.* Indianapolis: Bobbs-Merrill.

Nader, Ralph. 1965. *Unsafe at Any Speed.* New York: Grossman.

———. 1971. "A Citizen's Guide to the American Economy." *New York Review of Books,* 2 September, 14–18.

———. 1980. "Corporate Power in America." *Nation,* 29 March, 365–67.

———. 1984. "The Consumer Movement Looks Ahead." In *Beyond Reagan,* ed. Alan Gartner, Colin Greer, and Frank Riessman, 271–85. New York: Harper and Row.

———, ed. 1973. *The Consumer and Corporate Accountability.* New York: Harcourt Brace Jovanovich.

Nader, Ralph, Mark Green, and Joel Seligman. 1976. *Taming the Giant Corporation.* New York: Norton.

Nader, Ralph, and William Taylor. 1986. *The Big Boys.* New York: Pantheon.

National Safety Council. 1986. *Accident Facts—1986 Edition. Chicago: National Safety Council.*

Negin, Elliott. 1985. "Esther Peterson: The Grande Dame of Consumerism." *Public Citizen* 5 (Winter):17–21.

"Nestlé Audit Confirms Boycotters' Charges." 1983. *Nutrition Action,* October, 4.

"New-Product Debuts Reach Record Levels, Creating Market Pressures." 1987. *Wall Street Journal,* 11 June, 1.

Nickel, Herman. 1980. "The Corporation Haters." *Fortune,* 16 June, 126–36.

Nicks, Stephen J. 1986. "Lemon Laws in the United States: More Hype than Help." *Journal of Consumer Policy* 6 (March):79–90.

O'Donnell, Thomas C., Elizabeth Weiner, Hazel Bradford, Amy Borrus, and Dorinda Elliott. 1985. "The Counterfeit Trade." *Business Week,* 16 December, 48–53.

Okun, Arthur M. 1975. *Equality and Efficiency.* Washington, D.C.: Brookings Institution.

Okun, Mitchell. 1986. *Fair Play in the Marketplace: The First Battle for Pure Food and Drugs.* DeKalb: Northern Illinois University Press.

Ölander, Folke, and A. Lindhoff. 1974. "Consumer Action Research: A Review of the Consumerism Literature and Suggestions for New Directions in Theoretical and Empirical Research." International Institute of Management, Reprint ser. I/74–56, November.

Olson, Mancur, Jr. 1965. *The Logic of Collective Action.* Cambridge, Mass.: Harvard University Press.

Owen, David. 1987. "Octane and Knock." *Atlantic,* 2 August, 53–60.

Packard, Vance. 1957. *The Hidden Persuaders.* New York: David McKay.

"Panel Probing Substitute for the Pill." 1983. *Salt Lake Tribune,* 10 January, 4A.

"PC's Greatest Hits." 1986. *Public Citizen* 7 (October):25.

Peltzman, Sam. 1973. "An Evaluation of Consumer Protection Legislation: The 1962 Drug Amendments." *Journal of Political Economy* 81 (September-October):1049–91.

———. 1974. *Regulation of Pharmaceutical Innovation: The 1962 Amendments.*

Washington, D.C.: American Enterprise Institute for Public Policy Research.

———. 1975a. *Regulation of Automobile Safety.* Washington, D.C.: American Enterprise Institute for Public Policy Research.

———. 1975b. "The Effects of Automobile Safety Regulation." *Journal of Political Economy* 83 (August):677–725.

Peng, Khor Kok. 1980. "Value for People: The Potential Role of a Consumer Movement in the Third World." Reprinted. *Consumer Policy 2000: Background Reader,* 11–16. The Hague, Holland: International Organization of Consumers Unions.

Perry, Susan. 1982. "Cigarette Ads: Subtle Pressures." *Deseret News,* 26 July, 10.

Perry, Susan, and Jim Dawson. 1985. *Nightmare: Women and the Dalkon Shield.* New York: Macmillan.

Pertschuk, Michael. 1982. *Revolt against Regulation.* Berkeley: University of California Press.

———. 1986. *Giant Killers.* New York: W. W. Norton.

"Pesticide Problems Mount." 1988. *Shopper Report* 8 (February):2

"Pesticide Regulation." 1987. Letter in *Public Citizen,* January, 2.

Peterson, Esther. 1985. "International Consumer Guidelines." In *The Proceedings of the 31st Annual Conference,* ed. Karen P. Schnittgrund, 305–9. Columbia, Mo.: American Council on Consumer Interests.

———. 1987. "The Case against 'The Case against the UN Guidelines for Consumer Protection.'" *Journal of Consumer Policy* 10 (December):433–39.

Phillips, Lynn W., and Bobby J. Calder. 1979. "Evaluating Consumer Protection Programs: Part I. Weak but Commonly Used Research Designs." *Journal of Consumer Affairs* 13 (Winter):157–85.

———. 1980. "Evaluating Consumer Protection Programs: Part II. Promising Methods." *Journal of Consumer Affairs* 14 (Summer):9–36.

Pope, Daniel. 1983. *The Making of Modern Advertising.* New York: Basic Books.

Post, James E., and Edward Baer. 1978. "Demarketing Infant Formula: Consumer Products in the Developing World." *Journal of Contemporary Business* 7 (Autumn):17–35.

Prentice, Derek. 1978. "Local Advice for Consumers." In *Marketing and the Consumer Movement,* ed. Jeremy Mitchell, 61–71. London: McGraw-Hill.

Preston, Ivan L. 1975. *The Great American Blow-Up.* Madison: University of Wisconsin Press.

Purcell, Theodore V. 1979. "Management and the 'Ethical' Investors." *Harvard Business Review* 57 (September-October):24–44.

Rauber, Paul. 1986. "With Friends Like These." *Mother Jones,* November, 35–37, 47–49.

Reich, Norbert. 1986. "Product Safety and Product Liability," *Journal of Consumer Policy* 9 (June):133-154.

Reich, Robert B. 1987. *Tales of a New America.* New York: Random House.

"Report Urges FDA to Set Safety Limits for Fish Contaminants." 1987. *Food Chemical News,* 29 June, 19–21.

Ringle, Ken. 1984. "Lone Ranger: Public Interest Lawyer John Banzhaf Takes on Other People's Fights." *Washington Post,* 15 May, B1, B4.

Ripley, Randall B., and Grace A. Franklin. 1984. *Congress, the Bureaucracy, and Public Policy,* 3d ed. Homewood, Ill.: Dorsey Press.

Robertson, Leon S. 1977. "A Critical Analysis of Peltzman's 'The Effects of Automobile Safety Regulation.'" *Journal of Economic Issues* 11 (September):587–600.

Robertson, Thomas S., and John R. Rossiter. 1974. "Children and Commercial Persuasion: An Attribution Theory Analysis." *Journal of Consumer Research* 1 (June):13–20.

Roethlisberger, Fritz J., and William J. Dickson. 1939. *Management and the Worker.* Cambridge, Mass.: Harvard University Press.

Rose, Lawrence E. 1981. "The Role of Interest Groups in Collective Interest Policy-Making: Consumer Protection in Norway and the United States." *European Journal of Political Research* 9 (March):17–45.

Ross, Edward A. 1907. *Sin and Society: An Analysis of Latter-Day Iniquity.* New York: Harper Torchbooks ed., 1973.

Rossiter, Clinton. 1962. *Conservatism in America,* 2d. ed. New York: Vintage Books.

Rowe, Jonathan. 1985. "Ralph Nader Reconsidered." *Washington Monthly* 17 (March):12–21.

Sachs, Carolyn, Dorothy Blair, and Carolyn Richter. 1987. "Consumer Pesticide Concerns." *Journal of Consumer Affairs* 21 (Summer):96–107.

Sale, Kirkpatrick. 1986. "The Forest for the Trees." *Mother Jones* 11 (November): 25–33, 58.

Salisbury, Robert H. 1969. "An Exchange Theory of Interest Groups." *Midwest Journal of Political Science* 13 (February):1–32.

Sanford, David. 1976. *Me & Ralph.* Washington, D.C.: New Republic Book.

Sapolsky, Harvey. 1986. "The Changing Politics of Cigarette Smoking." In *Consuming Fears: The Politics of Product Risks,* ed. Harvey M. Sapolsky, 19–39. New York: Basic Books.

Scammon, Debra L., and Richard J. Semenik. 1982. "Corrective Advertising: Evolution of the Legal Theory and Application of the Remedy." *Journal of Advertising* 11, no.1:10–20.

Scanlon, Paul D. 1970. "Oligopoly and 'Deceptive' Advertising: The Cereal Industry Affair." *Antitrust Law and Economics Review* 3 (Spring):99–110.

Scardino, Vincent A., James C. Birch, and Kathy Vitale. 1976. *Impact of the FEA/EPA Fuel Economy Information Program.* Report prepared for the Federal Energy Administration's Office of Conservation and Environment. Cambridge, Mass.: Abt Associates.

Schlesinger, Arthur M., Jr. 1986. *The Cycles of American History.* Boston: Houghton Mifflin.

Schmitt, Jacqueline, Lawrence Kanter and Rachel Miller. 1979. *Impact of the Magnuson-Moss Warrant Act: A Comparison of 40 Major Consumer Product Warranties from before and after the Act.* Staff Report to the Federal Trade Commission, Washington, D.C., June.

Schorr, Burt, and Christopher Conte. 1984. "Coming of Age: Public-Interest Groups Achieve Higher Status and Some Permanence." *Wall Street Journal* 27 August 1, 9.

Schwartz, George. 1979. "The Successful Fight against a Federal Consumer Protection Agency." *MSU Business Topics* 27 (Summer):45–57.

Schwieterman, Joseph P. 1985. "Fare Is Fair in Airline Deregulation." *Regulation* 9 (July-August):32–38.

Segal, Mark J. 1986. "The Politics of Salt: The Sodium-Hypertension Issue." In *Consuming Fears,* ed. Harvey M. Sapolsky, 80–115. New York: Basic Books.

"Senate Passes Consumer Banking Legislation." 1988. *CFA News,* April, 1.

Senauer, Ben, Jean Kinsey, and Terry Roe. 1984. "The Cost of Inaccurate Consumer Information: The Case of the EPA Mileage Figures." *Journal of Consumer Affairs* 18 (Winter):193–212.

Sentry Insurance. 1977. *Consumerism at the Crossroads.* Study conducted by Louis Harris and Associates, and Management Science Institute.

Shabecoff, Philip. 1987. "Pesticides Called Manageable Evil." *New York Times,* 1 May, A24.

Shapiro, Stanley J. 1986. "Home as an Electronic Marketplace: The Consumer Protection and Public Policy Issues." *Journal of Public Policy & Marketing* 5:212–26.

Shephard, Thomas R., Jr. 1971. "Hello Consumerism, Goodbye America." Address at the Spring Marketing Conference of the National Association of Manufacturers, New York, 8 April.

Shodell, Michael. 1985. "Risky Business." *Science 85* 6 (October):43–47.

Silber, Norman I. 1983. *Test and Protest.* New York: Holmes & Meier.

Sim, Foo Gaik. 1985. "Being Sold Short." *New Internationalist,* May, 7–8.

Simmons, Henry L. 1973. "Competitive Problems in the Drug Industry." Statement before the U.S. Subcommittee on Monopoly of the Select Committee on Small Business, 93d Cong., 1st sess., February, pt. 23, 9372.

Sinclair, Upton. 1906. *The Jungle.* New York: Doubleday Page.

Slovic, Paul, Baruch Fischhoff, and Sarah Lichtenstein. 1979. "Rating the Risks." *Environment* 21 (April):14–20.

———. 1982. "Facts versus Fears: Understanding Perceived Risk." In *Judgment under Uncertainty: Heuristics and Biases,* ed. Daniel Kahneman, Paul Slovic, and Amos Tversky, 463–89. Cambridge: Cambridge University Press.

Smith, Betty F., and Rachel Dardis. 1977. "Cost-Benefit Analysis of Consumer Product Safety Standards." *Journal of Consumer Affairs* 11 (Summer):34–46.

Smith, Darlene Brannigan, and Paul N. Bloom. 1986. "Is Consumerism Dead or Alive? Some Empirical Evidence." In *The Future of Consumerism,* ed. Paul N. Bloom and Ruth Belk Smith, 61–74. Lexington, Mass.: Lexington Books.

"Smoking." 1986. *IOCU Newsletter,* no. 150 (February):7.

Snow, Arthur, and Burton A. Weisbrod. 1982. "Consumer Interest Litigation: A Case Study of *Nader v. Allegheny Airlines." Journal of Consumer Affairs* 16 (Summer):1–22.

Spano, Anthony T. 1987. "Sowing Confusion." *Best's Review* 88 (July):51.

Stampfl, Ronald W. 1979. "Multidisciplinary Foundations for a Consumer Code of Ethics." In *Proceedings of the 25th Annual Meetings,* 12–20. Columbia, Mo.: American Council on Consumer Interests.

"State and Foreign Consumer Action." 1986. *ACCI Newsletter* 34 (November):2.

Stein, Karen. 1979. "A Political History of the Proposal to Create a Federal Consumer Protection Agency." In *Proceedings of the 25th Annual Meetings,* 126–31. Columbia, Mo.: American Council on Consumer Interests.

Stewart, Charles J., Craig Allen Smith, and Robert E. Denton, Jr. 1984. *Persuasion and Social Movements.* Prospect Heights, Ill.: Waveland Press.

Stigler, George. 1961. "The Economics of Information," *Journal of Political Economy* 69 (June):213–25.

Stone, Christopher D. 1976. "Public Directors Merit a Try." *Harvard Business Review* 54 (March-April):20–34, 156.

Sun, Marjorie. 1982. "Depo-Provera Debate Revs up at FDA." *Science* 217 (July):424–28.

Swagler, Roger. 1979. *Consumers and the Market,* 2d ed. Lexington, Mass.: D. C. Heath.

Technical Assistance Research Program, Inc. (TARP). 1979. *Consumer Complaint Handling in America: Final Report.* Washington, D.C.: U.S. Office of Consumer Affairs.

———. 1983. *The Bottom Line Benefits of Consumer Education: A Preliminary Exploratory Study Conducted for the Industry and Consumer Affairs Department of Coca Cola USA.* Atlanta, Ga.: The Coca-Cola Company.

Thelen, David P. 1983. "Patterns of Consumer Consciousness in the Progressive Movement: Robert M. La Follette, the Antitrust Persuasion, and Labor Legislation." In *The Quest for Social Justice,* ed. Ralph M. Aderman, 19–47. Madison: University of Wisconsin Press.

Thorelli, Hans B. 1982. "Consumer Policy for the Third World." *Journal of Consumer Policy* 5 (Summer):197–211.

———. 1983. "Consumer Policy in Developing Countries." In *Proceedings of 29th Annual Meetings,* ed. Karen P. Goebel, 147–53. Columbia, Mo.: American Council on Consumer Interests.

Thorelli, Hans B., Helmut Becker, and Jack Engledow. 1975. *The Information Seekers.* Cambridge, Mass.: Ballinger.

Thorelli, Hans B., and G. D. Sentell. 1982. *Consumer Emancipation and Economic Development: The Case of Thailand.* Greenwich, Conn.: JAI Press.

Thorelli, Hans B., and Sarah V. Thorelli. 1974. *Consumer Information Handbook: Europe and North America.* New York: Praeger.

―――. 1977. *Consumer Information Systems and Consumer Policy.* Cambridge, Mass.: Ballinger.

Tolchin, Susan J., and Martin Tolchin. 1983. *Dismantling America: The Rush to Deregulate.* Boston: Houghton Mifflin.

"TPA: Tip of the Iceberg." 1987. *Wall Street Journal,* 2 December, 26.

"Two Guilty in Sale of Fake Apple Juice." 1988. *Salt Lake Tribune,* 18 February, 6A.

U.S. Bureau of the Census. 1975. *Historical Statistics of the United States: Colonial Times to 1970,* Bicentennial ed. Washington, D.C.: U.S. Government Printing Office.

U.S. Congress. Joint Economic Committee. 1974. *Federal Subsidy Programs.* Staff Study Prepared for the Subcommittee on Priorities and Economy in Government, 93d Cong. 2d sess. Washington, D.C.: U.S. Government Printing Office.

"U.S. Lowers Fuel Economy Requirement." 1985. *Grants Pass Daily Courier, 19, July 5.*

"Utility Bills Not Public Debating Forums." 1986. *Telephony,* 10 March, 19.

Viscusi, W. Kip. 1984a. *Regulating Consumer Safety.* Washington, D.C.: American Enterprise Institute for Public Policy Research.

―――. 1984b. "The Lulling Effect: The Impact of Child-Resistant Packaging on Aspirin and Analgesic Ingestions." *American Economic Review* 74 (May):324–27.

―――. 1985. "Consumer Behavior and the Safety Effects of Product Safety Regulation." *Journal of Law & Economics* 28 (October):527–53.

Vogel, David, and Mark V. Nadel. 1976. "The Consumer Coalition: Dimensions of Political Conflict." In *Protecting Consumer Interests,* ed. Robert N. Katz, 7–28. Cambridge, Mass.: Ballinger.

Wagenaar, Alexander C., Daniel W. Webster, and Richard G. Maybee. 1987. "Effects of Child Restraint Laws on Traffic Fatalities in Eleven States." *Journal of Trauma* 27 (July):726–32.

Walker, Jack L. 1983. "The Origins and Maintenance of Interest Groups in America." *American Political Science Review* 77 (June):390–405.

Ward, Scott, Daniel B. Wackman, and Ellen Wartella. 1977. *How Children Learn to Buy.* Beverly Hills, Calif.: Sage.

Wardell, William M., and Louis Lasagna. 1975. *Regulation and Drug Development.* Washington, D.C.: American Enterprise Institute for Public Policy Research.

Warland, Rex H., Robert O. Herrmann, and Dan E. Moore. 1984. "Consumer Complaining and Community Involvement: An Exploration of Their Theoretical and Empirical Linkages." *Journal of Consumer Affairs* 18 (Summer):64–78.

Warne, Colston E. 1982. "Consumers Union's Contribution to the Consumer Movements." In *Consumer Activists: They Made a Difference,* ed. Erma Angevine, 85–110. Mount Vernon, N.Y.: Consumers Union Foundation.

"Warning: Reagonomics Is Harmful to Consumers." 1982. Washington, D.C.: National Consumers League.

"Warning: The Suzuki Samurai Rolls over too Easily." 1988. *Consumer Reports* 53 (July):424–32.

Waruingi, C. 1980. "The Consumer and the Marketing System in a Developing Country: Kenya." Ph.D. diss., Indiana University.

Weidenbaum, Murray. 1978. *The Costs of Goverment Regulation of Business.* Study prepared for the Subcommittee on Economic Growth and Stabilization of the Joint Economic Committee of the United States. 95th Cong., 2d sess.

Weidenbaum, Murray, and Michael Munger. 1983. "Protection at Any Price?" *Regulation* 7 (July-August):14–18.

Wells, John. 1977. "The Diffusion of Durables in Brazil and Its Implications for recent Controversies Concerning Brazilian Development." *Cambridge Journal of Economics* 1 (September):259–79.

Whiteside, Thomas. 1972. *The Investigation of Ralph Nader.* New York: Arbor House.

Wiggins, Steven N. 1981. "Product Quality Regulation and New Drug Introductions: Some New Evidence from the 1970s." *Review of Economics and Statistics* 63 (November):615–19.

Wilkie, William L., Dennis L. McNeill, and Michael B. Mazis. 1984. "Marketing's 'Scarlet Letter': The Theory and Practice of Corrective Advertising." *Journal of Marketing* 48 (Spring):11–31.

Wilson, David B. 1986. "Fatalities up under N.J. Seat-Belt Law." *Salt Lake Tribune,* 17 January, A14.

Wilson, James Q., ed. 1980. *The Politics of Regulation.* New York: Basic Books.

Winter, Ralph K. 1972. *The Consumer Advocate versus the Consumer.* Washington, D.C.: American Enterprise Institute for Public Policy Research.

*World Advertising Expenditures.* Mamaroneck, N.Y.: Starch Inra Hooper.

"The World's Largest Industrial Corporations." 1986. *Fortune,* 4 August, 170–71.

Zald, Mayer, and Roberta Ash. 1966. "Social Movement Organizations." *Social Forces* 44 (March):327–41.

Zick, Cathleen D., Robert N. Mayer, and Laverne Alves Snow. 1986. "Does the U.S. Consumer Product Safety Commission Make a Difference? An Assessment of Its First Decade." *Journal of Consumer Policy* 9 (March):25–40.

Zimmerman, Gary C., and Michael C. Keeley. 1986. "Interest Checking." *Federal Reserve Board of San Francisco Weekly Letter,* 14 November, 1–4.

# Selected Bibliography

## Contemporary Sources

**Aaker, David A., and George S. Day eds.** *Consumerism: Search for the Consumer Interest,* 4th ed. New York: Free Press, 1984. A collection of forty-two articles representing a broad spectrum of perspectives on consumerism and highlighting its importance for marketing activities.

**Angevine, Erma, ed.** *Consumer Activists: They Made a Difference.* Mount Vernon, N.Y.: Consumers Union Foundation, 1982. Twenty-six chapters on the history of the consumer movement, written primarily by the people who made that history.

**Bollier, David, and Joan Claybrook.** *Freedom from Harm.* Washington, D.C.: Public Citizen and Democracy Project, 1986. An attempt to balance criticisms of government regulation by enumerating its substantial but largely taken-for-granted benefits. An appendix lists the major federal laws pertaining to health, safety, and the environment.

*Consumer Reports.* Mount Vernon, N.Y.: Consumers Union. A monthly magazine primarily devoted to comparative product testing. At least one article in each issue deals with a general topic of interest to consumers.

**Crandall, Robert W., Howard K. Gruenspecht, Theodore E. Keeler, and Lester B. Lave.** *Regulating the Automobile.* Washington, D.C.: Brookings Institution, 1986. An ambitious and largely convincing effort to use econometric techniques to quantify the costs and benefits of three areas of automobile regulation: safety, emissions control, and fuel economy standards.

**Creighton, Lucy Black.** *Pretenders to the Throne.* Lexington, Mass.: D. C. Heath, 1976. A history and evaluation of the consumer movement in the United States. Creighton is particularly critical of consumerism's reliance on classical economics and its failure to question the nature of consumer wants.

191

Forbes, J. D. *The Consumer Interest: Dimensions and Policy Implications.* London: Croom Helm, 1987. An examination of the development, nature, and influence of consumer activism. Covers consumerism outside the United States, particularly in Europe.

Griffin, Kelley. *More Action for a Change.* New York: Dembner Books, 1987. The story of student-oriented Public Interest Research Groups inspired by Ralph Nader. An appendix tells how to start one.

Holsworth, Robert D. *Public Interest Liberalism and the Crisis of Affluence.* Boston: G. K. Hall, 1980. An analysis and critique of the ideology of public interest reformers, especially that of Ralph Nader.

Maynes, E. Scott, ed. *The Frontier of Research in the Consumer Interest.* Columbia, Mo.: American Council on Consumer Interests, 1988. The proceedings of a landmark conference at which consumer researchers from around the globe convened to define and assess the state of policy-relevant consumer research.

Nadel, Mark V. *The Politics of Consumer Protection.* Indianapolis: Bobbs-Merrill, 1971. A pioneering analysis of the political aspects of consumer policy in the United States. Also contains three case histories of important pieces of consumer legislation.

Pertschuk, Michael. *Revolt against Regulation.* Berkeley: University of California Press, 1982. The memoirs of an advocate of consumer-oriented regulation and former chairman of the Federal Trade Commission. Traces the consumer movement from the 1960s through the late 1970s.

―――. *Giant Killers.* New York: W. W. Norton, 1986. Five accounts of cases in which public interest lobbyists were able to defeat powerful foes.

Preston, Ivan L. *The Great American Blow-Up.* Madison: University of Wisconsin Press, 1975. A history of the development of advertising and warranty law written by a communication researcher.

Sapolsky, Harvey, ed. *Consuming Fears: The Politics of Product Risks.* New York: Basic Books, 1986. An examination of the forces that act to present the public with what the authors feel is an exaggerated sense of product risks.

Silber, Norman I. *Test and Protest.* New York: Holmes & Meier, 1983. A careful recounting of Consumers Union's history from the 1930s to the 1960s.

Viscusi, W. Kip. *Regulating Consumer Safety.* Washington, D.C.: American Enterprise Institute for Public Policy Research, 1984. An assessment of the Consumer Product Safety Commission's performance that draws negative conclusions regarding both effectiveness and efficiency.

## *Classics*

**Caplovitz, David.** *The Poor Pay More.* New York: Free Press of Glencoe, 1963. A detailed and moving description of low-income consumers in New York City and the consumer problems they experience. The book was influential in bringing about reform in sales practices and rules governing the use of credit.

**Chase, Stuart, Frederick J. Schlink.** *Your Money's Worth.* New York: Macmillan, 1927. A somewhat puritanical plea for greater rationality and less waste in the marketplace. The authors oppose modern differentiation of brands that are much the same and call for product standardization and impartial information. The book's historical importance lies in the impetus it gave to the establishment of product testing organizations.

**Magnuson, Warren G., and Jean Carper.** *The Dark Side of the Marketplace.* Englewood Cliffs, N.J.: Prentice-Hall, 1968. A potpourri of consumer rip-offs amenable to legislative intervention during the late 1960s. Despite some laws shepherded through Congress by Senator Magnuson, most of the problems described remain unsolved.

**Mitford, Jessica.** *The American Way of Death.* New York: Simon and Schuster, 1963. An exposé of barriers to rational consumer choice when dealing with the funeral industry.

**Nader, Ralph.** *Unsafe at Any Speed.* New York: Grossman, 1965. An indictment of the American automobile industry that helped catapult Nader into the national spotlight. Best remembered for its allegations regarding the safety of the Corvair, the book was also a call for equipment to reduce injuries resulting from passengers colliding with the interior of the vehicle (the "second collision").

**Packard, Vance.** *The Hidden Persuaders.* New York: David McKay, 1957. A provocative account of how advertising manipulates people without their awareness to sell products, organizations, and politicians based on fears and fantasies.

**Sinclair, Upton.** *The Jungle.* New York: Doubleday Page, 1906. A fictional account of the horrible conditions faced by an immigrant family trying to earn a living in Chicago's slaughterhouses at the turn of the century. The novel was intended to elicit sympathy for the working man and promote socialism, but its lurid description of practices in the meat-packing industry turned it into the first consumer exposé.

# Index

42/65
46130074